# the sacred ibis speaks

# john houston

## the scots philosopher and mystic

Published by

**MELROSE**
**BOOKS**

An Imprint of Melrose Press Limited
St Thomas Place, Ely
Cambridgeshire
CB7 4GG, UK
www.melrosebooks.com


**FIRST EDITION**


Copyright © John Houston 2009

The Author asserts his moral right to
be identified as the author of this work


Cover designed by John Houston


**ISBN 978-1-906561-37-6**

Printed and bound in Great Britain by:
MPG Biddles, King's Lynn, Norfolk

**PEFC**™ PEFC - Promoting Sustainable Forest Management
PEFC/16-33-293

© **Mixed Sources**

**FSC**
Product group from well-managed
forests, controlled sources and
recycled wood or fiber
www.fsc.org  Cert no. TT-COC-002303
© 1996 Forest Stewardship Council

# Contents

| | | |
|---|---|---|
| Dedication | | v |
| Foreword | | vii |
| Quotation | | ix |

| | | |
|---|---|---|
| 1 | Basic Premises | 1 |
| 2 | Religion: A Sociological Phenomenon | 5 |
| 3 | The Problem of Evil | 13 |
| 4 | Sacrifice & Redemption | 23 |
| 5 | Religion Under Fire | 30 |
| 6 | Divine Providence | 38 |
| 7 | The Quest for Immortality | 45 |
| 8 | Diabolical Temptation | 54 |
| 9 | Ancient Secrets Resurface | 61 |
| 10 | Christ as Hermes: the Great Magician | 68 |
| 11 | *Mind Stuff* | 80 |
| 12 | Regaining Consciousness | 87 |
| 13 | The Universal Myth | 90 |
| 14 | The Legacy of the Greeks | 96 |
| 15 | The Attainment of Gnosis | 103 |
| 16 | The Dawn of Knowledge | 116 |
| 17 | Unity: Our Greatest Need | 132 |
| 18 | The Perfection of I AM | 144 |
| 19 | Chaos & Order | 151 |
| 20 | The Purpose of Humanity | 160 |

# Contents (cont.)

21  The Relationship: The Context of our Experiences          170
22  A Question of Politics                                     181
23  The Great Shepherd                                         192
24  Humanity: Reason Added to Instinct                         204
25  Considering Reflections                                    211
26  All-Attraction                                             215
27  Beehive                                                    218
28  The Quantum Self                                           220
29  Orthodoxy's Greatest Error                                 224
30  Humanity: The Expression of the Heavenly Principle         226
31  Preparation                                                230
32  Entering into the Relationship                             232
33  Self-Perpetuation                                          235
34  Ancient & Modern                                           237
35  Life in Reverse                                            248
36  The Pre-Destined Kingdom                                   259
37  The Necessity of Monarchy                                  282
38  Inclination                                                292
39  Our Milesian Foundation                                    294

About John Houston                                             305

Dedicated to the memory of my friend
Andrew James Collingwood

# Foreword

At this time the Human Race is standing at the crossroads of an *Epochal Threshold*. After this, life can *never* be the same again.

Great and unwelcome upheaval is presently affecting us. Everywhere there is apprehension about the future. There are many who do not know which way to turn. There is a very great need to see the restoration of balance.

This transition is *only one among many* undergone by our Race as we have evolved towards the Human stage. Strange as it may seem, this incredible journey is not yet over. It is for this reason that we should consider the significance of the *ibis*, a symbol ancient in its importance for us.

In Egypt, Thoth of the ibis beak was the god of literature. The Greeks referred to him as Hermes, whilst the Romans knew him as Mercury. In Egypt most scribes' palettes were under the protection of Thoth of the ibis beak, the god of letters.

Thoth was originally a shepherd. He was to invent the lyre, as well as weights and measures. He was recognised as the protector of merchants and the patron of poets and musicians. He was also seen as the god of dreams, indeed an *Immortal Magician*. The earliest records from Egypt go as far as to state that Thoth of the ibis beak was *the Creator of the planet Earth*.

What was so important about Thoth of the ibis beak was that he was the restorer of harmony and the *arbiter of all conflicts*. Thoth of the ibis beak is mentioned in *The Egyptian Book of the Dead*, where it states that he records the Divine Word on papyrus from the primeval marshes.

A rubric from *The Egyptian Book of the Dead* found at Khnum was believed to have been written by Thoth of the ibis beak. Thoth was a lawgiver and the

Archetype of other lawgivers appearing in other cultures just as he had done in Egypt. This includes *The Reforms at Lagash* around 3200 BC, or those of Sargon of Akkad around 2700 BC, or of Hammurabi from around 1800 BC, or those of the Biblical Moses, whose name is Egyptian.

Thus in Ancient Egypt, the symbol of the *ibis* was known to all who sought *initiation into the Greater Mysteries,* especially those who had reached the sixth, or penultimate, stage.

We know that, at this time, we require a new direction. Yet what we await is *a Person* who has been instrumental in guiding us this far. We are *dependent* upon this Person to guide us still further.

In centuries now gone Magicians knew that the *ibis* symbolised the phenomenon of *resurrection* through Cyclic or Aeonic return. The *ibis* symbolised *a passageway* from the known to the unknown.

It was known that the mask of the *ibis* was the most difficult and the most dangerous to assume. In so doing one was preparing to cross an abyss. The initial leap involved the acceptance that one's so-called existence, or life as we know it, is actually *non-existence.* Here we recall the words of Orpheus who said that, in common parlance, what we refer to as *life* is actually *death.*

We stand at a crossroads awaiting the *appearance* of our Ultimate Ancestor. Then there will be a *quantum leap* marking the end of the Human stage of our evolution.

Trapezuntius stated,

> It was known that Gemistos was so much a Platonist ...

> I myself heard him at Florence, for he came to the Council with the Greeks, asserting that the whole world would, in a few years, adopt one and the same religion, with one mind, one intelligence, one teaching.

> And when I asked: Christ's or Muhammed's? He replied: neither, but one *not* differing from Paganism.

This answer shocked Trapezuntius, who continued,

> I heard, too, from a number of Greeks who escaped here from the Peloponnese that he openly said, about three years before his death, that not many years after his death both Muhammed and Christ would be forgotten and the real truth would shine through all the shores of the world.

C. M. Woodhouse, *George Gemistos Plethon. The Last of the Hellenes*. Published as a special edition for Sandpiper Books Ltd., in 2000, p 34.

# 1: Basic Premises

In 1977 I matriculated at Glasgow University to fulfil what had been a secret ambition. I had wanted to study Philosophy and Systematic Theology. One year later, while working in a hostel for alcoholic men, it had become clear to me that the time had come for me to set my thoughts down on paper. As time passed it had become increasingly clear to me that I would have to write a series of essays which would constitute a radical re-interpretation of Plato. More to the point, I felt that it had fallen to me to reform Philosophy.

That part of my life was characterised by great transition. I had become involved in Christian house-fellowships and was reasonably happy for a while. In time, however, I was to become disillusioned and decided to leave not only the house-fellowships but the Christian faith as well. This was after a long period of self-examination. I did so because I had reached the conclusion that the Christian Era was now basically over, and that we in the West were witnessing the tail end of it.

But I was involved in a search for so it seemed *at the time*! Rather than all my spiritual problems evaporating away, they grew worse. Indeed it would be true to say that all my spiritual problems came to a head. I found myself face to face with the question which so many are now asking all over what was once Christendom: *where do we go from here?*

I didn't want to throw anything which I had formerly believed out of the window just for the sake of it. Therefore, I decided to *re-interpret* what I had previously believed. I felt that what was required was clarification, nothing more. As such I continued to study both the Old and the New Testaments as well as other writings, such as the Baha'i writings, Buddhist scriptures,

Hindu scriptures, the Koran, the philosophy of Martin Heidegger and that of Karl Jaspers, and the theology of Rudolf Bultmann; in fact, anything that came my way.

I felt that there was no profit in turning away from the Bible completely. From its pages I was able to gaze upon a Confession of Faith from a period of approximately 1000 BC until 100 AD in the Ancient World. Here there is an *interpretation* of history with an ancient people, Israel, seeking for freedom from oppression, for a land of their own, and to be a holy people with God visible in their midst.

Yet there was more to it than this. The fulfilment of their deepest desires was always out of reach, always on the horizon. Life was a pilgrimage and the Torah (the Books of Moses) was an invitation to participation in this pilgrimage.

This journey of faith takes place, as it were, between two poles. At the beginning of the Biblical narratives there is the creation of the heavens and the Earth, which is depicted in the opening chapters of *The Book of Genesis*. At the end of *The Book of Revelation* there is the vision of a new heaven and a new Earth.

This journey of faith, however, was not as straightforward as one would have hoped. At times the journeying was no more than aimless wandering in the wilderness, and the belief that there was a Promised Land was undermined by frustration and hopelessness. The people of faith had a task on their hands. Not only had they to overcome enemies but they had to contend with their own unbelief.

Although it would be impossible to give a summary of the Bible in one paragraph, there are certain things that *must* be said about it. The Bible is the product of a community of faith which emerged from the cultural background of the Ancient Near East. As such it is by *no* stretch of the imagination *unique* as to contents, as its approach to life was not uncommon among other peoples.

What it seeks to do is to speak *with authority* in an attempt to answer questions related to the most fundamental problems in its own way, in its approach to belief in God, or the gods, with the attempts of the Human Race to assert Its authority over the environment with the conviction that God had given to Humanity the leading role in what was a *Divinely-inspired Saga*.

As such, the Bible is concerned with what the Human Race has to do to fulfil this role correctly, because life was a bitter struggle against the elements, pestilence, more powerful warlike neighbours, as well as other considerations.

I was influenced by most of the theological writers that I read, but of them all I found that Rudolf Bultmann was by far the most stimulating. Bultmann had taken the step of trying to *demythologise* the New Testament. He felt that no one had paid sufficient heed to the understanding the New Testament narrators had of their own existences. This was indeed a theological landmark. Much light had been shed on the task of the theologian in these days; but here I felt that Bultmann had not gone far enough.

In our attempts to understand what it is that the Bible has to say to us we have not paid sufficient heed to the *basic premises* on which Biblical literalism and therefore Biblical theology are based. It is here that we have to come to terms with an unprecedented *crisis* in belief.

Our present generation, in the Western world at least, is like *no other* prior to us in the entire evolution of our Race. This generation is the very first, leaving aside legends concerning prehistoric Civilisations such as Lemuria and Atlantis, which has not had to concentrate all its energies on the basic struggle to progress or to *survive*.

Now, at the dawn of a New Millennium, work is figuring less and less in our daily lives and, in time, education will eradicate ignorance, meaning that lives can be lived *not* in seeking primarily to survive, but in finding *fulfilment*. It is precisely here that we differ most markedly from *all* the generations prior to us.

After serious study and meditation I became convinced that it was this *ease of survival* which differentiates us from *all* the generations of our fathers and mothers. All generations prior to us – and this for our purpose includes the narrators of the New Testament *par excellence* – were, due to their struggle for survival, to make an outrageous denial, a mistake which from our vantage point seems so great but, yet, so understandable.

We, as the Human generation at the very crossroads of possibility, are able to interpret our existences in a way entirely different from previous generations, and in a quite specific way.

*No* prior generation would seriously have considered the possibility of a loving God *deliberately* putting the Human Race in a situation where Humanity would be left to struggle to survive and gain insight into Its condition, and a struggle which would last for many millennia. Why should this be? They were of the opinion that *only a Devil* would have permitted us to experience the suffering we have experienced, and all this in consequence of being in a world such as this one (1).

This is significant for us to date, as regards Religion, and this includes the *literalism* on which the leading theistic faiths are based, these being Judaism,

Christianity and Islam, which have as their most basic premise the belief which *denies* that God created the Human Race *as It is,* in the world *as we find It.*

This is the basic premise which will seal their doom. This led me to ponder over a *diabolical temptation.* In the application of this it is hoped that the *anthropological* stage of Philosophical Theology is now concluded.

## NOTES

(1)    Without doubt, this is the legacy which Gnosticism has bequeathed to us for, in its most primitive stages Christianity, or *The Cult of Jesus Christ* to be more precise, may well have been a *Gnostic sect.*

There was *no one brand* of Gnosticism, with centres of Gnosticism in various parts of the known world. In general, they held that God was beyond conception and description because God was supremely perfect and infinite in attributes. They also held that it would be beneath the dignity of God to labour and, accordingly, God could not have created the world. Moreover, the fact that there was so much evil in the world was ample proof that *no* God characterised by love and compassion *could have created it.*

God lived in a pleroma of light and was totally inaccessible, although there were Emanations from God. These were *Aeons,* who descended in degree until the level of *the Demiurge.* This was the Creator of the world, with whom the Gnostics identified *the God of the Old Testament,* who was known as *Yahweh.*

They considered the Christ to be an *Aeon,* having been sent into the world to restore *The True Religion.* Some believed that the Aeon had entered the Christ at his baptism and left at the point when the Christ was being taken away to be crucified, so that *it was only the man who suffered.*

Gnostics believed that salvation was only for a tiny elect. There were Gnostics who believed that salvation was only possible for Humans of the male gender.

# 2: Religion:
# A Sociological Phenomenon

## I

Religion is as old as the Human community, indeed older. The turning of Humanity to the gods for help has its roots, to a great extent, in Human desires and fears, particularly those associated with self-preservation. For many the only thing to give life meaning from one day to the next is no more than the desire to simply remain alive.

Religion has to do with the desire for worship, and perhaps even with the desire to rise above the present level of awareness. The desire of an individual, irrespective of what it may be, will arise from and be conditioned by the cultural background of which the individual is a part, even if it is no more than *a reaction against* that particular cultural setting. It involves the understanding an individual has of his or her own existence, and is shaped further by the ease or struggle for survival experienced by the individual.

When we look back down through the centuries, religious practices may seem to be rather superstitious, even *inhuman*, with attempts to ward off evil, with sacrifice, and with a plea for a future hoped-for redemption from life as we know it with its characteristic fears, frustrations and anxieties, its unfulfilment and limitations.

Every ancient people believed that certain personages had a peculiar power which meant that they could consult the deity and, thereby, reveal the will of the deity. Every man could sacrifice, but not everyone could render the oracle of God, for this pertained to a *select* group or individual. Each tribe had its own god, and it was through the medium of the tribe that the god was able to become *effective on Earth*. The god was the patron of the tribe, the supreme magistrate and the leader in war. The piety demanded was no more than the loyalty due to the tribe and to the tribal ritual. No real cognisance was taken of the character of the worshipper or his or her inner feelings or thoughts.

In religious beliefs and practices the Human being looks *beyond* his or her senses in a particular way, for no Human being does so in an *isolated* manner. In the past, in the quest for truth and understanding, one identified with the tribe to which one belonged and on which one depended for survival, for religious beliefs were never self-contained. This communal aspect to Religion should be stressed as fundamental. The religious approach to life is *not* characterised by a coincidence of individual actions, although not all actions will have an apparently communal aspect, for within the outlook of a religious community there will be a diversity of roles or ministries. Aspirants will be seen to possess different gifts. All individual actions, within the faith, are related in some way. Even when a monk sits alone in a cell he is still part of a movement with shared ideals and practices.

# II

Religious outlooks have altered with the passage of time. Science and Technology, and many other benefits of education have greatly increased our Knowledge and, accordingly, religious beliefs have been refined and continually modernised, although this usually happens only very slowly. For the best part of 2000 years our basic approach to Religion has remained unaltered. Within Christendom, it was proclaimed that Jesus Christ was *the embodiment of the dealings of God with the Human Race.*

We are told that the Human Race had gone astray due to wilful rebellion against God, thus rendering Humanity unable to live in harmony with God and with Itself.

In the New Testament we see Jesus Christ proclaimed as having been sent by God into our world to undertake a work of reconciliation, thus removing forever all barriers which existed, *supposedly*, between the Human Race and God.

We should realise that a *continual assessment and reappraisal* of our beliefs need not be avoided, for this is quite natural. With progress and increased knowledge, outlooks must change. With the growth of the feet, shoes which were once comfortable are found to be too small, so much so that the feet become cramped and the growth of the feet will be stunted unless action is taken. There are many beliefs which were accepted as true without question at certain stages in the development of Civilisation on this planet, but we must accept that *no* beliefs can continue to exist with their validity unquestioned *ad infinitum*.

In these days Religion has lost a considerable amount of popularity, and some talk of Religion as though it were synonymous with *Superstition*, although this is somewhat unfair. The origin of a particular belief or practice does not determine the validity of its present form or what, in time, it may become. No one thinks any the worse of Science although its roots are also to be found in Superstition, so this should not be overlooked when we look at Religion.

Down through the centuries religious outlooks have altered, indeed religious development has proceeded in certain recognisable stages. One of the most significant developments has been the transition from tribal to national worship. The national god is considerably more powerful than the tribal god, just as the national king is more powerful than the tribal chief. There is a much greater need for reverence and adoration as the god is more powerful, but also more distant.

As Human Civilisation has been developing, a multitude of different needs have had to be satisfied. Yet there are some needs which exist irrespective of the cultural background or the Age in which one lives. Every individual and every nation has ideals, and when we look closely at Human development we see that there has been an advancement from lower to higher needs.

Initially material needs are of fundamental importance. Thereafter, one aspires to satisfy the needs of the nation to which one belongs, under the guidance of the National Temple.

This, as it happens, is the stage we are now on the point of forsaking and, simultaneously, individuals are beginning to realise that they have an importance and also ideals which cannot be found in the National Temple. All over the planet people are seeking to find fulfilment and realise Destiny, with such becoming an individual passion in an individual way.

The religion of the tribe belongs to that stage of Man's development in which his energies are entirely occupied in their struggle against Nature and other tribes.

Patriotism and religion are one, and the offices of worship are upheld by the entire power of the State, and the gods speak with authority to the spirit of the believer.

The individual has become aware of wants and longings which are *not* satisfied in the National Temple. The further progress of religion is apt to appear *as a revolt* against a system which has grown so strong. The individual sets out to seek a consistent intellectual view and so figures as a sceptic, appearing to preach a doctrine *contrary to patriotism*.

Thus the individual stage of religion succeeds the national; yet the individual stage is also, in part at least, the universal stage. (1)

What we have been witnessing in the West has been a breakdown of this *national form of worship*. Remnants remain, however. This is to be seen in the United Kingdom, for example, on occasions such as Armistice Day, State funerals, Coronations and so on, where we see the hierarchy of the Church and State, along with the Armed Forces, arrayed in solemn fashion before their Monarch who is not only the principal citizen but also *The Defender of the Faith*.

# III

The Christian faith did not appear from nowhere, but rather *emerged* as part of the evolution of certain traditions which constitute the basis of religious belief as we know it. Christianity has its roots in the Hellenistic or Greek Age, with great influence being applied from *The Apocalyptic Movement* which lasted from approximately 200 BC until 100 AD.

The greatest influence upon the primitive Christian community was probably Iranian Eschatology and Apocalyptic belief, the basis of which was the belief concerning the contrast between two rival gods, namely *Ahura Mazda* and *Angra Mainzu*, with the entire history of the Human Race seen as a struggle between these two gods and conditioned thereby, and varying in intensity until the end of the world. The Final Judgement coincides with great triumph, the Powers of Darkness having been overpowered by the Powers of Light. Parallels to this are to be seen quite clearly in the New Testament.

By the time of Jesus of Nazareth who is the Jesus of the New Testament, however, the mixed origins of the Apocalyptic Movement had become something strictly *Jewish*. It belonged, in general, to the Inter-Testamental Period which lasted between the end of the Old Testament and the beginning of the New Testament. It was *a mystery* to those outside the community by whom the method was employed.

The Eschatology within the Jewish tradition had four major strands: there was a dualism, a struggle between two Cosmic powers; there were world epochs of 1000 years; there would be a resurrection of the dead; the world would be destroyed by fire.

All this was presented in a *mythological wrapping* to which, in the telling of the tale, the narrator *would have had to resort* in order to relate the content of the story to others. In this way others would be able to relate to the new faith and possibly understand it, and thereby *a new tradition* would grow out of older traditions, and thus become another variation on a very Ancient and quite fundamental Theme.

The early Christian apologists could contrast what they considered to be a true story; the story of God's saving activity in Israel through Jesus Christ, using the Mythology of those whom they considered to be Pagans. In effect, this enabled them to depict Jesus Christ as the most recent advent of a *Suprahistorical Person* who has been *incarnated* on Earth at crucial stages in the development of Civilisation in order to provide guidance for Humanity.

It is therefore very important that we should understand that the Christian faith has its roots in the pre-Christian Era. The twentieth century, in particular, has furnished us with information concerning late Jewish speculation, as well as Gnosticism and other Mystery Cults which were contemporary with *The Cult of Jesus Christ*. As such it is possible for us to see more clearly in the New Testament the setting of the Greek world, and the various affinities which Christianity shared with other Religions.

Certain theologians – Johannes Weiss, for example – related the teachings of Jesus of Nazareth to *Jewish Eschatology*, those teachings which were concerned with the end of the world. This was expected *within a generation* of the death and resurrection of Jesus Christ, with the inauguration of a *supernatural* Kingdom on Earth.

The Jesus of the New Testament saw himself as the one who would return to Earth *within a generation* to establish such a Kingdom. His preaching was Apocalyptic and proclaimed the arrival of *The Kingdom of God*. His preaching pointed to the end of the Ages. His hearers would have accepted his message as a test of the love of God in a world from which its inhabitants *sought redemption*. The post-paschal *kerygma* understood the resurrection of Jesus Christ as an anticipation of the end of the world, the curtain raised on the final act of Human history.

The young Jewish rabbi certainly seems to have captured the imagination of many. His followers had a story to tell, and they were prepared to risk life and limb in the telling of it. They were to speak of a young rabbi, but the story did not end there for their story also concerned God, because they claimed that God had raised this young rabbi from the dead, thus vindicating him and ratifying his message. Now *all* the ancient promises to Israel had been fulfilled.

Another great influence on the primitive Christian faith would have been Gnosticism, whose impact would have been two-fold, for there were very distinct differences between the Gnostic and the Christian view of the world. In *The Gospel According to John* we see the use of discourses remarkably similar to those found in certain Mandaean writings which probably came from Syria-Palestine, a place where primitive Christianity flourished. These similarities involved the use of sayings which characterise the Gnostic Redeemer as the Good Shepherd and the Real Vine.

> In John, Jesus descends from heaven like the Gnostic Redeemer to bring to Man the saving message, and he returns to the Father after completing the work. In face of his words, light and darkness separate themselves, before them life and death are decided. He who is of the truth hears his voice; to the blind, however, the Messenger of Life remains hidden.

The second characteristic relationship of *The Gospel of John* to Gnosticism consists of the fact that in its Gnostic form a pointed anti-Gnostic theology is expressed. Man's *lostness* in the world is not the lost condition of a heavenly substance in the power of darkness, but the spiritual turning of the creature from the Creator. The Redeemer therefore does not bring a knowledge that illuminates Man as to his true nature; rather it reveals to him his sin. (2)

There are considerable problems to be faced here. The Biblical narrators had an approach which has become totally alien to our own, and it is essential that we should grasp this. Only then will we be able to act positively in our attempts to understand what these Biblical narratives *mean* to us when they talk of the Human world experiencing Divine intervention.

The basic premises of the narrators of the New Testament are as follows: the Human Race was created in a perfect environment where the Human Race was perfectly happy; initially the Human Race possessed a *potential* for Immortality; the Human Race had been *destined* to enjoy the fullness of fellowship with God; Humanity had originally lived under the protective care of God.

It was told that God had withdrawn because of some sort of *disobedience* by Humanity. In so doing Humanity had turned Its back on the grace of God; thereafter, fellowship with God was no longer a privilege to be enjoyed by Humanity.

The aforementioned premises permeate the teachings propagated by the Christian Church down through the centuries, although as we all know there is a whole host of different traditions within the Christian faith.

In the New Testament these premises appear most markedly. They are expressed as the symptoms of a Human condition, a lostness which Jesus Christ had been sent to rectify.

Yet, this is all based on that initial premise that God would not have *deliberately* put Humanity into a world where the first thing the Human Race would have to do was to learn to survive (3).

In our spiritual development, Jesus of Nazareth (or more correctly, *how* the primitive Christians *portrayed him* in their writings) has played a very significant role. It is unlikely that Jesus of Nazareth was *an historical person* as such, but whether he was historical or not, we are still able to grasp *the significance* of the words ascribed to him by his disciples. When looking at this message we see that his most important contribution was the proclamation that the gates of Heaven were *now open* for us.

Down through the bloodthirsty centuries, no doubt that message gave hope to countless millions of believers, but for us today there is an all-important *difference*, for we are able to bring another aspect into play.

Whereas Jesus of Nazareth believed that the gates of Heaven were open for us – and such is an integral part of the message of the New Testament – we can consider the possibility, due to our ability to survive with relative ease, that *they were never closed in the first place.* It only *appeared* to the Ancients that the doors to Heaven were closed due to the harshness of Existence.

## NOTES

(1)   Allan Menzies, *History and Religion.* Published by John Murray, London, 1918 edition. p. 426.

(2)   Rudolf Bultmann, *The Gospel According to John.* Published by Blackwell Press, 1971. p. 9.

(3)   In this age of *going forward* at meetings to become a Christian we tend to lose sight of the fact that, in the Ancient World, there was a process of *Initiation* which had to be undergone by devotees of a particular sect or cult. There is no reason for assuming that *The Cult of Jesus Christ* was any different in this respect.

Having been initiated into *The Ancient Mysteries* the aspirant would then be given *the secret message* which was *contained* in the text, to which the sacred writings were merely a mirror or representation.

This *secret teaching* within the New Testament may have involved the belief that a Civilisation existing on Earth in prehistoric times had disappeared in a very dramatic way. It may also have involved information about Civilisation on Earth being due to the benevolent intervention of beings from another and higher world.

This is true of *The Ancient Mysteries* of Egypt, of Babylon and of Greece, of which *The Cult of Jesus Christ* would have been a localised adaptation, which taught *Initiates* that Civilisation on Earth was the outcome of the arrival of beings, considered by our ancestors to have been *gods*, whose home was on a planet which orbits *Sirius*.

# 3: The Problem of Evil

## I

Every thinker, and every theologian in particular, has to come to terms with what we refer to as *evil*, and it is here that the theologian faces the greatest problem. What the theologian must attempt to do is, after admitting that there seems to be such a thing as *evil*, go on to explain how this *evil* is possible in a Universe governed by a God who is both All-Powerful and Benevolent.

This is what theologians refer to as *theodicy*. When facing such a problem, the first point for the theologian to tackle is to explain what is meant by *evil* and then to provide, in addition to this, the reason why such a belief was brought to light in the first place.

There have always been people, although perhaps not as many now as there once were, who believed that they were threatened not only by enemies who were visible, but by others who were *invisible*. Human existence had the characteristic of standing under a *threat* which had various constituent parts. It contained the notion that Humanity was hedged in by an Incomprehensible Power which seemed, at times, to play a game of hide-and-seek with us.

There was the frustration brought about by the limitations of being apparently finite and mortal. There is anxiety about the future, guilt about the past, solitude and even loneliness in the present, all of which contribute to a sensation of unfulfilment. One may live in fear of dreadful illnesses which may take the lives of those that we love, or the life of a loving parent thus leaving children unprotected from poverty. One may have no real friends and life, therefore, may have no real meaning.

We seem to come unwittingly into a world where problems await us. All around us in the midst of life there is death. Yet we do not simply live and die. We need to seek *an approach to life* which will inject *meaning* into our lives. We are all too aware of the fact that life may not work out according to plan and, therefore, adjustments may be necessary.

We experience a sense of urgency and in the urgency of life there is the experience of crisis. For many people in ordinary everyday life one crisis follows another. There is, above all, the crisis in belief which has now come to a head in these days at the very dawning of a New Millennium. This crisis in belief has nothing to do with *mere morality* or even with any religious persuasion as such. We are dealing here with something of which we are aware as transcending *all* sociological phenomena.

There is the crisis of care for tomorrow our good fortune may change. Tomorrow, our lifestyle and our safety may be at risk. We have an inbuilt sense of duty and we are only too aware that others have a right to us. We hope to find beauty, truth and love. We are pulled this way and that along a path which is often the dividing line between self-assertion and duty. Our family, our nation, our church or political party and others all make claims upon us and upon our time and, because of this, discipline is necessary.

It was undoubtedly due to the obstacles in the path of progress, fulfilment and prosperity which led the Ancients to conclude that the gods had abandoned this world to live in another world far above our heads (1). The gods, while seeming to demand so much from us, appeared to be *no more than spectators* in our plight. If there were to be any intercourse between the world of Humanity and the world of the gods then a *Representative* would be necessary.

This is the most fundamental theme of all Human Religion. The *Representative* of a higher world forsakes self-interest in that world to *descend* from the realms of light to our world *here below*, which was enshrouded in darkness and gripped by despair and spiritual death. Life on Earth was not so much to be enjoyed as endured.

And this fleeting life is a life of trouble and torment. As in the case of other peoples, the tormenting idea also emerged in Israel, that Human life stands under a curse; that we have lost something that once belonged to us. The Paradise Myth tells us how things were in the beginning, for a short time. Man who ate the forbidden fruit was driven out of Paradise; and, henceforth, women must bear their children in sorrow; the ground is cursed so that it brings forth thorns and thistles and Man must eat his bread by the sweat of his brow. The Greeks had something corresponding to this in the Prometheus Myth. The necessities of life once accrued to Man's benefit themselves,

'But Zeus with angry purpose hid the source of food
for once Prometheus deceived him'. (2)

The Human Race, or more correctly that which has reached *the Human stage of Its evolution*, has had to overcome many obstacles on the way to coming to terms with the world, to create the circumstances which will assist evolution to continue. With this in mind we must eventually realise that we have to come to terms with ourselves, for the most important relationship we can have is the one we have with *ourselves*.

This is something uniquely Human. We can accept ourselves or reject ourselves. We can *be* ourselves or imitate another. This is brought about by the bewilderment of having *possibility* which makes us *more* than we really are at any given time, for we are never actually *complete*. Indecision is brought to a head by the necessity of finding some sort of fulfilment while, at the same time, avoiding chaos. Sitting on the fence is rendered virtually impossible if we want to live an authentic life.

# II

The Ancients, in spite of the harshness of their world, were, nonetheless, convinced that God cared for them. The Ancient World was full of tales about how Messengers, or Angels, had come to Earth to deliver messages of hope and salvation. It was by means of *Representation* that one was informed of the will of God.

According to the Biblical narratives the will of God is made known by a progression of bearers of tidings, for revelation was *progressive*. There were angels, then prophets, the greatest of whom was Moses who had met Yahweh, the god of the Hebrews, on the summit of a holy mountain. This story is strikingly reminiscent of tales of other leaders from other cultures, from whom the Hebrews *borrowed* the story.

The greatest of revelations was yet to come, however, and according to the Jews this would involve the re-establishing of the Davidic dynasty which was, in itself, a forerunner of greater things to come. The Christian community considered this to have been fulfilled in the person of Jesus Christ, whom they regarded as the saviour of the world, having come here from the very presence of God to impart the grace of God to us.

Problems have to be dealt with in life; of this we are all too aware. But how should we view these problems? Is there any means available to us which would be able to permit us to interpret our lives in a more positive and meaningful manner?

Religion has always tended to look the other way when faced with the *diabolical temptation* to suggest that our appearance on Earth, as we experience it, was *no mistake* but according to a plan of evolution which we were unable to comprehend fully. We need to reconsider what the Bible says about the structure of Nature being altered by the rebelliousness which brought about what the Bible refers to as *The Fall* (3).

> And to Adam he said
> Because you have eaten of the Tree
> Cursed is the ground because of you;
> In toil you shall eat of it
> All the days of your life.
> In the sweat of your face
> You shall eat bread. (4)

It was believed that from a particular point onwards, obstacles had fallen on our path. It was much more than a question of guilt. There was what appeared to be a systematic attack upon us by an enemy which was nothing short of a powerful unseen army. In spite of penitence and sacrifice it was still there. It seemed as though *a final deliverance* was necessary for the force was depicted as standing somewhere between Humanity and God, as well as being between one Human and another.

In time, this force was *personalised* into an army of fallen angels or demons, with a leader whose position was that of the Arch-enemy of God. This is the Devil, or the Satan. Christian apologists have always stressed the need to beware of this powerful unseen army (5).

> Again, the air is the sphere of the Devil, the enemy of our Race who, having fallen from Heaven, endeavours with other evil spirits who shared in his disobedience both to keep souls from the truth and to hinder the progress of those who are trying to follow it. (6)

This was, in effect, only the *personalising* of the forces of Nature, which were often so unpredictable, such as rain for harvests and so on. This was a response to the Biblical idea that, whether on an individual or national basis, there was *no* real idea of rule or order in the world. Such forces would have to be kept at bay. There was a *future Kingdom* which God would inaugurate at an appointed time. One day, it was believed, God would rule in the midst of all our circumstances. Until then, we would have to be patient and wait and work for its coming.

In the Ancient World there were those, even then, who had lost all belief in the benevolence of God, or the gods. To some, life was such that all we could do was make the best of it. According to Epicurus, the root of all *evil* was fear, that unnecessary fear with which so many of us are troubled. If there are gods then they had shown *no real interest in us*. Death was just a long, untroubled sleep. *Evil* could be avoided by means of Justice but if it came, then one would simply have to endure it. Happiness could be experienced through living quiet, sober lives which were lived in the cultivation of friendship.

# III

Here we need to look a little closer at this most vexing question. It is in the encountering of the harshness of life, and the hopelessness with which so many live their lives, that the problem of *evil* comes to our attention and demands notice.

If the belief that God *deliberately* put us in a world where we would have to learn to survive and develop unaided is correct, albeit *with interventions at crucial stages of development* as is nonetheless fundamental to the Christian message, as well as other leading Religions, then it is probably incorrect to consider ourselves as *fallen*.

This means that the premises presented to us traditionally can now be considered *false*. If this is the case then we must conclude that Religion is at the crossroads. Our interpretation of the Biblical narratives will have to alter, quite simply, because the most basic premise of the Biblical narratives will have altered.

The point in question is quite simple: did God create us *as we are* and put us into the world *as we find it?* The answer we give to this question could drastically alter our approach to the life of faith.

It is precisely here that Philosophical Theology waits at the crossroads, for our basic assumptions can now alter from those which were held in the past. Until these days this *evil*, which is the term employed to encompass a multitude of trials and tribulations, anguish and suffering which one could experience in life, was always viewed *as a punishment*, for it was what we were supposed to deserve because of our disobedience to God. In previous generations, in popular Religion at least, the love of God was *not* to be found in the *removal* of the harshness we had experienced, but that one day through faith we might be rescued or *redeemed* from it.

This view is unrealistic. The truth of the matter is that *that which has now reached the Human stage of Its evolution* and is set to evolve still further, was given an obstacle course for a birthday present. This would have to be overcome as it contained the key to our development. In the overcoming, all our faculties would have to be employed to the full. Thereby, we would find fulfilment, experience the full awareness of our worth and, at the same time, experience the reality that the power by means of which the worlds were created abides within all of us *as a permanent endowment*. These may just possibly be the facts of our existences and, ironically for atheists at any rate, these are *truths* cited by them in arguments contrary to Religion.

This problem of *evil* has always been very difficult for religious communities to handle, for life was harsh in an inexplicable manner. At the same time it was proclaimed that the Godhead was nonetheless Benevolent and Omnipotent. Somehow or other we ended up by *blaming ourselves* for the sometimes pitiable conditions of our everyday circumstances. We seemed to see ourselves as culprits.

We have had to struggle so much and there has been an indescribable amount of suffering in the process. Yet here we have to consider *The Ancient Mysteries*, which were not concerned with God in any readily recognisable popular religious sense, for *The Ancient Mysteries* were concerned with *what it means to be Human*, and *why* the Human Race actually exists.

*The Ancient Mysteries* proclaimed that *God had become the Human Race* so that Humanity could learn what it meant *to be* God. This would involve the process of evolution, the perfection of Form, the experience of *Deification*.

There has been a continuous growth of Civilisation on the planet, but the circumstances have not yet been created to permit Civilisation to take hold *fully*. These circumstances would be a Social Order operating on a global scale whereby the Human Race lives in harmony with Nature, where people do *what they do best* in service to the rest of Humanity or to the planet, enabling us to realise that the Human Race is a Collective Consciousness. This would permit us to rise *above* the present Human stage to the *awakening* of the Christ Principle which is dormant within all of us.

An entirely different approach to the *interpretation* of Existence is now possible for us because we are able to approach what we refer to as *evil* from a perspective somewhat different from that of our forefathers and mothers.

That power which has hedged us in need no longer be a threat to us. We need no longer feel abandoned for that power which *seemed* to be so heartless, which left us to struggle and survive in life and death conditions, learning the rules by trial and error, can now be seen in a different light.

This *evil* was a thorn in the flesh which made us desire a better world for this *evil* was the experience of overcoming an apparently incomplete world in sometimes horrific circumstances.

*Evil* is the experience of trying to survive while, at the same time, trying to find fulfilment in a world where we felt threatened and deprived of certainty. At this stage in our development it would be a good idea to stop for a breath of fresh air, and then gaze down into the abyss from which we have crawled.

## NOTES

(1)   *The Ancient Mysteries* informed initiates that attempts had been made by Extraterrestrials to establish Civilisation on this planet. These beings whose home, according to *Esoteric* Tradition, was a planet which orbits Sirius, were trying to assimilate Humanity into a Galactic Confederation of *Extraterrestrial* Humanities.

At certain times they have *intervened* to assist Humanity to become more civilised, and fundamental to *The Ancient Mysteries* was the story that a Civilisation being established on Earth had disappeared in a rather dramatic fashion.

Many see this as a reference to Atlantis. Why this happened is far from clear. Possibly, this was part of these Extraterrestrials' overall plan, to lay the foundations for Humanity to have the possibility to progress by means of learning fundamental lessons, until such time as we would be ready to be assimilated into a Galactic Confederation. It would be like a coming of age!

If this is the case then the end of Atlantis was *brought about by these beings* who did not want a fledgling Humanity to have access to *such great possibility which It did not have the wisdom to utilise properly.*

(2)   Rudolf Bultmann, *Philosophical Essays*. Published by SCM Press in 1955. p. 121. From the essay 'Adam, where are you?'

(3)   The Bible does not actually explain what is meant by *The Fall*, and this only highlights what is known by those who have studied these things, which is that the Bible is written in such a way as to be *incomprehensible* to those who have not been *initiated* into *The Ancient Mysteries*.

In the first chapter of *The Book of Genesis* Adam and Eve are featured as is their subsequent expulsion from Paradise.

Both the Old and the New Testaments are the product of a community which had been subjected to Greek culture for more than three centuries.

With the majority of the Jews living outside Palestine in the Diaspora and therefore Hellenised, it should come as no surprise that their sacred book should begin with an allusion to the Myth of Orpheus and Euridice.

Orpheus and Euridice lived in Paradise and, after a bite from a serpent she descends into Hades or Hell, which is the Earth, the place where the souls of the departed are to be found. Orpheus followed her here to redeem her by means of his *Music*.

The Myth of Orpheus and Euridice probably relates to an attempt by an Extraterrestrial Civilisation to establish Civilisation on Earth as part of a process of *Reproduction*, with planets interacting with each other to overcome their isolation so that, eventually, the Cosmos may return to Its origin, which is the Original State of Consciousness.

In addition to this there was a very powerful Egyptian influence upon Israel, which is demonstrated with the use of the Myth of Osiris and Isis; Osiris is the first King of Egypt and Isis is a Virgin Goddess.

Osiris was the husband of Isis and, after he had been murdered by his evil brother, he was raised from the dead by Isis. She had used very potent magick to receive his seed and conceive. When her son was born *she hid him in the marshes*.

This is where the story of Moses comes from. Here, too, we should not forget that the name Moses is Egyptian, and means *son*.

All of this points to the fact that the message of the Bible is very ancient, with the Bible being a later development in a process which is common to Humanity of all Ages. Thus we see that the message of the Bible is *not unique*.

(4)  *The Book of Genesis*, chapter 3: 17.

(5)  Since the dawn of Humanity there have been occasions when Civilisation has been approached but not fully realised. This is because there has never been the establishment of a Common Purpose on a global scale which will permit Humanity to operate *authentically* as a *Collective Consciousness*.

With the failure of the Common Purpose to establish Itself cultures have *continued to compete* with each other. To secure stability the ruling class was characterised by *heredity* which, in time, can create conflict due to excessive rigidity, with The Laws of Nature *demanding* constant change.

With the ruling classes requiring to unite the masses under their leadership, they were forced to provide a belief system to which the masses could relate. This would have involved some sort of inclusion of the Popular Mythology of the masses, which would have been superstition, and not the least bit scientific.

Civilisation has nothing to do with beliefs as such, and *The True Religion is Civilisation*. For *The True Religion* to become established we would require the Common Purpose which would be a Humanity *united for the sake of the establishment of Civilisation*. Then people would do what they do best for the Common Good, thereby rendering devotional service, and thereby further freeing Humanity from the struggle for survival to which we are all so accustomed.

Thereby the Christ would begin to become *manifest from within* and the Human stage of our evolution, as we know it, will be over.

(6)    *St. Athanasius on the Incarnation*. Translated by "A Religious of C S M V". Published by Mowbray & Co., London, 1979.

# 4: Sacrifice & Redemption

## I

For various reasons, in the Ancient World there was a preoccupation with appeasing the gods. This had a lot to do with the uncertainty involved in connection with the forces of Nature. It was this fear which led people to indulge in sacrifice.

The sacrificial act was *not* an end in itself; it was to *ensure forgiveness*, thus restoring the favour of the gods in the hope that, in time, a *complete redemption* from the harshness of life, as it was experienced, would be realised. In the sacrificial act there was the hope, implicit in the act that it would eventually lead to a better world.

> The state of madness through which Humanity passed in the first stages of its existence has bequeathed to Man many errors. But of them all, sacrifice is the oldest, the worst and the most difficult to uproot. Primitive Man, whatever his race, thought that the way to quieten the unknown forces around him was to win their favour as one wins the favour of men, by *offering* them something. This was logical enough, for the gods whose favour he sought were malevolent and selfish. This appalling absurdity had become an act of subjection, with Man, as it were, the liege of the deity. (1)

We see then that primitive Humanity felt threatened by the gods. They in turn seemed to ask so much, for life was indeed precarious. No sacrifice seemed to be too great to offer, not even the sacrifice of *another Human being*. In the sacrificial act the offerer is seeking for forgiveness whereby sinfulness and unworthiness may be overlooked. Once again, this could not be seen as unreasonable, for the gods were deemed to have been entitled to everything that we have.

There are various theories in this respect. With sacrifice the offerer may be attempting to be reunited with the gods by appeasing their anger, the promiscuity of the offerer having been removed. In the eating of the sacrifice by the Priesthood, the god was believed to have been brought closer by means of the removal of barriers. In the immolation of the victim the unworthiness of the offerer is represented and, thereafter, it was believed that a fresh start was available to the offerer (2).

Sacrifice is the essential act of *external* worship. It is *the enactment of a prayer*, a symbolic action which expresses both the internal feelings of the offerer as well as the response of the god.

In Israel, as elsewhere, the principal act of the National Cult was *sacrifice*. Over the centuries, the sacrificial act had undergone a process of development, to the extent that the sacrificial act was subdivided into various categories, with different sacrifices to suit different depths of guilt or degrees of malpractice.

There were sacrifices such as holocausts, with the victim being consumed by fire, with the smoke, it was believed, *going up to God*. Nothing was left for the offerer. There were communion sacrifices as well as sacrifices of an expiatory nature, for sin and reparation. There were vegetable offerings and offerings of incense and, in the Temple, there was the Shewbread.

Some scholars believe that, in the earliest of times, the Human Race was not so concerned with, far less preoccupied with, sacrifice or ritual as was the case in later times. Initially, it was believed, the concern was *not* with *how* a sacrifice should be offered, but rather the prime concern was *to know the deity* to whom the sacrifice was offered.

This was probably the case in Israel down to *The Reforms of Josiah* in 621 BC, when a new period of history began for the Jews. The essential change was that all sacrifice had to be offered at the Temple in Jerusalem because of the *centralisation* of the National Cult. This was to preserve the Cult from unwanted outside influence. This was what was referred to as *The Deuteronomic School*.

With the exile to Babylon attitudes altered still further. The fear of loss of their identity led many Jews to become passionately concerned with ritual purity. It was at this time that Ezekiel introduced two sacrifices which were not mentioned in texts prior to this time. There was also the appearance of the Priestly Code, which contains all the texts relating to sacrificial worship. The ritual was given definite form in the days of Ezra, and this Code of Rites continued until the Fall of Jerusalem in 70 AD.

# II

A development of the sacrificial act can be clearly seen in the Old Testament. This corresponds to the fact that the faith of Israel did not appear *once upon a time* but, rather, developed and altered over a period of many centuries. The outline of the faith of Israel was shaped, to an incalculable extent, by the cultural background of the Ancient Near East.

There is evidence from the Old Testament that would seem to suggest that *Human sacrifice* was practised at one time within Israel. There is reference to this in *The Book of Joshua* (3). We can also read of how Abraham did not seem to be unwilling to put his son to death as a sacrifice to the god Yahweh (4). There is also the story of the foolish Jephthah who made a promise to Yahweh, the god of the Hebrews, which was not inconsistent with faith in Yahweh, according to Jephthah at least.

> If Thou wilt give the Ammonites
> Into my hand then whosoever comes forth from
> The doors of my house to meet me
> I will offer him up for a burnt offering. (5)

This sacrificial activity is based upon a plea for redemption and salvation, for in all forms of Religion, Humanity seeks to rise *above* Itself. Deliverance is sought from conditions in which, apart from redemption, life will be spent involved in the mundane and the commonplace.

The central theme of Christianity is the Doctrine of Redemption and Salvation, involving a special *interpretation* of *The Myth of Adam*. Initially Adam, who is a symbol for Humanity, which exists as the bridge between two worlds (6), is close to God, indeed in perfect union with God. When Adam leaves Paradise, he is turned out *as our Representative*, according to the narratives, so that when he *fell* we also *fell with him*.

When we bear in mind that the Bible is endeavouring to impart a *secret teaching* which would have been revealed only to *initiates* we can easily understand why there is considerable disagreement among contemporary scholars who are trying to interpret these narratives.

Some take the serpent as a symbol for the Satan, or the Devil, whereas Adam and Eve are viewed as historical characters. Some interpret *The Tree of the Knowledge of Good and Evil* as purely symbolic but, on the other hand, the driving out of the Garden of Eden was nonetheless real. Others would maintain that the narratives contain a picture wherein lies a Great Truth concerning the history of and the *purpose* of the Human Race.

The Biblical account of *The Fall* has parallels elsewhere and the Old Testament draws on them. An earlier source is *The Epic of Gilgamesh* which comes from a period of around 1500 years prior to Homer. *The Epic of Gilgamesh* depicts a tragedy whose main strand is the conflict between the desires of the gods and the aspirations of the Human Race. The gods are seen to possess both a benign and dangerous aspect to their nature and, as such, they had to be approached with the utmost care (7).

In *The Epic* there is a depressing vision of death and, in the vision, all the angels were demons. The vision also included lions with an assortment of monsters for company, such as the sphinx and the eagle griffin with Human hands and feet. With death, ordinary mortals go to the house, where they sit in darkness. There they eat clay and dust, sitting around like heavy moping birds, voiceless, with draggled feathers. In this condition, however, mortals are not alone for they have the companionship of *The Annunaki*, or *Great Ones*, who had been banished from Heaven by Shamash due to their misdeeds. In the Underworld, these *Annunaki* occupy a position somewhat similar to that of *The Titans* who, in a tale from another culture, had been banished from Heaven by Zeus.

In *The Epic of Gilgamesh* another strand of the story is also seen, for we see how Humanity has been deprived of *a true Humanity*, of the love of God and of Immortality. Parallels to this are to be clearly seen in the Old Testament.

The sins of Adam are passed on to his offspring, which is the entire Human Race, by means of procreation. Thus Adam is the prototype as well as the ultimate generator of Humanity. In the *Genesis* narratives the powers possessed by Humanity, like those of Adam, are tainted. The conditions for a correct relationship with God are sadly lacking.

The primitive Christian community believed that by means of Jesus Christ the calamitous *Fall* of Adam had been reversed, with Jesus Christ fulfilling the role of the Second Adam. It was believed that through the First Adam the Human Race had inherited death, with the subsequent loss of the *potential* for Immortality.

The Second Adam, as it happens, has *assumed* the substance and the powers of Humanity, by means of the principle of *Representation*, thus enabling Humanity to experience the eternal life which Adam now possesses and is able to impart. For the expiation to be effective there has to be an act of salvation and, in this, there is the need for *Incarnation*, something about which the New Testament speaks with clarity.

> Therefore as sin came into the world
> Through one man and death through sin
> So death spread to all men
> Because all men sinned. (8).

In another place the New Testament says,

> The first Adam became a living spirit
> The Last Adam became a life-giving spirit
> The First Adam was of the Earth, a man of dust
> The second man is from Heaven.
> Just as we have borne the image of the man of dust
> We shall also bear the image of the man of Heaven. (9)

Primitive Humanity could not easily have come to terms with the state of freedom which It *seemed* to experience. When we experience freedom or firstly become conscious of being *potentially* free, that is, possessing the ability to realise Destiny, we are gripped by the awareness of a situation which appears to be dangerous indeed.

We experience a double threat which is rooted in some sort of finite freedom and expressed in anxiety. In effect, we experience the anxiety *of losing ourselves* by *not* actualising our potential and, at the same time, the anxiety of losing ourselves *by* actualising our potential. With so many *inhibition* rules.

With this dread of the future we are trying to cling to the past, and we dig ourselves in to defend our position. This dread is actually a dread of God, that mysterious power which governs our lives. There are understandable aspects to this dread, for we are afraid of the uncertainty of the future.

This leads us to an unresponsiveness to the future, and anyone who is unwilling to *surrender* to what is *a mystery* will be controlled by dread, and this will result in clinging to wealth and position.

It has been ordained that we should live on a future basis. If we do otherwise we fall prey to the great fear of Nothingness and Death for we cannot bear to look into the void. Our vulnerability often forces us to cling frantically to what we can do to justify ourselves and in seeking to become accomplished. This is the great tragedy. It can lead to us misusing the created world and all because we are relying on our works to win the respect of others and the favour of God.

## NOTES

(1)  Roland de Vaux, *Ancient Israel; Its Life and Institutions*. Published by Darton, Longman & Todd in 1961. p. 436.

(2)  This sacrifice was not fundamental to *The Ancient Mysteries*. What we are talking about here is *Popular Religion*, the sort of Religion which is propagated by the State as a means of providing *a Cult* with which to unite people.

Sacrifice is barbaric from our point of view, but the sacrifices which are mentioned here are, no doubt, *an improvement* on what had existed prior to them.

(3)  *The Book of Joshua*, chapter 6: 26.

(4)  *The Book of Genesis*, chapter 22: 10.

(5)  *The Book of Judges*, chapter 11: 30.

(6)  The Bible, as well as other sacred books, is providing us with some sort of insight into *The Cosmic Drama*.

In this Drama, worlds are reproducing themselves, with Earth, our planet, producing the Human Race as we know It, being the outcome of the cross-fertilisation of the Earth with another world which, according to tradition, orbits *Sirius*. This is the message of the great Myths, such as the Myth relating to Osiris and Isis and the Myth relating to Orpheus and Euridice.

God is within *all of us* and, by means of the experience gained on many worlds, such as this one by means of Humanity, the Godhead is able to discover from experience what True Self-Expression is for God. This True Self-Expression *of* God is the same thing as True Self-Expression *for* God; ultimately this will correspond to the expression of Divine Predisposition, which is the Predisposition *of* God to *be* God.

Also fundamental to *The Ancient Mysteries* was the belief that within the Universe there was only *one* Person, and that is God.

(7)    There is the case of Ishtar, or Innanu in Sumerian, who was worshipped in the Temple at Uruk with Anu. As the Queen of Heaven she was the goddess of both love and war.

*The Cult of Jesus Christ*, in preaching *the atoning death of Christ*, was actually removing any ambiguity felt by the community in connection with the attitude of the gods towards Humanity.

This *atoning death of Christ* was, in effect, *the sacrifice to end all sacrifices* and therein it was proclaimed that all offence between God and Humanity had been *removed forever*. Full and free forgiveness was now readily available for Humanity. Sacrifice, or *the need* for sacrifice, *no longer existed* because of the life, death and subsequent resurrection of Jesus Christ.

(8)    *The Epistle of Paul to the Romans*, chapter 5: 12.

(9)    *The First Epistle of Paul to the Corinthians*, chapter 15: 45.

# 5: Religion Under Fire

## I

We live at a time of great transition for Humanity and this no more so than in the realms of Religion. The twentieth century, in particular, was to see the churches emptying more and more and, simultaneously, an ever-increasing amount of people armed with a preparedness to openly admit that they were either an agnostic or an atheist. Here it is our purpose to examine the main criticisms of Religion as it has been practised to date, and to ascertain whether these criticisms are a justification for believing that Religion, or a religious approach to life, is either unnecessary or outdated.

The criticisms can be grouped into various sections. There are the claims of certain atheists, for example, that the need for belief in God can be explained *psychologically*. Then there is the understandable urge to condemn churches who do not practise what they should be preaching, as this does nothing to encourage authentic belief. Others protest that Religion should be abandoned as it does not recognise Human Consciousness as *supreme*.

The dreadful extent of Human suffering prevents many from accepting any form of religious belief. Furthermore, an old-fashioned peddling of an outworn Biblical literalism has caused a great deal of misunderstanding, and tends to make serious Bible study appear to be uninteresting.

To atheists such as Ludwig Feuerbach, Religion was simply an illusion. The basis for this claim was that the individual who was religious had misunderstood the distinction between the individual Human being, so-called, and the Human Race *en masse*. Whereas the individual is apparently mortal and finite, the Human Race, on the other hand, appears to be Immortal and Infinite. When a religious man or woman finds himself or herself in the presence of an Omnipotent Being which is considered to be God, what is happening is that the believer is projecting Humanity into the skies by means of a process of *extrapolation*.

Emile Durkheim suggested that the gods worshipped by Humanity are *imaginary* beings. They are *unconsciously fabricated* by Society as instruments to control the individuals within the community. Durkheim felt that when a man or a woman considered that they were in the presence of a power which transcended their lives they were indeed in the presence of an Omnipotent Being *experienced as a greater environing Reality*. This Reality, however, is really nothing supernatural; in fact, it is no more than a fact of Society.

Sigmund Freud, the originator of psychoanalysis, had an interesting approach to Religion. He saw it as an attempt by the Human Race *to fulfil our deepest desires*. It was a *mental defence* against the more threatening aspects of Nature such as sickness, natural catastrophes and, inevitably, death.

These forces are remote and will remain so forever. When Religion faces them, however, it endeavours to transform them into mysterious *personal* forces.

The problems do not end there. Due to the harshness of Human existence, there has been the development of a curious situation whereby Human beings have been fashioned into *culprits*, for surely the Human Race is *the source* of the harshness of existence and the cause of all the pitfalls which have plagued us!

Traditionally, the Human Race was viewed as *fallen*. It is here that atheists point out that what has been projected into the skies is then, in turn, identified as something *alien* to ourselves.

Now on a global scale we are seeing the development of a turning away from a religious outlook which teaches Human beings that they are inherently sinful, worthless in and of themselves and unclean in the eyes of God. The Human Race need no longer see Itself as a loser and as a sufferer of the effects of an undesirable teaching which stated that the Human Race was actually *guilty of being Human*.

Man now holds his human nature as an alien one; he is alienated from himself. Through belief in God he denies the greatness of his own human nature. If Man, therefore, is to find himself, he must once more recognise that what he has ascribed to an alien divine existence is, in fact, Man's own fullness of being. Along these same lines Nietzsche, Nicolai Hartmann and Jean-Paul Sartre have demanded that we leave every thought of God behind for the sake of the liberty of Man; human nature being irreconcilable with belief in God. (1)

# II

None of the preceding points of view could truly be described as completely outrageous. Each has a point to make and should be viewed from *a positive perspective*. In fact, we could learn a great deal from such claims, particularly when we bear in mind that a great deal of religious activity in the past ended in apostasy. Then, of course, there is the fact that Religion is impregnated by an outworn *Mythological* view of the world and of our existence. This has made a lot of it out of touch with Science and, for many, no more than a dead letter.

Example after example could be cited of churches which, while posing as authentically Christian, have behaved shamefully and acted contrary to what one might have expected from authentic Christianity.

Churches have not always stood their ground against injustice and slavery. Some actually *encouraged* it, probably not wanting to offend the flock that paid for the upkeep of the ecclesiastical organisation. Even in Europe prior to the Second World War most churchmen and women remained silent while the Nazis were gaining power. Many Jews, for example, were shocked by the fact that, in general, churchmen and women were *not* convinced that the Nazi attack on the Jewish community was *wrong*, in and of itself (2).

Most churchmen and women would prefer to preach about the heroism of the martyrs of the past, *rather than becoming martyrs themselves*. This is quite understandable. For most of us the important thing is to remain alive, and we are not prepared to go beyond a point which will place us in danger, even although we are crucially aware that we are being completely hypocriti-cal about the whole thing.

In this clergymen and women are *no* different from others, as the will to survive is common to all creatures at all times. When science was gaining strength to the detriment of the Church, the lives of many people were put at risk.

> Galileo who held a certain scientific truth to be of great impor-tance abjured it with the greatest of ease as soon as it endan-gered his life. In a sense he did right. That truth was not worth the stake. (3)

Many atheists and agnostics, especially in the earlier parts of the twentieth century, grew up living under a tyranny which was upheld by the National Church of that country. Their distrust of Religion, *albeit an inauthentic form* of Religion at that, can be understood. In the face of such injustice, Religion could just possibly be seen as a worthless mysticism, unable to offer even the smallest crumb of comfort to those who saw the world as being on the way to complete destruction.

Today the greatest barrier to Religion and to the religious approach to life, for many people, is this question of *evil*, for the depth and extent of Human suffering makes the notion of a loving God and caring Creator ridiculous for many. At this point in time there will be no great advancement in this con-nection in the short term. This means that this problem of the unaccepta-ble extent of Human suffering is one of the greatest tests of faith. Then there are other considerations. There is the violence inflicted upon the animals and there is the insane destruction of the environment.

The authors of the Biblical narratives were faced with a similar problem. However, from their point of view it would be *contradictory, even blasphemous,* to suggest that a loving God would have deliberately put the Human Race into such a world for, as we see from the Biblical narratives, *a Perfect God cre-ates perfect worlds* was their response.

It is for this reason that a *culprit* had to be found. The Human Race and the serpent took the blame. This gave rise to the belief that this present world was *not* the creation of God. This is not an acceptable answer in these days, however, especially when we can envisage the possibility of a global Human Civilisation where poverty and ignorance have been eradicated and *evolution is able to take yet another quantum leap.*

It was against such a background of oppression that Karl Marx sought to strike back. Experience in life had provided Marx with the stimulus to develop *a Materialist-Atheistic Tradition* which used the figure of Prometheus as the Archetype.

The use of Prometheus provided a pattern of *defiance of the gods*, this figure having stolen fire from Heaven in order to use it on Earth in the interests of Human culture. Marx thus developed a Creed whereby he hated the gods who repaid the Human Race in evil for the good that they had done on Earth. The figure of Prometheus was opposed to *all* the gods in Heaven and on Earth who *failed* to recognise Human Consciousness as *supreme*. No such God should be permitted to stand in the way of the Human Race. Such was the polemic of Marx.

The god of an outworn religious point of view may indeed be a threat and a barrier to progress but that need not, in any way, *equate the focal point of such a Creed with God*, in the true sense. Besides, some actually maintained that Marx was, in fact, formulating a New Religion. There were those who had actually *unconsciously fashioned it into a form of Religion*, with the Communist Party and the State as the focus of the Creed, with the founder a pseudo-messiah with his disciples.

One such communist had very devotional recollections of the funeral of Lenin.

> Our hearts flew up to the Communist Heaven, to Lenin. For Lenin is surely sitting up there. He has become the great Father, who from Heaven guides the Earth, which is indeed the function of the Heavenly Father. Lenin is glorified. Below, on Earth, everything that he has said or written is being collected; the Newest Testament is being written. (4)

In our journey towards a global Human Civilisation which will exist to create the circumstances for that which has reached the *Human* stage of Its evolution to evolve *still further* in accordance with Its predisposition, many errors have been made, but nonetheless, our history is characterised by *progress*. We have been *guided* this far and that guidance must continue; indeed this guidance which we receive is actually *interaction with the Divine*.

For millennia we have been struggling to put poverty and ignorance behind us. In time, these problems will have been eradicated but evolution will continue; our developing *self-knowledge* will give us greater ability to *interpret* our existences.

*What we require now is further revelation.* We still have to ask ourselves why such an arduous uphill struggle was so necessary. It is possible to understand this a little better by referring to the Biblical narratives.

The Bible teaches that at the root and origin of the Universe, which is so vast, and in relation to which we appear to be infinitesimally small, there abides a Conscious Spirit *who* wills and knows everything. The Human Race has been the chief work of this Conscious Spirit, for whose sake the planet Earth was brought into existence. Creation was not complete until the arrival of Humanity for, by means of Humanity, the Cosmos becomes Self-Conscious.

In *The Book of Genesis* we see the creation of the heavens and the Earth. At the end of *The Book of Revelation* we see the creation of a *new* heaven and a *new* Earth. We see a people who were once in bondage journeying across a wilderness in confusion. Yet the story does not end there for they were on their way to the Promised Land.

These people were at the mercy of the elements as well as other considerations. There was the plea for a Messiah, a righteous king who would establish the Kingdom of God, which is Theocracy, on Earth, thereby installing peace and justice. Christians believe that this was the task of Jesus of Nazareth and that, after his return from Heaven, the Kingdom would be established by him, with Jesus of Nazareth ruling on behalf of God, *as God*.

Yet still we have to ask ourselves a very important question. To what extent is the Bible of relevance to us today? There are certain things that we should bear in mind, for there are parallels between Christianity and other religious outlooks, particularly the struggle between two Cosmic forces. The Human Race is depicted as having progressed amidst the struggle between the Powers of Light and the Powers of Darkness, with the winner taking all.

In the New Testament, Jesus Christ is depicted as entering into battle against the forces of the Arch-enemy of God, having been sent into the world *for that specific purpose*. This, of course, highlights the mythical element of the New Testament which, if not recognised, can make it difficult for the text to speak to us, especially if an uncompromising literalism is employed.

There are many problems concerning Jesus himself. We should never lose sight of the fact that this Jesus of the New Testament lived almost 2000 years ago, assuming that he is actually *an historical character*. Thus there are problems about the beliefs which Jesus actually held.

From our point of view, if Jesus is God and *God in the Christian sense of the word*, then Jesus could not possibly have had false beliefs. Perhaps the most important question facing the Christian community over the next decade or so is: is Christianity flexible enough to allow that the Son of God could either have had *false beliefs* or even have been *mistaken*?

In the case of Feuerbach, his criticisms of Religion are centred on the belief that God cannot be authentically referred to in *anthropological* terms, that is, *Human* writ large. Yet this in no way dispenses with the possibility of the Human Race having a Creator. In the case of Durkheim, his criticisms stand or fall on that aspect of Religion which was completely *national* in outlook, where Religion and Patriotism are one and the same. This approach is not so nearly relevant today, as there is a growing awareness that Religion is only authentic if it seeks to unite *all* Humanity in a Kingdom of God, which is Theocracy. We bear in mind that *no* nation has a monopoly on God.

The arguments of Freud were more a criticism of *superstition*, which would have had a lot to do with Religion and religious rites in former times. Now, with education and the Age of Science we are better able to understand the world and ourselves. Now that we need not be at the mercy of the Elements, as we once were in the West even as recently as the earlier parts of the twentieth century, the outlook of Freud has lost a great deal of relevance.

This is not to suggest that life in the future will be problem-free; there will be a tribulation to undergo as we enter the New Age and guidance will be necessary for the Human Race.

In the past, when a religious community called out to God for deliverance from harshness and suffering, they knew it was possible that they might not receive an answer. If this actually happened then it was concluded that something was *amiss*, and the community looked for some sort of sacrifice for the purpose of expressing penitence. Watching this, the atheist would have been greatly angered and thought that the reason why this produced no results was that the community was deluded because there was *no* God such as the community believed in.

We are only now beginning to understand the significance of our existences and what it actually means to be *Human*. The Human Race is the outcome of millions of years of experience, whereby that which used to live in the oceans was to take refuge in the undergrowth and then up trees, until such time as it was possible for the awakening of the innate knowledge of the Cosmos to progressively take place. The Human Race actually exists to create the circumstances *for this Awakening to take place*.

We need no longer think of ourselves as *fallen* or abandoned. We need never be ashamed of ourselves in the presence of God, who is actually *Omnipresent*. Despite all the difficulties of the situation, in spite of all the obstacles in our path, we have overcome. We have won a decisive victory and now the whole of Creation is at our feet. We now no longer have anything to prove to anyone. Now is the time to put down all our weapons. All our enemies have been defeated.

## NOTES

(1)   Wolfhart Pannenberg, *The Apostles Creed*.  Published by SCM Press in 1972. p. 18f.
       The relevant chapter is discussing *belief in God*.

(2)   A. Roy Eckhart, *Elder and Younger Brothers*. Published by Scribners, New York in 1967. p. 8.
       An account of the rise of Hitler is given with reference to the reaction of the various churches.

(3)   Albert Camus, *The Myth of Sisyphus*. Published by Penguin Classics in 1975. p. 11.

(4)   Hans Gerhard Koch, *The Abolition of God*.  Published by SCM Press in 1961. p. 137.
       A book about a Christian pastor in a Communist State.

# 6: Divine Providence

Is there such a thing as Divine Providence, and if there is, what is it? In this somewhat brief analysis we shall concern ourselves with the words ascribed to Jesus of Nazareth as found in the New Testament.

As we embark upon this study there are certain points which have to be borne in mind. It is easy to read all sorts of things into the words ascribed to Jesus by the writers of the New Testament narratives. Our analysis comprises a somewhat panoramic view of the beliefs of Jesus, and approaches the study from the angle that Jesus saw everything as being in relation to *an imminent end of the world* which he *seems* to have expected, with the coming of the Son of Man in power with the Angels of Heaven from beyond the clouds. This is why in reference to the Ascension in *The Acts of the Apostles*, chapter 1, the risen Christ rises up from the Earth and goes to the realms of light situated somewhere *out there*. For Jesus this was the goal of History, the consummation of the Ages, and lives were to be lived in accordance with this.

First of all there is a very important question we must ask: how does Jesus' attitude to Divine Providence hold water today, inasmuch as Human suffering, as well as the wanton destruction of the environment, are probably the two greatest barriers to the *acceptance of the belief* in the existence of an All-powerful, loving and merciful God who is *passionately concerned with our welfare?* Such is the same God Jesus proclaimed all those centuries ago.

In this connection the first thing to do is to define *Providence*. One scholar saw belief in Divine Providence as being the most fundamental part of a religious outlook.

It has been stated that faith in providence is religion itself, and again, that the denial of providence is the denial of all religion.

Providence is *not* seen as something quasi-philosophical but as,

A confidence that Man's personal life is the concern of a wisdom and power higher than his own. (1)

The scholar also saw the need to define Religion, although he claimed that there could be *false* religious experiences, but this is not our present concern. Religion arises from faith *as a response to revelation from God* and, if authentic, it flows from the heart of the believer. Faith in Providence, in other words, is another aspect of *the awareness of God as personal* which, as it would most definitely appear, lies at the root of *all* religious experience.

Providence, therefore, is the participation of God in the finite experiences undergone by the Human Race. Great care must be exercised here that we do not make the mistake of thinking of the *relationship* as being similar to that which exists between a manufacturer and a manufactured article. Providence is intimately involved with or linked with Creation; indeed it is true to say from the words of Jesus that Divine Providence is at the very heart of Creation.

God operates in such a way as to show that one is to *understand the relationship* as being between a Father and a Son. Such is the intimacy of the relationship as described by Jesus. It is a relationship which is upheld, governed and determined by God who, at no time, should be envisaged as *a mere spectator*.

It has generally been the case that, in theological works, the Doctrine of Creation is followed by an examination of Providence. This is due to the fact that God, the Creator, is normally deemed to be able to govern such affairs without difficulty.

By asserting Providence, therefore, one is in effect implying a belief in the *constant* creating and sustaining activity of God. In such a case, then, Creation has a goal or Destiny which is as yet *unreached*. Providence, then, is the involvement of God in a progression surely and steadfastly towards a richer and even fuller stage of life.

Karl Barth, one of the leading Christian theologians of the twentieth century, saw Creation as the place where *the glory of God would one day be made manifest*, with the Human Race as the guests of honour in the witnessing of such an event. Karl Barth had the belief that,

Creation was the external working of the Covenant, and the
Covenant as the internal working of Creation. (2)

Creation is the place where Providence is *experienced*, and this gives rise to yet
another question: does Divine Providence appear *as part of the natural order
of things*? Perhaps we could put it another way: would it be true to say that
although Divine Providence may exist, it can *only be recognised* through the
eyes of faith? Could it possibly manifest itself as an event which would have
*absolutely no significance* for someone else? Let us look at a passage from the
New Testament.

> Now as Jesus came into the district of Caesarea Philippi he
> asked his disciples,
>
> 'Who do men say the Son of Man is?'
>
> And they said, 'Some say John the Baptist, others say Elijah, and
> others say Jeremiah or one of the prophets.'
>
> He said to them, 'But who do you say that I am?'
>
> Simon Peter replied, 'You are the Christ, the Son of the Living
> God.'
>
> Jesus answered him, 'Blessed are you, Simon Bar-Jona, for flesh
> and blood has not revealed this to you but my Father in Heaven.'
> (3)

What it was that gave Peter this insight was not intellectual superiority but
*Divine Revelation*, in the narrative at least. This Providence is, therefore, *not
a speculative hypothesis* founded on a large-scale observation of History, for
Nature *offers no such evidence*. These things cannot be made the subject of scientific enquiry for belief in Divine Providence is founded *existentially*.

This existential or personal basis for belief in Providence prevents us from
regarding Human experience as being part of a mere mechanical process. It is
not even a matter for metaphysical speculation, but *solely an act of faith*.

Let us continue by looking at those Biblical narratives concerning Joseph,
the lad with the coat of many colours, to see if we can understand this a little

better. Joseph had been sold into slavery by his brothers who were jealous of him, but later on he was to perceive *the hand of God* in his enslavement.

> 'I am Joseph, your brother, whom you sold into Egypt. And now do not be distressed, or angry with yourselves, because you sold me here; for God sent me before you to preserve life.' (4)

Joseph was to realise, therefore, that there had been a Divine over-ruling, and that his training for the future had taken place *in gaol.*

How could such a reaction be possible? How could he have arrived at such a conclusion? What proof did he have of this? When he *interpreted* his existence *he had all the proof he needed*, and more besides.

For the sceptic, however, this belief which Joseph had in Divine Providence, particularly when Joseph was a slave and in a position of apparent hopelessness would have appeared as ridiculous.

At any rate it was against a background of intense sorrow and, no doubt for a time, hatred perhaps, with plans for escape and then revenge against his brothers, that Joseph *recognised* Providence. The faith which Joseph had, however, did not transport him to another place or another time. What it did was to enable him to see that although there was darkness all around there was, nonetheless, *light at the end of the tunnel.*

Providence gives us a vision of a Greater Reality *beyond time and sense*, as it were. This enables us to understand, although somewhat embryonically, that life has a purpose. Providence enables us to understand that the Godhead is concerned with us and there may indeed be a place for us, *at the end of the tunnel,* perhaps.

Our part *in this context* is to discipline ourselves and to find fulfilment through Co-operation with others in the overcoming of all obstacles in the way. Bit by bit, thereby, the Promised Land, which is the Kingdom of God, is beheld. Our present condition is seen as part of a preparation for the Absolute in terms of Consciousness, although as regards our development we are still at comparatively early stages.

Jesus Christ saw the Providence of God as being inextricably involved with the Revelation of God to the Human Race. By means of this Divine Providence we can come to a knowledge of God.

'Do not labour for the food which perishes but for the food which endures to eternal life, which the Son of Man will give to you for on Him has God set his seal.'

Then they said to him,

'What must we do to be doing the works of God?'

Jesus answered them,

'This is the work of God, that *you believe in Him whom God has sent.'* (5)

According to Jesus it was *the work of God* that people should recognise that it was he, *himself*, who was *the one sent by God*, and to understand thereby that God was bringing Covenant Promises to fruition. To Jesus, Providence was the supply by God to Humanity *of a Revelation* for that particular Age, indeed for a generation which Jesus *erroneously presumed* to be the very last before the end of the world.

Jesus had a polemic against anxiety. It was that first and foremost we should have a correct relationship with our Heavenly Father. In fact, this should be our priority in life. Jesus, however, makes no attempt to mask that there is a whole lot of suffering going on all around and that, as such, we must face life with resolve, but with the knowledge that life as we experience it is *not* an end in itself. To Jesus, authentic belief in God is also *the gift of God*, and it leads us along a path which takes us to the very goal of Creation. Here we need to recall that preoccupation with Creation is just as damaging as having to suffer hardships which, to Jesus, were the birthpangs of a New Age.

In *The Gospel according to Matthew*, chapter 24, we have from Jesus a warning about an impending tribulation which would herald the end of the Ages. For those of the community of faith there was to be *no* supernatural protection or deliverance from this, indeed many of the Christians would have died in that tribulation.

> Let him who is on the housetop not go down to take what is in
> the house; and let him who is in the field not turn back to take
> his mantle. But alas for those who are with child and for those
> who give suck in those days. Pray that your flight may not be in
> winter, or on the Sabbath.

Perhaps one might be excused for asking what all this has to do with Divine Providence. Could not a New Age have been ushered in, in a more humane way? There are other considerations: why did the world as we know it *not end* at the time of the tribulation which *Jesus predicted*? Is it not correct to say that the predictions of Jesus, the Apocalyptic Prophet, were soon found to be *false*? Why his prophecies about an imminent end of the world did not come to pass have been an embarrassment to the Christian community ever since.

We take heed of the fact, though, that not all the teachings of Jesus were Apocalyptic. To understand the message of Jesus we must strip away all time-conditioned elements. If truth always corresponds to the facts, then we should look at the message of Jesus, *not* from an Apocalyptic standpoint, but from the standpoint that life is to continue and that if there is to be a Golden Age, then it will be ushered in by means of some different method.

At the very heart of the Gospel we see the message from Jesus to all Humanity to seek the eternal, as well as the temporal, but with the eternal always having pre-eminence. The same approach is the answer to the mundane problems in life. From the words of Jesus, the Providence of God is experienced as *an assurance of ultimate deliverance from spiritual ignorance*, as opposed to *supernatural protection* from any shortage of provisions and the presence of danger.

Jesus saw Divine Providence as a pointer to the eternal purposes of God which, according to the Jewish tradition from which Jesus emerged, involved the resurrection of the dead, whereby all the injustices in life can be rectified. We are all aware, are we not, that entrance into life can *seem* to be haphazard? One can be born into a wealthy, caring and educated family, as well as being in sound health, physically attractive and intelligent.

For another, however, the reverse may be true in every case. We can detect the blessing of God in the first instance, but what of the second? This is why it is understandable that our present existences should be viewed *as a preparation* for another life where all the wrongs and unfairness can be rectified.

It appears, then, that the Jesus of the New Testament saw himself as the *embodiment* of Divine Providence. Here we see certain aspects woven closely together. Providence enables us to hear, or understand, the proclamation of the prophet. This is an encounter with the Living God and not merely the adoption of a particular life-style. This leads to an understanding of one's life and its significance. It leads to that Fundamental Transformation referred to as being *born again*, which is the *Awakening* of those powers within us which constitute *the next stage* in the process of our evolution.

The world of the Jesus of the New Testament is now utterly removed from us, yet still there is belief in Divine Providence. It still manifests Itself *as the proclamation of the prophet* to those who seek to understand by means of the prophet.

This proclamation of the prophet can be likened to a light which shines on the path which the Human Race is *pre-destined* as well as *predisposed* to walk. It permits the Human Race to understand Itself and Human Destiny in a clearer way, thereby empowering Humanity to overcome the trials in the long obstacle-course of life.

## NOTES

(1)  H. H. Farmer, *The World and God*. Published by Nisbet & Co. in 1935. p. 92.

(2)  Colin Brown, *Karl Barth & the Christian Message*. Published by Tyndale Press in 1967. p. 89.

(3)  *The Gospel According to Matthew*, chapter 16: 1.

(4)  *The Book of Genesis*, chapter 45: 4-5.

(5)  *The Gospel According to John*, chapter 16: 27f.

# 7: The Quest for Immortality

## I

When we read the pages of the Bible, whether the Old or the New Testaments, is there a message which the Bible consistently imparts? When we take into consideration the various strands of thought which come from the various stages in the development of the faith of Israel, is there an outlook which remains unaltered?

What is the belief which cements together the various layers of Biblical thought, which is found in all the books, and which *determined why the canon of scripture should be as it is*? There is an answer to these questions, and it is that the Human Race has an *inbuilt* or *innate* desire to become Immortal, this being due to the fact that Humanity has an *existential* awareness of having *the potential* to experience Immortality. This existential awareness is actually founded on *Predisposition*.

It is significant in no small way, this existential awareness of having the *potential* for Immortality. What is significant for Orthodox Theology today is that when we look at the various teachings from the Ancient World, passed down to us in *Mythological Form*, such as the Myth of Adam and Eve, we see that the purpose of these stories is to tell us, *in picture form*, how it was that a potential for Immortality was *lost*. A God-given potential had apparently been forfeited because of the wilful disobedience of Adam, meaning that we should become subject to death because *temporality was the outcome*.

As we consider this question relating to Immortality we must bear in mind that the Biblical narrators appear to have compiled their narratives from the standpoint of a *contrived* position. The misunderstanding which led to such a contrived position was due to their inability, in producing a popular Religion for the masses, to accept that a loving God would have *deliberately* put the Human Race into a world such as this one, where Humanity would have to struggle to progress and survive for many millennia.

These narrators, in order to preserve and maintain their belief in the *benevolence* of God while, at the same time, providing a tribal or National Cult with which to unite the population in a manner to which they could relate, compiled their narratives from the specific perspective that the Human Race lived in circumstances which had been brought about because of some sort of catastrophe. The conclusion was that we had brought disaster upon ourselves because of rebellion against God (1).

In the narratives we had become the culprits, with the harshness of Existence brought about because we had stepped out of line with God. We had been living under a curse, not only forcing us to struggle for survival, but we had to come to terms with the fact that our *potential* for Immortality had been forfeited. Thus in the *Genesis* narratives we see Adam, who *represents* the Human Race in this Mythological Saga, unable to approach *The Tree of Life* and hence *experience* Immortality.

*The Tree of Life* is by far the most important symbol in the Biblical narratives. The whole of Biblical Theology is concerned with being able to approach *The Tree of Life* afresh. All other themes are *subordinate* to this, because we know that from our perspective, and from the perspective of the Biblical narrators, the most important thing is Immortality.

Whether there is to be a Messiah or not, or whether He will establish the Kingdom of God on Earth, these things, important though they may be, are *not an end* in themselves, but act as *landmarks* in the evolution of Consciousness which will result in the Human Race being able to sample the fruit of *The Tree of Life* and experience Immortality.

According to the Myth of Adam and Eve, in the earliest of days the Human Race enjoyed a state of Innocence, until the *supposed* disobedience which resulted in *The Fall*. Thereafter the fruits of *The Tree of Life* were withheld. The former coveted position was now no longer available. The way to *The Tree of Life* was guarded by the Cherubim lest Humanity should partake of the fruit and become Immortal in a sinful condition.

In the past it was concluded that there could be no Immortality in surroundings characterised by such suffering, hardship and the awareness of a condition of *lostness* brought about by anxiety. In such conditions who would want to be Immortal?

Somehow or other, however, the belief that one day we would be able to approach afresh *The Tree of Life* always seemed to be able to persist. In *The Book of Revelation* there is a vision of the end of the world and *The Tree of Life* is there for all to see.

> Then he showed me the river of the water of life, bright as crystal, flowing from the throne of God and of the Lamb.
>
> Also on either side of the river *The Tree of Life* with its twelve kinds of fruit. (2)

So we see that the Ancients felt that the harsh conditions and historical circumstances of their temporal lives were the result of *disobedience* to God, inasmuch as Adam had been offered a choice and he behaved foolishly. The condition of the Human Race was symbolised by and depicted as *a refusal* of *The Tree of Life* with the unfortunate acceptance of the fruit of *The Tree of the Knowledge of Good and Evil*. Here a further clarification is necessary.

> For the Ancients the good was not just an idea; the good was what had good effect; as a result in this context 'good' and 'evil' should be understood more as what is 'beneficial' and what is 'salutary' on the one hand and 'detrimental' and 'damaging' on the other. So the serpent holds out less the prospect of an extension to the capacity for knowledge than the independence that enables Man to decide for himself what will help him or hinder him.
>
> This is something completely new in that as a result Man leaves the protection of divine providence. God has provided what was good for Man and had given him complete security. But now Man will go beyond this and decide for himself. The question in mind is probably whether the coveted autonomy might be the greatest burden of Man's life. (3)

In the description of the condition of the circumstances which the Human Race encountered in life, there is the symbolism of two Trees. There is *The Tree of the Knowledge of Good and Evil* which represented what had come to be considered as the *historical* circumstances of the Human Race. Then there was *The Tree of Life* which, nonetheless, was deemed to hold the key to Human Destiny.

Those of us who are alive at the dawn of a New Millennium can view Existence in a manner utterly alien to those narrators from the Ancient World, for we can, for example, envisage our lives as part of a future Global Civilisation where poverty and ignorance have been eradicated as far as possible; yet this future Global Civilisation is, nonetheless, one and the same as that Kingdom of God prophesied in the Sacred Literature from the Ancient World. We are, in fact, on the threshold of realising what has been *anticipated as possible* for the Human Race.

In what way is the Human search for Immortality to be seen in the Biblical narratives? What is the Old Testament if the belief that 'salvation is of the Jews' is undermined? And what of the New Testament if Jesus is anything other than 'the way, the truth and the life'?

# II

Jesus Christ saw himself as the *fulfilment* of what was proclaimed in former times. Furthermore, he saw himself as *the key to the regaining* of Immortality for the Human Race.

We should not lose sight of the fact that the narrators of these passages are *interpreting their existences*, not only for themselves as individuals, but on behalf of their nation, their community of faith, as a *chosen* people, separated from all the others, as instruments of the grace of God.

Every nation and every ethnic group has its own individual characteristics which, when written down, will provide a particular outlook within an historical setting. From this literature, or writings, there will be a scaling-down to get to the very heart of the message of the traditions of the people. This will involve the direction the community is travelling in relation to spiritual goals, that is, *how they envisage the unfolding of Human Destiny* and their role, as a nation, in that unfolding.

This is where the idea of the need for *a canon* appears, something which is considered to display the Mind of God and which claims to speak with authority *for* God, as opposed to mere Human beliefs and attitudes. Canon has *authority*, the word being derived from the Greek, the root implying a rod, a straight line, or some sort of instrument for measurement. Whatever problem the nation may encounter in the fulfilment of their commission as servants of God, the solution will be found in the canon.

The canon develops slowly rather than appearing *once upon a time*. The need for canon has its roots in crisis, a national crisis as it was in the case of the nation of Israel, and with the Christian community a crisis involving the need for a strategy to face the future, with all the Apostles either dead or dying and the return of Jesus Christ *no more than an unfulfilled promise*.

In the canon History is *re-interpreted* in such a way as to preserve the hopes and aspirations of the people until a new day has dawned. Then Destiny will be realised, and the nation in question would be vindicated as the servant of the Most High God.

In *the canon* there are certain tensions which are a reflection of the situation which the nation has experienced in its dealings with other nations. On the one hand, there is the plea for deliverance from temporal problems whilst on the other hand, there is a corresponding plea for the things of Eternity, as symbolised by *The Tree of Life*. These tensions colour the writings, but they do not exist in any other way than as *part* of the whole, as though they were pieces of a jigsaw puzzle.

In her entire history Israel played a relatively insignificant part in the development of the cultural setting of the Ancient Near East, from which Israel emerged. The cultural setting of the Ancient Near East is very much in vogue in the Old Testament.

The future of Israel always seemed to be balanced on a knife-edge. This led to increased tension within Israel, especially since the promise of an inheritance made to Abraham, and then the promise of a Davidic Dynasty without end, were yet unfulfilled. They were always on the horizon, always out of reach.

There was a tendency to look to the past for guidance for, in a sense, it was as though Israel had always been in the wilderness, for they were not masters in their own land. They believed that all that would change when the Messiah appeared.

By the time of the Jesus of the New Testament, the traditions of Israel had been greatly influenced by *The Apocalyptic Movement*. It was generally held that the world was soon to end, and for many there was no doubt about it.

Jesus of Nazareth goes as far as to predict that the end of the world would take place approximately *one* generation *after* his death and resurrection (4). Jesus of Nazareth says that there are many who had heard him preach who would not experience death, as they would witness the Kingdom of God being inaugurated before their very eyes. This same Jesus would enjoy playing the role of honour.

Even if those predictions had come to pass, *and they did not*, they would *not* have been an end in themselves; thus in The Book of Revelation we read:

> I am Alpha and Omega, the first and the last, the beginning and the end. Blessed are those who wash their robes, that they might have the right to the Tree of Life, and that they may enter the city by the gates.

# III

Let us return to this quest for Immortality. How do we interpret the Biblical narratives which, as we have seen, are based on *a false premise*, which is that Human existence *as we experience it*, was never actually intended by God and that we are, because of disobedience to God, living our lives under a curse whereby a once-cherished *potential* for Immortality has been removed?

All this talk of God has its source in an innate knowledge of God, experienced *existentially* as part of the way in which we understand things.

Admittedly, there is an approach from the side of Human existence, but this is essential for we can only truly speak with authority from that perspective, for it is our experience. This means then that, *in this context* Systematic Theology or Philosophical Theology is the art of *interpreting* the inner experiences, feelings or realisations of the Human Race in the light of Being, or God. This demands an attempt to define the relationship of the finiteness of our experiences with the Infinite which is God; thus in The Book of Genesis we read:

And the Lord commanded the man saying,
You may eat freely of every Tree in the garden;
But of the Tree of the Knowledge of Good and Evil
You may not eat, for in the day
You shall eat of it you shall die.

This is the basis for the supposition that life as we experience it is lived void of any *potential* for Immortality. Yet it is here that we have to disagree. This claim has as its foundation the belief that Humanity was created *once upon a time*, but this is not the case.

If the Human Race had appeared on the scene of Time with full Knowledge of the true extent of our Humanity and our potential then, even if expelled from the Garden of Eden, surely the Human Race would have possessed the expertise to enjoy a relatively sophisticated life. For one thing, the Age of Science would not have taken so long to appear.

The Biblical narrators made a grave error when they were formulating a theological outlook. Their foundation was a totally *false premise*, which was that the Human Race had been created perfect and went downhill thereafter (5). This does not correspond to the facts because for centuries we have been learning and storing Knowledge, none of which was known previously (6).

*The Tree of Life* is an Eternal Principle of which we are all the roots, bark, branches and fruit. This *Tree of Life* was germinated in the soil and left to grow. The difficulties It has had to overcome to develop roots in the soil are the lessons to be learned from the experience of the Cosmos, for the learning of the lessons permits *the perfection of Form* by means of evolution.

The Cosmos has provided *The Tree of Life* with the possibility to develop by means of interacting with experiences gained. The Cosmos gives rise to the possibility of Knowledge gained during the process of History which, according to Biblical literalism, was not intended by the Godhead.

This *Tree of the Knowledge of Good and Evil* has a particular role to fulfil, for *it is the temporality* which we experience as characteristic of our *present* existence here on Earth. It is the *conditioning* which makes mistakes possible, for one has to *learn from experience*, which is the true way to progress (7).

Yet this *Tree of Life* has within Itself the ability to recall Its Divine Origin and, because of this It will bear fruit which will exist forever and Its fruit will be for none other than the Godhead.

## NOTES

(1)   This must surely be an allusion to a great Civilisation, such as the legendary Atlantis, which is believed to have existed on the planet millennia ago.

Plato, the *greatest* philosopher of all, mentioned Atlantis in *The Timaeus* as well as in *The Critias*.

This would have been common knowledge among the esoteric circles of the Human populations, whom *Extraterrestrials* had been assisting. In this connection some reason would have been necessary to explain the struggle for existence as the outcome of the legendary *disappearance* of an Ancient Civilisation.

The decline of Civilisation and the return to barbarism could no doubt be adequately described as a *Fall*. Yet it may not have been abandonment as could be supposed from the narratives, which may or may not be giving a totally accurate picture in this *mythological representation*. The Extraterrestrials knew that the Human Race, which is a comparatively recent phenomenon, was not yet ready to be *assimilated* into a Galactic Confederation.

What that secret teaching was, and what was revealed to initiates within the primitive Christian community is not known.

(2)   *The Book of Revelation*, chapter 22: 1.

(3)   Gerhard von Rad, *Commentary on Genesis*. Published by SCM Press in 1972. *The Old Testament Library*. p. 89.

(4)   *The Gospel according to Matthew*, chapter 24: 36 is most explicit.

(5)   See the opening chapters of *The Book of Genesis*.

(6)   As the chapters unfold it will become clear to the reader that, according to our philosophical heritage, Knowledge *is* Recollection. Our Self-Discovery comes through *recognising* reminders. It is through experiencing our History that we are *empowered* to remember *who* we are.

(7)   Those Extraterrestrials who were referred to by our Ancestors as *gods*,
      would have created the circumstances which would have enabled the
      Human Race to have the ability to become civilised, should they be able
      to learn certain very important lessons. These higher powers are depicted
      as having the ability to *assume* Human form to communicate with us in
      a meaningful way.

# 8: Diabolical Temptation

## I

In our analyses so far we have looked to the Bible for guidance in our attempts to understand how a particular religious community understood itself all those centuries ago. It was part of a cultural setting which, as it happens, has influenced the Religions of the world, providing them with the same fundamental Mythology. This involved *assistance* from a higher world which communicates with our world to provide instruction to enable us to become more civilised.

Once we have actually read the Bible, or other sacred books, we must be satisfied that we understand what is being related to us. We must remember that there will inevitably be considerable differences in outlook between us today and those Ancients. We must realise that our understanding of Existence is radically different from that which is found in the popular Religion of Biblical literalism, for there are certain time-conditioned elements which have to be abandoned.

First of all, we have to be perfectly clear as to what it is that the Bible is actually saying to us. We realise that the Bible is the product of a community of faith, and is concerned with *how* the Human Race can recover *a lost potential* for Immortality, the losing of which spelt disaster both materially and spiritually.

Those Ancients who are responsible for the traditions which appear in the Bible, particularly the Old Testament, believed that the *regaining* of the potential for Immortality would be the eventual outcome of the process *symbolised* in the Biblical narratives as the Exodus from Egypt to the Promised Land.

In the earliest of times the Hebrews were nomads, wandering in the desert. For a part of their history they may have been slaves in Egypt. They had received a promise from God, however, that the outcome of their wanderings would be the Kingdom of God, a Theocracy where everything is done according to the will of God. This Kingdom would be a unity with the political setting such that it would permit the Human Race to create those circumstances which would render possible the sampling of the fruits of *The Tree of Life*.

But what disagreements do we have with the Bible? Let us try to be as precise as we possibly can. Our main disagreement is centred on the belief current in the Ancient World *in popular Religion at least* that the Human Race is *fallen* and that the Human Race, as It is, is not the creation which God desired, and that the world, as It is, is not the way that God created it.

We disagree with the notion that there needs to be some sort of atonement to make us acceptable to God. We also disagree that there is the need to *regain* Immortality for Immortality was never lost. *Immortality cannot be lost.* That which is immortal will always be immortal because that is its *nature*. We bear in mind that all this talk of being *fallen* is derived from a worldview formulated when the Human Race was engaged in a relentless struggle for survival.

How then do we interpret the Biblical narratives? First of all we have to take into consideration that Theology has *already* been undergoing various fundamental changes. We have to consider the Bible continually in order to re-assess it. This is something which has been done already during the twentieth century due to the approach of Rudolf Bultmann in particular.

> The forms in which the Gospel is presented must take account of the contemporary Man's understanding of his own existence. This is why he insisted on the need to 'demythologise' the Gospel. The Bible, he says, is written within the framework of an ancient and now incredible world-view; the three-storey Universe, supernatural beings coming to Earth from above and below. He wants to separate the positive content of the Gospel from the Mythical World-View, which is now an obstacle to the grasping of the real substance.

> Demythologising, he maintains, will not involve the rejection of
> the authority of the Bible as the Word of God, it is the only way
> in which it can be set free from outworn beliefs. (1)

During the twentieth century we became much more aware of other faiths, particularly those of the East. Do any of these other faiths have any real relevance for us? And what of Judaism? In general, Christians have paid only scant attention to why certain Jews would have found it impossible to have faith in Christ.

Yet the reason for this is very simple, for there was one specific point of departure between the Jew and the Christian, quite apart from the fact that *the predictions made by Jesus Christ* about the end of the world had been *totally discredited.*

The orthodox Jew, in considering the Christian faith by interpreting the inheritance of thought within Israel, would have concluded that the Christian faith was built upon *a false premise.* To the Jew, Jesus may or may not have been a great Teacher, but no more than that. To the Christian he was the Lord.

This alienation came to a head when it was proclaimed that Jesus had ascended to the throne of God to live there *as God*, and not simply as *one of the gods*, as had been claimed of others such as Herakles (Hercules), the Son of Zeus.

Yet this was not all there was to it for there was a much more fundamental dispute. The Christian faith seemed, *to the Jew,* to undermine the grace of God, the Jewish argument being based on the ability of any man or any woman to *return* to God.

> The Jewish doctrine holds that a man can at any time return to
> be accepted by God at any time. That is all. The simplicity of this
> idea is deceptive.

> The concept of return has been at the heart of Judaism, and it
> is for the sake of this idea that Jonah is read aloud on the high-
> est holy day of the year. But the theology of Paul in the New
> Testament is founded on the *implicit denial* of this doctrine, and
> so are the Roman Catholic, Greek Orthodox, Lutheran and
> Calvinist Churches.

Paul's elaborate language concerning the impossibility of salvation under the Torah and for the necessity of Christ's redemp-
tive death *presupposes* that God cannot simply forgive anyone
who returns.

If the doctrine of the return is true, Paul's theology collapses
and Christ died in vain. Nor does any need remain for baptism
and the Sacrament of Confession, or for the bread and the wine.
Man stands in a strict relationship to God and requires *no* medi-
ator. (2)

# II

In the New Testament narratives the Christian scribes depicted their own
plight as well as their hopes, using the figure of Jesus Christ most graphically.
Jesus Christ is a picture of the Human search for fulfilment and salvation, as
seen from the specific point of view of those narrators.

In the beginning Jesus Christ is with God, but *assumes* Human form in
order to undergo a process which was the fulfilment of a very important task.
After this had taken place he returns to God, taking up the position which
God had ordained for him.

This is all an expression of an innate awareness of Destiny, and of being,
when all is said and done, aware that a Divine Mission is being brought to fruition on Earth *by means of the Human Race.* This is at the heart of all Human
thought and activity and this belief in the Divine Mission is very important.

Nothing seems to have been able to alter this persuasion, and even in
the direst of circumstances this inbuilt awareness always proved to be a great
source of strength and comfort. In the face of hopelessness Humanity always
clung to this belief. This is a great attribute and displays that it is the question
of Destiny, or God, which is the most important for the Human Race.

The God of the New Testament is a vision of light *at the end of the tunnel.*
This God is all that is Perfect, depicted as male because the community was
Patriarchal. This is the God which the Human Race wants to serve and wor-
ship. The Human Race *belongs* to this God and the Human Race *knows* this.

In this picture we see a reflection of our deepest desires, for our visions are affected by our thirsting for the realisation of Destiny.

When we try to understand the appearance of life on Earth, and the subsequent beginnings of Civilisation, we have to bear in mind that our understanding is not yet complete; indeed it is still at early stages of development.

God is experienced existentially, *as part of the way in which we understand things*. Our Destiny, which is at the end of a long and arduous journey of overcoming, is presently out of reach, just like the God and Father of Jesus Christ, of whom we only ever appear to catch the merest of glimpses.

If in our arduous struggle through historical circumstances we discover that it was all ordained by God, with all our Human fallenness and lostness being part and parcel of it, and we still maintain that God is nonetheless Omnipotent and Benevolent, what do we do with the Devil?

Can an Omnipotent God have enemies? Is this Devil the awareness of a God who remains an *apparent spectator* while we struggle through an obstacle course? We have to complete this if we are to survive, with no assistance on the way, except by means of the prophet, who appears at crucial stages of development to provide us with guidance and to *ratify* the existential awareness that we have.

This awareness is fundamental to our nature. We possess Knowledge of everything we require for the *fulfilment of Destiny*. Our task is therefore about Recollection, about *remembering* our Divine Origin and Purpose.

The Devil is an enigmatic character, to say the very least, for he has been enshrouded in darkness and is hated, feared and referred to as evil. Yet this is no villain or heartless character at all, for this is *how* the Human Race has interpreted Its existence at a certain time and from a certain perspective. It stems from that part of our development when the Human Race was having to struggle for survival.

It was *ordained* that our progress here on Earth would *appear* to be unaided, apart from the gift of Prophecy. It is for this reason that some felt that we were standing under a curse. Humanity, or that which has *reached the Human stage* of Its evolution, has progressed in accordance with the ability of an Internal Principle which, in fact, is none other than *Predisposition*. We have the innate ability to be brilliant, and we are as such because of Divine Ordination (3).

And what of the foreseeable future? *The True Religion* will appear and this will express Itself initially as the desire for Civilisation and, thereafter, with Its sustaining. Each one will do what he or she does best *in service* to the whole. Humanity will be united by a Common Purpose which will facilitate the maintenance of Civilisation. The people of the Earth will eventually be *guided* by a Divine Priesthood.

This unity will free us from the struggle for survival and, with the release of the captives those powers which exist within us as a permanent endowment, by means of which the worlds were created, *will awaken to a new and higher level of realisation.* That which is now at the Human stage of development will take a quantum leap and evolve still further.

We need not concern ourselves with looking to the past for a Golden Age. We need not pray for some sort of reconciliation which is now known to be unnecessary, for nothing has been withheld from us.

What we presently await is the appearance *from within us* of a new level of awareness and understanding. We shall discover new depths to our being and, when the time has fully arrived, the Knowledge latent within us will burst forth into full bloom.

## NOTES

(1)  Alec A. Vidler, *The Church in an Age of Revolution.* Published by Pelican Books in 1961. p. 222.

(2)  Martin Buber, *I and Thou.* Translated by Walter Kaufmann. Published by T & T Clark, Edinburgh in 1970. p. 37.

(3)  As within the Cosmos there is *only one Person,* who is God, who is everything, then all our experiences are to be understood within the context of Self-Discovery for God, and *realised* by means of True Self-Expression for God.

Thus the arrival of the Common Purpose on Earth for Humanity is a stage in the appearance of the Common Purpose for the Cosmos. The Common Purpose on Earth, a Human Theocracy, will be the Common Purpose of the planet.

In achieving this level of Civilisation the powers of the planet, *animated as Humanity,* will be able to raise themselves to a higher level of Realisation.

Initially it was our Ultimate Ancestor, who is God, who began the process of Self-Discovery. The Godhead, being the only existence there is, had to discover the means of reproducing Itself *as a Collective Consciousness.* This was the only way in which the Ultimate Ancestor could relate to Itself, as It and *only* It actually exists.

For this to be possible an environment had to be created, and this is why the Cosmos exists. This is the good end of a process which is referred to as the growth of complexity in Nature. This process has its origin in the Predisposition of the Original Godhead to *be* or to *become* God. This process is only possible because the Godhead is actually *predisposed*.

With this in mind the Reproduction of the Human Race and Its continued evolution is a very important stage on the way *to the appearance of Heaven.* The Predisposition to be God is possible by means of the Human Race which is actually predisposed to create the Divine Identity.

This Predisposition has brought us this far but, with the Human Race having been endowed with Reason, it is our task to create the circumstances for the process of evolution to continue, which demands *Reason.* This will culminate in the creation of Heaven, the perfect environment for that which *Humanity will become* when the Predisposition to *be* God has been fully realised.

The next stage in Human Civilisation is to enter the Rational Stage of our evolution; as the Rational Stage grows in strength it will be at the expense of the Irrational Stage which will wither and die.

This will culminate in the creation of Heaven, the perfect environment for that which the Human Race will become.

# 9: Ancient Secrets Resurface

There has been a great deal of disquiet among us because of the rather chaotic condition of international politics, with the very real threat of annihilation having hovered over our heads like the lid of a coffin for so long. At a more grass roots level there is the fear of unemployment with the dreadful spectre of poverty in its wake.

Yet this disquiet goes much deeper than *mere politics* for it is integrally involved with how we *see* ourselves, for we have to come to terms with the fact that life can never be the same again. This process of the *disappearance of work* will continually increase as the New Millennium develops. What we have to come to terms with is that life has been changed *forever* and that, in spite of our ever-increasing ease of survival brought about by Science and Technology, our search for understanding is not yet over and that, to a considerable extent, we are still in the dark.

When we consider the evolutionary path which our Race has travelled we can easily see why there has always been the contention that there is an element of mystery in life, which is believed to have begun on Earth around 3000 million years ago. The very first organisms able to evolve are likely to have differed from those organisms which presently exist, and it is possible that those earliest systems may have been crystals of clay.

The process of evolution *has not been linear*; at one point in time a species of fish migrated landwards to improve its chances of survival. It was to live in the undergrowth before taking to the comparative security of the trees. Around 17 million years ago it was *manifesting* itself as *Sivapithecus*, but there were developments from there and, in due course *Australopithecus afarensis*, for example, evolved into *Homo erectus*, the first hominids to control fire, who migrated from Africa one million years ago. The most recent development has been the appearance of *Homo sapiens sapiens*, of whom skeletal remains are to be found from the last Ice Age onwards. This is the Human Race, the *form presently attained.* This will eventually be abandoned for something much more appropriate, whatever that may be.

Five thousand years before the Christian Era the Zagros Hills and the Tigris Valley were inhabited by Neolithic farmers and cattle-breeders living in villages of pressed mud, using Stone-Age tools and practising Stone-Age Magick and living in social groups the size of clans. Two thousand years after this, however, the scene has altered dramatically. *History has dawned.* Civilisation has appeared in Egypt and, in Mesopotamia, the Empire of Sargon of Akkad has been established.

Society is now complex and highly organised. Geographical areas are divided into separate States centred on large towns or cities. Agriculture is based on irrigation and produces a surplus of food to maintain civil servants, scribes and specialised priests. Art in the form of Architecture, Sculpture and Metal Work has achieved excellence. Religion pervades every aspect of life and, as was the case in Egypt, in Mesopotamia, Sumerians and Semites alike worship the same gods. Religion greatly influences public and private life, modelling institutions and providing inspiration in realms such as Literature.

Egyptian and Sumerian society crystallised around the Temple on a Theocratic basis. The land was deemed to be the property of the gods and the crowned heads, at the end of the day, were only the humble servants of the gods.

Religion was home to an awesome pantheon of deities, with Divine society organised as a replica of Human society and, as happens within Human communities, the gods were not all of equal status. Some wielded great power whilst others were mere supervisors of the plough or the pick-axe.

The real power lay with a trinity of *male* deities. *An*, the Principal Deity, was 'the overpowering personality of the sky'. With the passage of time *An* had tended to become more remote and was represented by *Enlil* who, as the second Principal Deity within Sumerian society, was worshipped as the Creator of the Earth. He had been responsible for separating it from the sky.

Subordinate to *Enlil* was *Enki*, 'the god of sweet waters' and hence life. He was to perform a mediatorial role, being also the god of Intelligence and Wisdom, who possesses 'a deceptive mobility and a treacherous charm'. He was also 'the broad-eared one who knows all who have a name'. *Enki* is the originator of Arts and Crafts, of Literature and Magick.

Such a world is alien to us. Since that time many Empires have come and gone. At the same time other great figures, philosophers and religious teachers have emerged to *reinterpret the fundamental Mythology* which was accepted unquestionably as true by previous generations. These teachers considered themselves to be recipients of Divine Revelation, and this simply as part of a growing spiritual awareness which is now recognised as having existed *even in the days of the Neanderthals*.

The earliest known belief system which still has any remnants, and these within cultures which are basically illiterate is *Shamanism*, whose traces are still to be found in Siberia, parts of Africa and Greenland.

Each primitive culture would have had a priest and a medicine man. They would also have had a *Shaman*, who was able to communicate with the dead and their world, and who was imbued with an authority to speak on all occult matters. To them, as with all pre-literate societies, the world in which we live had an invisible dimension to it, with the world best symbolised by a triangle.

Shamanism was probably superseded by *Druidism*, whereby it was the belief that life was governed by one single *internal* principle. It is with the Druids that we have specific mention of a *Suprahistorical Person* referred to by them as *The Messenger of the gods*, who had *assumed* Human form.

Those who are united with him are able to enter into Life and Light. The Druids, according to legend, were to influence Hermetism, which was the Higher Religion of the Hellenistic (Greek) world, into which Socrates and Plato, among others, had been *initiated*.

The world of today still vibrates with the power of Greek thought, and it is impossible to understand modern thought without some research into its origin and development. Yet we have to bear in mind that there was an Esoteric Tradition, *an inner teaching*, which was kept safe behind a veil of secrecy and available only to initiates.

Greek philosophers possessed remarkable insight, so much so in fact, that their beliefs are of relevance to us today. Greek philosophers were moved by a sense of wonder at what was perceived. They, like us, were no longer satisfied with a Mythological explanation about the world and about life and death. They wanted something which was much more *rational*. In the West as in the East, Esoteric Schools appeared, *teaching in secret*.

In the East the Buddha, also known as Sidartha Gautama, was born in 563 BC in what is now Nepal. From writings and oral traditions handed down we know that the Buddha stated that there had already been certain stages of development and that, in time, the Human Race would enter a Fifth Round.

The Buddha, we are told, attained the level of *Nirvana*, or Enlightenment, his body radiating with an unearthly beauty. He implied that with the arrival of *The Fifth Round*, the memory records of all past existences, presently latent within the subconscious would then become active.

At this time, he was to imply still further, Humanity would not have to contend with mere belief or faith, but that the Human Race would *know Itself*, by possessing Knowledge. This is also taught by *The Ancient Mysteries of Egypt and Greece*, with this being part of *a natural process of evolution*.

In the West, development was characterised by adamancy concerning *the supremacy of Mind*. The Cosmos was viewed by means of the analogy of Work and Art, and *no* work of Art can become a reality until it has taken shape *within the mind of the artist*. Ultimate Reality, accordingly, must be an *Archetypal Pattern* or Image in the mind of the artist, which in this case is God.

Greek philosophy continued to develop and there appeared a plethora of Esoteric Schools but, to a certain extent this only led to confusion because many of the theories were conflicting (1).

Socrates was a landmark in the development of Greek philosophy and in the thought of the entire Human Race. He turned from Natural Philosophy to the study of Humanity, Itself. It had become evident to him that Nature did not offer any readily available explanations as answers to the questions which plague the minds of philosophers.

He had gone to Delphi, where the Oracle had informed him that his actual task was to *know himself*, and this encouraged him to turn his gaze inwards, not necessarily to find the meaning of life, but to discover those norms which govern and define subjectivity.

He realised that he would achieve nothing *until he knew himself*. In relation to this need for Self-Knowledge, all other considerations were comparatively irrelevant. He was to consider all conceptions, examining them for the sake of Truth. This was how he lived his life, a dedicated servant of the State, without official position, neither engaging himself in politics nor striving for honour.

Western thought reached new heights with Plato, born in Athens in 427 BC. He was the greatest disciple of Socrates. Plato taught that the greatest task of the Human Race, or that which now *appears as the Human Race* after a process of evolution which has lasted 3000 million years, is to climb from the world of Perception to the world of Ideas. These Ideas govern our thoughts but they need not be thought out by us. They present themselves to us in thought *as they are*. The things of Perception share in the Original Ideas and, accordingly, Perception is able to awaken Ideas held *before this life*.

Our striving towards Knowledge, or *Gnosis*, in the beholding of Ideas is, therefore, a liberating of oneself from the passions of the body which must be controlled. The highest Idea is the Idea of the Good, and all other Ideas are known through this one.

The soul which strives to know or behold this Idea in life will rejoice in the vision of It *after death* as it did *before union with the body*. Continued Existence and Immortality are, therefore, a part of each other and life *on Earth* is but a passing episode.

Plato also sought a remedy for those ills which persistently beset Society, although *not in politics* but in a practical philosophy, *as a Religion*. It was his lasting conviction that those ills would not cease until either rulers became philosophers or philosophers became rulers.

Plato, who in some dialogues puts his thoughts into the mouth of Socrates, stated that the Human Race had shared in *the portion of the gods*, and that in this Humanity was alone among creatures.

By means of their art Humanity had invented houses, clothes, shoes and bedding, and articulate speech with names. Initially they lived in scattered groups as there were no cities. They were at the mercy of the Elements and of wild beasts that continually devoured them. They were the weaker because they knew nothing of the Art of Politics. In time, they decided to protect themselves but because of a lack of political skill they injured one another and they were scattered again.

Plato goes on to say that Zeus (God), therefore, fearing the entire destruction of the Human Race, sent Hermes, *The Messenger of the gods*, to impart to Humanity the qualities of respect for others and a sense of Justice to bring order to our cities and create a bond of friendship and union.

At the end of the day what the Human Race sought was *Knowledge*, as the Buddha and Plato both maintained, although they both stipulated that this *Knowledge* could not be *taught*. How, then, could one come to possess such *Knowledge*?

Here Plato puts his thoughts into the mouth of Socrates to propound the theory of *Knowledge as Recollection* and in *The Meno* Plato states that,

This is bound up with the doctrine of certain religious teachers that the soul is immortal. It does not perish at death but
migrates elsewhere and in due course is born in another body.
In the course of its wanderings, both here and *in another world*
it has learned all there is to know, the more easily because the
whole of Nature is akin. In this life, therefore, it is possible, starting from something which we *consciously* know to be *reminded* of
all the rest of the Knowledge stored latent in our minds, and this
is the real nature of the process we call learning.

There was a resurgence of such Ancient Wisdom during a period approximately 500 years after the birth of Plato. An Esoteric School was established
in Alexandria, and it began to influence the known world during the first century of what we refer to as the Christian Era.

These teachings were to decline again, however; yet they were to re-
emerge with what we refer to as the Renaissance and, once again, the Human
Race regulated Its bearings by means of an *Esoteric Tradition* of which Plato
had been one of the major custodians.

That was 500 years ago, or thereabouts. It now looks as though we are
moving into a process of unprecedented transition, with our Race moving into
a New Age. This will be nothing short of a *Great Renaissance.*

This has a significance for us because this time *Knowledge may indeed
dawn,* and teachings will no longer have the importance attached to them as
in former days. More importantly, we may now be on the threshold of rising
to levels of Awareness which we are not yet capable of comprehending, and
this may mean the end of the *Human* stage of our evolution.

Powers presently *slumbering* within us, by means of which *the worlds were
created*, will have been aroused and, after that, things may never be the same
again.

## NOTES

(1)  With the development of Greek thought there were conflicting theo-
     ries. Philosophers were trying to ascertain Reality, which was synony-
     mous with *Meaning*.

The Eleatic School, led by Parmenides, who was born in 540 BC, considered
Change to be illusory and only that which was at rest is real but, to account

for the world of illusion Parmenides introduces the spiritual principle called Eros.

Heraclitus, born in 535 BC, advocated that the only thing constant is Change, thus identifying Reality with Change, which was considered to be controlled by Reason.

Next there were the Atomists who deemed that the only Reality was the mechanical force which sets material particles in motion.

Thereafter came the cosmologies such as that of Empedocles; the four Elements of Earth, Water, Fire and Air were set in motion by forces of love and strife.

Anaxagorus postulated the existence of Seeds which were purposefully controlled by Reason.

# 10: Christ as Hermes:
# The Great Magician

## I

During the first century of the Christian Era there was a great deal of spec-
ulation concerning the appearance of a Divine Messenger, known as *The
Messenger of the gods*, the Son of God, and referred to by the Greeks as *Hermes*.
This belief was widespread and *not* restricted to one particular culture.

This god, whose arrival among us was anticipated, was in fact the *same
Suprahistorical Person* who has appeared at crucial stages in the development
of Civilisation on this planet. It was in relation to him that the primitive
Christians tried to draw parallels when recording the Gospels, in an attempt
to depict Jesus of Nazareth as *The Messenger of the gods*.

The world was actually undergoing a process of spiritual development at
the time, leading to a much greater understanding of those most fundamental issues in life. It was at this time that the Christian faith was born; with the
primitive Christians persuaded that History had altered Its course for one
great and final time.

Most of us are familiar with the New Testament narratives depicting a
scene where Three Wise Men, for they were *Magicians*, had been searching the
heavens to ascertain where a very special baby would be born. This was a baby

boy who, when fully grown would provide the Human Race with Knowledge which would permit the Human Race, or that which has reached the Human stage of Its evolution, *to rise to even greater levels of Consciousness.*

Some certainly appear, from Esoteric Tradition, to have expected *The Messenger of the gods* to appear approximately 500 years after the birth of Plato, who was born in 427 BC, so the period centring on or around 70 AD may have a special significance for us. As it happens, this is around the time when the primitive Christians, as we see from the New Testament, expected the return of a *glorified Jesus,* as is evident from the Gospels.

Within a few decades, however, with the return of the Jesus of the New Testament no more than an *unfulfilled* promise, *The Cult of Jesus Christ* ceased to identify itself with Judaism, or be basically Jewish, and became a Gentile phenomenon.

With the Fall of Jerusalem in 70 AD and the *failure* of the Jesus of the New Testament to *return* to Earth to establish a supernatural Kingdom with the assurance of Justice for all, many would have to suffer that shattering experience of the loss of faith but, as it happens, there is good reason for assuming that a very special baby boy had been born *in Alexandria.*

A School of Philosophy was to be established there and its founder was, in time, to be hailed by his followers as *The Messenger of the gods*, deified as the god Thoth of the ibis beak, the Egyptian Hermes, *the same Suprahistorical Person* who has appeared amongst us at crucial stages in our development in order *to guide* Humanity. He was to bring philosophy to an unprecedented higher level (1).

Meanwhile, in the East, the Patriarch Ashvaghosha was committing to paper the essential teachings of Mahayana Buddhism, as prior to him the fundamentals were passed on *orally by initiates*, direct from the time of the Buddha.

It would appear that all over the planet those who were illumined were expecting to see the development of something which had been foretold and was very special. In this connection Ashvaghosha produced a quite remarkable treatise known as *The Awakening of Faith.*

Ashvaghosha taught that originally True Reality is only One, but the degrees of Ignorance are Infinite. As from True Reality one realises that there is *no objective world* and, accordingly, the various means of following and obeying this Reality arise *spontaneously*, without thought or action, by means of which Ignorance gradually disappears.

He also maintained that phenomena are originally in the Mind and that they have no real outward form, with the phenomena of the worlds of desire, form and non-form being Mind-produced. Without Mind there can be no objective existence. Existence is the result of false or imperfect ideas in the Mind. As such Mind and Matter are eternally the same. The essence of Matter is Wisdom, and the essence of Wisdom is Matter, being the *embodiment* of Wisdom.

This time in the middle of the first century of the Christian Era also saw something very important happening among the Celts. It is indeed possible that, at this time, the Druids, the spiritual hierarchy of the Celts, were disbanded. They may have known that *one greater than they* was now amongst us.

These revered Guardians of *The Celtic Mysteries* had proclaimed that only through the cycle of birth and death can we reach that *destined state of perfection* from which we are presently so far removed.

Although the Druids were literate, writing was restricted to use in the keeping of accounts and for inscriptions on coins. Their concept of History, Law and Knowledge was such that these things were considered to be sacred in origin and, if committed to writing, it could lead to possible devaluation and sacrilege. Their body of Knowledge was gathered bit by bit during their wanderings, containing the notion that the Ancient Scots were intimately related to the Pharaohs of Egypt.

In the Ancient World the Druids were far from unknown. They were the advisors of kings. They meditated on the nature and the size of the Cosmos. Many famous people met them, but they were to divulge almost nothing of their discussions.

Tradition has it that they instructed Pythagoras. Diodorus Siculus stated that they taught that the soul is immortal and that at an appointed time after death it enters another body. Julius Caesar cited their cardinal doctrine as *transmigration of the soul*, which was a supreme incentive to valour, eradicating the fear of death. Cicero mentioned that, in 60 BC, a young Druid named Davidiacus visited Rome and so great was his wisdom that the educated people who flocked to hear him fell upon his every word, proclaiming him to be *Plato re-incarnate*.

By the end of the nineteenth century, when Edward Dwelly set about compiling his *Scots Gaelic to English Dictionary*, he was to define the term *Druid* as 'A Magician. A Conjurer. A Philosopher'. Dwelly was then to refer to the Druidic Art as *Druidheachd*, maintaining that 'no direct native information is available in either Scotland or Ireland concerning Druidism, with the pre-eminent masters of the Druidic Art, *The Tuatha de Danann* only dimly remembered by Scottish Highlanders' (2).

# II

At this point in the first century AD, the groundwork was done to enable the remoulding of Greek thought, making it different from anything which preceded it, and this is best accounted for by the arrival of the Great Master, believed to have been none other than the Great Magician.

Some of the Hermetic Literature dates from this period of the first century AD and they were original Greek works. What was common to this body of literature is the attitude it exudes. It has no interest in speculative philosophy. It sought to justify the religious life, aiming to provide the Human Race with a very pure and spiritual philosophy which would bring Humanity to a knowledge of God.

'Learn this', they said. 'That within you which sees and hears is the Logos of the Lord. *The Mind is God.*'

To know God demands *Rebirth* and not just the adoption of a particular lifestyle. It was necessary to be *born in Mind*.

*The Messenger of the gods*, Hermes, was deemed to be equal to God and, being the express image of the Heavenly Father, *Hermes was very beautiful.* God is depicted as loving Hermes as his very own. Because of this God gave everything to Hermes to be its Guardian. Hermes was referred to as *Thrice Blessed,* or as *Hermes Trismegistus.*

The suggestion seems to be that Hermes is *Suprahistorical.* He is portrayed as the Ancestor of the Human Race. But is this only symbolism? This Divine Man who is of Divine Origin, and who is capable of redemption from the taint of Matter is, in essence, that which exists within all of us, or that which has reached the *Human* stage of Its evolution.

Hermes is depicted as having *assumed* Human form to *undergo a series of trials.* He has identified himself fully with that Collective Consciousness which has reached the Human stage at this level of Absolute Consciousness. He is seen as an overcomer as though he is overcoming himself. Somehow or other he does this not for himself but for the Human Race.

We are, thereby, enabled to become *as* Hermes, as a Collective Consciousness. The Ultimate Goal is to create Heaven so that the Absolute may experience Its Absoluteness in terms of Consciousness. This is the Heavenly Vision which is pursued by Hermes.

Hermes may have been intended for this and only this. Those who compiled the tractates, being no doubt disposed to taking their Platonism seriously, would have believed in Eternal Archetypes. In this connection Hermes is the Platonic equivalent of *the Idea of Humanity*. He is portrayed as the light of the world and he is able to impart life to Human beings. After his passion he is able to return to his home among the Stars. This is Hermes, *The Messenger of the gods*.

While here on Earth Hermes had undertaken to lead his own sons to Enlightenment. Hermes had been talking to Tat about spiritual things. Tat starts to relate to Hermes about difficulties he had been undergoing. This had led to considerable frustration and discouragement due to what Tat considers to be a lack of progress. Hermes tries to reassure Tat. He reminds him that 'this kind of thing cannot be taught, but that God brings it to Mind when God wills'.

Tat is still dissatisfied and continues to plead for guidance. Hermes then makes another reply.

> I have nothing to say but this: seeing in myself that *an Uncreated Vision* has come to pass by the mercy of God, I have passed out of myself into an Immortal body, and I am no longer what I formerly was, but have been *born in Mind*.

Hermes goes on to say that the body of colour and touch and sense is *not* the True Self. Tat must pass *out of himself* like people who dream in sleep but without sleeping (3).

The fact that the Great Magician is referred to as *Thrice Blessed* is very significant. As handed down by the Wise Men of the East, *The Manu Laws* state that,

> He, whose firm understanding obtains a command over his words, a command over his thoughts, and a command over his whole body may justly be called a Triple Commander. The man who exerts this triple self-command with respect to all animated creatures, wholly subduing both lust and wrath, shall by those means attain Beatitude.

Such a person will have dominion over Matter and, in effect, will be the Lord of Nature, the Ruler by Divine Right, Universal Emperor, God and Creator.

Something similar to this must have occurred during the life of the Buddha. When the Mind has achieved a state of balance, a state of peace and harmony due to the counteracting, by means of a change of attitude of the effects of previous actions, the karmic effect *crystallised* in bodily form may still oscillate for a long time. Then complete harmonisation takes place, producing the form of bodily perfection.

Authorities state that this can lead to a *spiritualisation*, indeed to a *transfiguration* of the body. This is reported to have happened to certain great masters. It also happened with the Buddha whose body, as legend states, was of such unearthly radiance and beauty that the golden robes then offered to him, when placed against his skin, lost their lustre.

Belief in *The Messenger of the gods* has been baptised into all cultures to provide the basis for religious belief as we know it. All our major Religions tell of the Representative of a higher world who has come here to guide us.

By the time of the Greeks and then the Romans, the situation existed for the first time on Earth, leaving aside those legends concerning Lemuria and Atlantis, whereby there was a cross-fertilisation of cultures on a scale which was without precedent.

In Alexandria Mystics were to gather from all over the known world, to such an extent that Alexandria was to become like a gigantic philosophical reservoir. Zoroastrians, Chinese Buddhists, Hindus, the Druids of the Celtic world, Jewish Kabbalists, the beliefs from Black Africa, as well as a plethora of Mystery Cults, were to meet face to face.

The result was the realisation that they were all talking about the same thing. There arose among people the keen desire to discover what is *The True Religion*. Many perceived this to involve a very Ancient Secret about the Human Race and *why* the Human Race exists. It did not end there, as for some strange reason there was a relationship with that Star which we refer to as *Sirius*.

What we have to understand is that when *The Christian Faith* was to reach out to the greater world outside Palestine, they were forced to come to terms with the fact that their message was *not* unique.

They realised that if their message was not portrayed in a particular form, then it would not be possible for the Gentiles and the Hellenised Jews to relate to it, and *The Cult of Jesus Christ* would have died in its infancy, as had countless other Cults.

It is for this reason that the Jesus of the New Testament, who is *not* an historical character as such, but an adaptation from quite a few traditions in order to provide the Roman Empire with a belief system to assist political unity, is portrayed *as* Hermes, *The Messenger of the gods.*

When the Christian faith began to lose ground in the land of its birth, because it was evident that the claims that the Jesus of the New Testament had made were *patently discredited*, they turned to the Gentile world as their mission field.

Here they were to contend with a dilemma: *how would they portray Jesus?* They alluded to Hermes, but their difficulties were not satisfactorily resolved until they used a blueprint of Socrates who, as was common knowledge, was considered to have been the wisest man to have lived in the Ancient World, with whom the Gentile masses could more readily identify.

Jesus, like Socrates, is depicted as one who is not intent upon looking for laws which would secure private rights, but for those which bind all of us to Society. The initial assumption here is the authority of Law *over* the rights of the individual. Socrates believed that the laws in operation demanded an unqualified acceptance, *even when wrongly applied.* Thus we see in the unjust condemnation of Jesus an unmistakable allusion to Socrates, with the mock trial and its thirty pieces of silver, and the acceptance of death when he could have escaped.

The death of Socrates, almost four centuries earlier, was accepted by Socrates as *compliance* with the belief in the authoritative character of the Law. In the Gospels, this is transformed into a Divine Messenger choosing to give his life as a ransom for many, and this in spite of the fact that he could have called upon the Angels of Heaven to rescue him, had Jesus so desired.

To understand the development of Greek thought we must seek further to understand what took place in Alexandria at that part of the first century AD. We can only attempt to summarise this from the writings of the philosopher known as Plotinus, who came into contact with this *Wisdom of the gods* from Alexandria.

Plotinus (203-262 AD), widely recognised to have been one of the greatest of the Greek philosophers, went to Alexandria at the age of twenty. In Alexandria he was instructed by one known as Ammonius Sakkas, a porter of bales at one time as his name implies who, although humbly born managed to receive an education and, in time, founded his own School of Philosophy.

As for Plotinus we know almost nothing, except that Sakkas was his tutor. At all times he refused to divulge his true identity, or the identity of his parents, and was just as secretive about the place and time of his birth.

Yet we do know that he went to Alexandria, which was like a gigantic philosophical reservoir, a gathering-ground for teachings from East and West, with Greek philosophy existing side by side with Oriental Mysticism, the Teachings of the priests of Egypt, Jewish Kaballists, Gnostics, *The Cult of Jesus Christ*, the Druids and many many more.

Plotinus sought a more exalted approach to life. His teachings *differed* from those of his predecessors, including Plato and Aristotle, due to their Infinity and Inwardness.

Prior to Plotinus, the Greeks had regarded Infinity as imperfect. Greek thought had been directed towards the outside world, towards external things, even with Plato and Aristotle, both of whom sought *an explanation for material things*.

For Plotinus, however, only the *inner* experience of union was real and valid. He viewed the external world as a means to this end but also, at the same time, a constant threat.

At the very heart of the teachings of Plotinus there is the thought of God, which is the Good towards which *all striving tends*, and in which all things share. This idea of God is basically inexpressible, although words can be used to indicate God's being.

Thought appears with the World Mind (Nous) which emanates from God and which, somehow or other, is no longer One. Thought seeks to return to God but it is as though a differentiation has occurred.

The ideas present in the Mind are mental prefigurations of things. The World Soul (Psyche) emanates from the World Mind (Nous) and seeks to return there after considering the Ideas. Psyche has animated Matter and has produced a multiplicity of things which are Forms *depicting Ideas* while, at the same time guaranteeing the *unity* of all things.

In this process of *returning to the Beginning*, as it were, it is the task of the Human Race to lead the way. It is here, though, that Human beings discover that they are inwardly divided between the Material and the Mind. Some Human beings have become lost in material considerations, and are so absorbed in them that they are unable to find either energy or inclination for anything else. As such they are forgetful of their own deepest being. Humanity must learn to turn from Matter *as* Matter to uncover the idea *in* Matter.

By means of a process of evolution, to which the Cosmos has *subjected Itself,* It is trying to unite Its various tendencies in a higher union. This unity is what Greek philosophy has as its highest goal. This unity is *experienced* as the process of the *perfection of Form*, culminating in the Cosmos discovering, through experience, what actually is True Self-Expression for the Cosmos.

For the Greeks the constitutive principle of the Cosmos is *not* Matter but *Form*. Within the Universe there is the tendency for phenomena to go from one opposite to another. In this process the Cosmos discovers what True Self-Expression is *for* the Cosmos, and this *demands* Form. The various tendencies should be united on a higher level which is *beyond the need for Reproduction*, which is the Immortal state.

The Inner Teachings of the Greeks proclaimed that this unity was to be brought about on Earth by means of the Human Race. Once Humanity had attained Cosmic Consciousness, union would be possible *between worlds*.

We see, then, that *within* the Universe and *by means of* the Universe a quite fundamental Reproduction is taking place. This process of Reproduction has reached the *Human* stage of evolution, Ancient Authorities considering such the Final Act in the Divine Saga during which Reproduction is necessary.

# III

As mentioned, when the Christian apologists were attempting to portray Jesus of Nazareth as *The Messenger of the gods*, they were forced to draw on Socrates as a model, with whom the Gentiles could identify.

Thereby, they were identifying themselves with *The Ancient Mysteries*, Ancient Wisdom, an Esoteric Tradition which was kept from the eyes and ears of ordinary Humanity, of which they now considered themselves to be the prime custodians, for they had been witness to its latest revelation. What Socrates had been, Jesus would become!

Socrates had given his life willingly for philosophy after a mock trial, and in accordance with Greek philosophy would have accepted belief in the Immortality of the soul, with life following life until a level of perfection is attained.

In the resurrection of Jesus, which is designed to display Jesus as having *become Immortal*, we have the Christian sequel to the *spirit–body* which is able to return to be with God after separation from the entanglements experienced here. The New Testament informs us that Jesus ascended to the throne of God witnessed by his disciples (4).

In many ways it was a matter of what we consider to be the Truth, for we all see things differently. When with his disciples Jesus of Nazareth was adamant that he was 'the way, the truth and the life' and, as such, the *only* pathway to God (5).

When Jesus was to appear before Pontius Pilate, however, and here we are considering this from the perspective of a literal interpretation, it was a completely different story.

> Pilate entered the praetorium again and called Jesus, and said to him, 'Are you the King of the Jews?'
>
> Jesus answered, 'Do you say this of your own accord, or did others say it to you about me?'
>
> Pilate answered, 'Am I a Jew? Your own nation and the Chief Priests have handed you over to me; what have you done?'
>
> Jesus answered, 'My kingdom is not of this world; if my kingship were of this world, my servants would fight, that I might not be handed over to the Jews; but my kingship is not of this world.'
>
> Pilate said to him, 'So you are a king?'
>
> Jesus answered, 'You say that I am a king. For this I was born and for this I have come into the world, to bear witness to the truth. Everyone who is of the truth hears my voice.'
>
> Pilate said to him, 'What is truth?' (6)

The New Testament appears to be attempting to portray Pilate as being fundamentally ignorant, in spite of the power and prestige of his office, and the wealth and education to which, no doubt, he would have had access. Jesus' apparent ignorance of Greek philosophy and his poverty, however, become virtues.

Yet Pilate was no well-heeled barbarian for here he is asking a legitimate question, a question often on the lips of one schooled in Greek philosophy. To understand the real significance of this we must look a little closer at Greek thought.

In 399 BC a public action was brought against Socrates, accusing him of 'corrupting the minds of the young' and 'practising religious novelties' rather than 'worshipping the gods of the city'.

Socrates advised his accusers not to kill him, for if they did so 'no one would be found to take his place. It is literally true', he said, 'that God has appointed me to this city to rouse, reprove, persuade all of you, like a gadfly'.

He continued by repeating that they would not find another like him. He said,

> I suspect, however, that before long you will awaken from your drowsing, and in your annoyance you will finish me off with a single slap, and then you will go on sleeping till the end of your days, unless God in his care for you sends someone to take my place.

The Athenians convicted him and he was sentenced to death, yet even here he refused to compromise. He was offered an attempt to escape from prison before he drank hemlock, but he vehemently refused to overturn the laws of the land to his own advantage, or to either forsake philosophy or Athens. 'The difficulty,' he said, 'is not to escape death, but to escape doing wrong.'

What is this *truth* of which Pilate made mention? When Pilate asked this question of Jesus he received no reply, and we are left to consider the possibility of the answer being a *Messianic Secret*.

Yet it is nothing of the kind, because it was known as part of a series of questions and answers, and used by the students of philosophy in Alexandria, and mentioned later by Plotinus.

Q What does philosophy aim at?
A At Absolute Truth!

Q What kind of truth is that?
A Truth for *all* intelligence; a truth which any intellect is necessarily shut out from knowing is *not* an Absolute Truth.

Q  What is the truth for all intelligence?

A  *Unity!* The *oneness* of all things!

Q  How so?

A  Because while the *diversity* of things is addressed to that which is *peculiar* to each order of intellect, their *unity* can be taken up only by what is *common* to all orders of intellect. Unity is thus the object of philosophical enquiry inasmuch as it is the truth for all; in other words, the absolutely true.

Q  What is this unity?

A  Alexandrian philosophy is driven in upon the answer that *thought is the unity of the Universe,* hence the knowledge of Self, the thought of thought, the reflection of Reason upon Itself is inculcated by Plotinus as the highest duty, and the noblest source of Purification and Enlightenment.

## NOTES

(1)  These dates are tentative for it seems as though the Romans interfered with the chronology of the period. Assuming that there was an actual historical person called Jesus, who is introduced to us in the New Testament, then he would have been born sometime between 7 BC and 4 BC.

(2)  *Dwelly's Illustrated Gaelic to English Dictionary* or Faclair Gaidhlig gu Beurla le Dealbhan in Gaidhlig, usually spelt *Gaelic.* Published by Gairm Gaelic Publications, in Glasgow, Scotland.

(3)  Hermes also had a son called Asclepius (sometimes Asklepios).

(4)  *The Acts of the Apostles,* chapter 1: 11.

(5)  *The Gospel according to John,* chapter 14: 6.

(6)  *The Gospel according to John,* chapter 13: 33-38.

# 11: *Mind Stuff*

## I

The twentieth century saw many great advances, particularly in the realm of modern Physics. Men such as Einstein and Planck, to name but two, have forced us to radically alter our approach to understanding the nature of Reality. Using only mathematical symbols they placed all previously recognised conceptions of the Universe in a state of obsolescence.

Concerning the Universe certain points can now be considered as fundamental:

- space is curved;
- the Universe is *finite but unbounded*, in the form of a sphere;
- *The General Theory of Relativity* states that if we take a speck of Matter and accelerate it to the speed of light, it would acquire almost infinite energy. If it was possible for someone to sit on top of the speck, however, such an Observer would think that it had no energy at all;
- Mass and Energy are basically the same;
- Matter is comprised of waves and these are characterised by *possibility*;
- the Ultimate Unit of Reality is *Planck's Constant*, that is, the most fundamental property of the Universe is one electrical wave, consisting of one positive half-cycle and one negative half-cycle;

- the combination of these two half-cycles gives the foundation of *a binary information system*;
- the Universe is composed of *electricity* in the form of electrical wave patterns which are Data or *Memory*.

When we observe the Cosmos we see that it is expanding because, irrespective of the direction that our gaze takes us from our planet, we see other Galaxies receding from us. The more distant the Galaxy, the more rapid the acceleration in a direction away from a now bygone centre.

Using the most simple logic it is evident that were this process to be *reversed* we would witness the spectacle of a Cosmos growing smaller and smaller and becoming more and more dense until the point is reached, similar to what must have happened many millions of years ago, when all the Matter of the Universe existed at one infinitesimally small and dense point. This could be referred to as a *Singularity*.

This is a state of affairs which our Mathematics finds impossible to describe because when Matter is condensed to infinite densities, Time and Space are infinitely distorted and the Laws of Physics break down.

In spite of all the solid objects in and around us, before World War II a scientist named Sir Arthur Eddington felt compelled to propose that the Universe was *Mind Stuff*.

Initially this may appear as absurd and ridiculous to many. Certain developments in the fields of Molecular Biology and Electronic Computing, however, certainly appear to have given their support to this hypothesis of Eddington.

Molecular biologists, in analysing the basic building blocks of life, have no problem in considering them to be *Information Complexes*. It seems that there are distinct parallels between *The Laws of Chemistry* and the fundamentals of Electronic Computing. This is especially so as we seem *forced* to concede that the Universe is one gigantic process of Cosmic Radiations.

This is an analogy to which Westerners can easily relate as we are all accustomed to Man-made radiations such as television and radio. Like Cosmic radiations, these are a means of *Data Transmission*.

The assertion that the Cosmos might be *Mind Stuff* is really nothing new to the sages of the East. This is a truth made abundantly clear to those who have taken a closer look at the teachings of the Buddha.

A great deal of what he knew remained *secret*. What he did reveal was 'out of compassion for those whose eyes were hardly covered with dust'.

He taught in a specific way. He *avoided* questions concerning that Supramundane State of Realisation, or other problems going *beyond* the realms of the intellect. He concentrated all his energies on providing practical assistance for those who listened, corresponding to the capacity of the hearer to understand.

He taught that in order to find the Jewel, or *Mani*, that symbol of the highest value in the Mind we must, first of all, consider the nature of Consciousness.

In the first verse of *The Drammapada* of *The Pali Canon* we see the assertion that 'all things are preceded by the Mind, led by the Mind, created by the Mind'.

In *The Abhidamma*, which is the earliest attempt at a systematic representation of Buddhist philosophy and psychology, the world is viewed exclusively from the point of view of the *phenomenology of Consciousness*.

To the Buddha the world was that which *appears as such* within Consciousness. He rejected any concept of *Substance*, even when he considered material and physical conditions. For him, they could in no way be considered as contrasting with psychic functions. He regarded them as an inner and outer appearance of the same process which was only of interest to him as it fell within the realms of Direct Experience.

Accordingly, the Buddhist does not enquire into the essence of Matter, but only into the essence of *Sense-Perception*. These experiences create in us the idea of Matter, with the External World, according to *Karma*, a constituent of Personality.

Mind is envisaged as producing a net of relations which is Supra-Individual. It spreads over all realms of Sense-Perception whether spiritual, mental or sensuous.

As the process unfolds there arises gradually, from the chaos of mundane Consciousness, an intelligible Cosmos whose fundamental property is Space. This is an all-embracing principle of a higher unity. Its nature is *emptiness*, and because of this it is capable of embracing and containing everything.

Infinity of Space and Infinity of Consciousness are *identical*. When Enlightenment is reached it is then realised that there exists a Supra-Individual *karmic* Inter-Relatedness comprising the Human Race, the planet Earth, the Solar system, the Galaxy and then Galaxies.

There is an Infinite mutual Relationship linking *everything that is*, constituting the Universality of Consciousness.

# II

The Greeks, too, sought to appreciate these things. In *The Phaedo* of Plato we are informed concerning Socrates that he once heard someone reading from a book by Anaxagorus, asserting that it is *Mind* which produces order and is *the cause of everything*. Apparently this explanation pleased Socrates.

Greek philosophers had been endeavouring to understand Nature. These Sophists considered Nature to be the Supreme Court of Appeal for Human values and actions. They considered Science to be necessary for the investigation of and the interpretation of Nature.

The importance of this was paramount to them. Yet they were not primarily concerned with outer appearances for, to them, *Nature was Reality* and *only Nature was deemed to exist*. It was the foundation from which phenomena originate, from which Existence is derived in a process of *becoming and decaying*.

This all applied to Socrates, who was considered by many to be a Sophist, as Aristophanes maintained. What Socrates sought was *The Ultimate Reality*, and he attempted to uncover it by enquiring into the intrinsic validity of things by means of rational criticism.

For Socrates what was True was also expedient, meaning that what was good for the individual must be good for the community, as the Common Good is where the expedient and the Good coincide.

Socrates' quest for *Ultimate Reality* was in connection with the practicality of *The Ultimate Sanction* behind all Human judgements and activities. Socrates was not searching for *the beginning of things* as such. His aim was to reduce the Cosmos to an *Ultimate Reality*, thus rendering it rational.

There have always been those who are fascinated by questions about life and death, or with good and evil. Such people often sought to discover Fate or Destiny.

Mythologies have always existed to provide some sort of answer to all of this, but these Mythologies were concerned with Temporal Beginnings, with some Great Inauguration which had taken place, supposedly, 'once upon a time'.

Other philosophers, these being *Ionians*, sought to discover the Original Substance out of which all other things were composed. What they sought was not the Beginning that once was, but that constant Reality *behind* Matter.

But what was this Ultimate Reality? What is this Element which, in Itself, is not subject to change but which makes change possible? Thales thought it to be water. Anaxamines thought it to be air. Anaximander postulated the existence of a *Basic Element* whose characteristic was *boundlessness*.

It was in this connection that Socrates noticed that any theory which attempts to answer this question without accounting for *the origin of purpose* was doomed from the outset. For Socrates, it seemed that Existence stemmed from *the Form given to Formless Matter*. This displays the characteristic dualism of Mind and Matter. The Constitutive Principle of the Universe is not Matter but *Form*.

For Socrates the Cosmos is ultimately conceived as *an analogy of Work and Art*. No work of Art arises spontaneously but is produced, bit by bit, from an image or idea which is *pre-existent* in the Mind of the Artist. As such the work of art is *a communication* of the Mind of the Artist.

Behind the *form* of the Cosmos we must bear in mind that what we are experiencing is really Electrical Wave Patterns which are Data or Memory. These processes, when subjected to a systematic analysis of their inter-reactions, have produced bodies of Knowledge known to us as Chemistry and Biology.

The hydrogen atom represents the Ultimate Natural Memory. It can be compared to a single binary unit, or as the most elementary letter of an alphabet.

Chemists endeavour to render this intelligible, in an outer sense at least, because, ultimately, the world around us is as it is because of a process of Data Transmission. Most of us are unfamiliar with many of the letters of the alphabet, but this need pose no problem for us because Nature, when spelling out the message *of which we are a part*, uses a shorter alphabet of four letters from which words and sentences are formed. These four basic letters are Carbon, Hydrogen, Oxygen and Nitrogen.

The photosynthesis of green Matter and the structure of living things are due to the specific programming by the Data Patterns of Solar radiation. The chemistry of the surface of the Earth is completely dominated by the Data Programming of the radiations of the Sun.

Cosmic radiations appear to be by means of radiation of which sunlight is typical. Such information is readily available, being simultaneously present throughout Space as frequency patterns in Eternity.

All *ways* of living, or *forms* of life, are receiving sets for such radiations, in the same way as a radio ham is able to tune in to a specific selection of transmitted radio waves. The Data Programmes of Nature are like seeds, in exactly the same way as Human sperm is the programme for a Human being. This is possible because life is organised at the molecular level with DNA and RNA the ultimate programmes of life in Molecular Biology.

Progress made in Molecular Biology has furnished us with definite conclusions:

- the secret of life is to be found at the molecular level;
- the pattern of the molecules, as an Information Complex, *determines the identity of the creature*, whether it is to be a shark or a canary;
- as an Information Complex the pattern of the molecules involves concepts such as Data, Programmes, Codes and Memories.

The most fundamental commodity of the Cosmos is probably Data. Should it be influenced by *Intelligence*, which is qualitative, then the result should be *purposeful behaviour*.

Great consideration should be given to *Data* and to the process Its dissemination has produced. This will involve a *Programmer*, which is someone who, for whatever reason, wants to transmit Data.

This demands a process of Transmission. Also required is Memory or Memories such as those which are to be found in the memory banks of a computer. This all culminates in a result which is the outcome of the Transmission. It may even involve a response from a Receiver.

The Ancients of both East and West believed that it was Mind which fashions all things. Those who were Hermetists, who were disciples of Hermes, the Great Magician, declared that *God was the Mind in Humanity* and that the soul undergoes a process of Purification, or Katharsis, *through bodily experience*.

A New Age will dawn for Humanity. It will be characterised by the Supremacy of Mind which will then be able to attain Its true potential. Thereafter, It will continue on a radically different level. With this dawning we will have looked *beyond* Matter to the realisation of the Idea inherent *in* Matter, as Plotinus advocated. Yet, at the same time this will be something that simply *happens to us*.

Our understanding of the Cosmos with the assistance of Messrs Einstein & Co. has forced us to admit to certain irrevocable conclusions:

- there are *no* events *in themselves*;
- the prime category of Reality is *Experience*;
- only *Experience* can give meaning to the structure of everyday life, such as the Laws of Nature;

Meaning can depend on the opinion of the Observer.

We need not see ourselves as something *other* in the Cosmos. We are integral to the Cosmos and participating within It. The Self is moulded by the experience which it encounters, just as the Self also produces experiences which can be witnessed by others.

There is no such thing as *a thing in itself.* It has no reality of its own. It is only part of the Whole. In exactly the same way there is no such being as *a Self in Itself.*

Everything is part of an All-Embracing Relativistic Event, which takes place within the Divine Mind. Here we can use the analogy of a gigantic electrical impulse computer which enables us to enjoy an *objective subjectivity.* Nothing is external to the Mind.

The Divine Mind, by means of considering Its diversity which ranges in terms of form between Male and Female, and between Maximum Expansion and Maximum Density, is able to discover, through experience, what *Form* is most conducive for *True Self-Expression* for the Divine Mind.

This, of course, is where the Human Race comes in. Here is the *as yet imperfect* embodiment of that Archetypal Pattern which is the Beginning and the End of Everything. The Origin of Purpose is also at the same time the Origin of *our* Purpose. Here we have the Chief Secret of the Ancients. Here we have the basis of the question which was on the lips of every Initiate. This was an Ancient Truth, indeed it was Knowledge about *why the Human Race exists.*

# 12: Regaining Consciousness

As we study the Ancient Wisdom which has been imparted to us by gods such as Hermes, Orpheus, Osiris and Krishna, and from sages such as the Buddha and Plato, we see that there are distinct parallels in their messages. In effect, they were all proclaiming what was fundamentally *the same thing*. They stated that we are presently undergoing a process of life after life, in an approach to the *full* experience of life. This journey is to be understood by using the analogy of Night becoming Day, of Winter becoming Summer, of Unconsciousness becoming Consciousness, and of Death becoming Life.

This is perfectly illustrated in the Hermetic Literature, whereby, this passage *to* life is described in terms relating to an ascent which corresponds to what was believed to have been a primal *Fall*. This ascent involves a journey through the spheres, during which time those passions inherent in the material body would be returned to the planets from which they had been received. This culminates in the pilgrim reaching the place where the Powers praise God, the good end of a process of *Deification*.

Rising from the very depths of Existence, with Its characteristic torments, is far from an easy task, *but it is possible*. In the achieving of this the pilgrim is able to enjoy an experience which *satisfies* the ultimate needs of the soul. In seeking to embark on this journey, Tat, who is a son of Hermes, duly asks his father for guidance. This he receives in due course.

> Draw it unto yourself, and it will come; will, and it happens; reduce to *inactivity* the senses of the body, and then *the birth of deity* will be.

Such is the attribute of Mind to be adopted. As it happens, this is also an integral part of a process of Purification which is designed to cleanse the soul from the irrational torments of Matter. These torments include ignorance, lust, guile, injustice, envy, wrath and malice.

It is in the overcoming of these that one experiences *Rebirth*, whereby the *Immanent Man* is liberated, by the grace of God, being no longer governed by the body but governing it. When the time comes the soul knows where to go and flies aloft.

Tat, who is a son of Hermes, experiences Rebirth under the guidance of his father. It is after this that he is heard to utter *The Confession of the Reborn*.

> Father, being made steadfast by God, I now perceive *not only* with the vision of the eyes, but with the intellectual energy which is through the powers. I am in Heaven, on Earth, in water, in air, in animals, in plants; in the womb, before the womb, after the womb; I am *everywhere*.

We see, then, that the Hermetic Literature taught that *any* person, who seeks sincerely and conscientiously, may indeed undergo an experience enabling liberation from the life of the senses which are inherent in the body. This *provides* one with an experience of Immortality and Deification.

With this experience *another body* is produced. This is a *Spirit-Body*, as is clear from the treatise known as *The Key*, whereby the pious soul, after separation from the body and from the limitations of bodily existence, becomes entirely *Nous*. It is then clothed in a body of *pure fire*.

In the Hermetic Literature the soul is never depicted as though it were a sort of feeble ghost, but as that which is the *most real* of all. It is depicted as the originator and source of *all* phenomena.

This belief is not restricted to the Hermetic Literature for, in *The Orphic Mysteries*, which are very ancient and whose origins are lost in obscurity, we have a similar idea.

*The Orphic Mysteries* were founded by one known as Orpheus, who is described in *The Orphic Mysteries* as a Divine Teacher who has been sent to instruct Humanity. He is portrayed as a philosopher, an enlightened poet, a wonderful singer but when it came to playing stringed instruments he was, without doubt, the greatest of all because his musical ability was *unsurpassed*.

His life is often symbolised by the swan, and so, since time immemorial, the swan has symbolised Music and Song. If the figurative language of Plato is to be correctly interpreted then it may imply that this Divine Teacher would be reincarnated as a philosopher, poet, singer and musician.

Orpheus believed that although Humanity *had fallen* this in no way altered the lofty truth that Humanity was *akin* to the gods. Humanity could still rise again by means of a system of *Purifications* in order to win redemption from sin and death. Thereby one could live forever with the gods.

Orpheus taught that the soul is Immortal. Therefore it exists not only *after death* but *before life*. Orpheus, in fact, would have been quite adamant that, as far as common parlance was concerned, the words *life* and *death* were improperly used.

For Orpheus, what we refer to as *life* is actually *death*, with the body *a tomb* for the soul in which it is kept in custody, life after life, until life in the true sense is reached. It is thus that one is freed from *the wheel of birth*.

# 13: The Universal Myth

## I

Those prophets who have gone before us knew that before they could relate their proclamations to their hearers they had, in the first instance, to express themselves in terms with which the hearer could identify and understand. *For this reason a Mythological approach was necessary.* Fresh Revelation would have to be expressed by means of Popular Mythology, something which was already known. One tradition thus grew out of another, while providing solutions to problems from one Age to another.

As such it should come as no surprise that when we look at the Mythologies passed on from Age to Age there is, as is clearly evident, a striking similarity between them, involving the use of the symbolism of *The Exile, the River and the Star.*

The Ancient Egyptians employed the Myth of Osiris and Isis. Osiris was the principal Egyptian Deity, the brother and consort of Isis and the father of Horus (1).

There were subtle variations on the theme. To many, Osiris symbolised the Sun and the Stars, whereas Isis symbolised the Moon and the Mother Earth, as well as the Nile. Osiris, who corresponds to the Apollo of the Greeks is, according to legend, reputed to be the last god to reign on Earth. As such he was considered to be the progenitor of the Pharaohs.

There was a deeper significance to all of this, for *Osiris was the god of the dead*. He had taken it upon himself to visit the realms of the dead, to provide the dead with assistance to return to *life*. It is for this reason that Osiris was the greatest symbol of *resurrection*, of living again. He had come to Hades, *which is life as we know it*, the place where the souls of the dead are to be found *entombed* in bodies, from which they require to be released in order to *return* to God and to life.

In the days when the Pharaohs ruled in Egypt it was commonplace for them to undergo a ceremony which was symbolic of death. This recalled the tales of the ritual and barbaric murder of the prehistoric kings of Egypt when senility approached. During the ceremony the Pharaoh would wear the shroud of Osiris, the god whose murder in Mythology was followed by the birth of his Son, Horus. This represented that principle which guaranteed the eternal existence of all things.

In the ritual murder, Osiris would be seen to reappear *as* Horus, as the Rising Sun, as the bright and morning Star, to begin a new cycle. The Son of the Pharaoh, as a co-regent, would symbolise the rejuvenated powers and then, when mature, he would undertake the work of theological reform, in order to define more clearly the relationship which exists between Humanity and the gods.

In Egyptian mythology Osiris appears most clearly as the Human-faced bird. He was the first god to be *incarnated on Earth* so that the Human Race would be able to perpetuate Itself.

With the death of Osiris, the falcon, which was a glorious and dynamic image of his Son, Horus, appears on the horizon representing new life. The death of the Father and the resulting birth of the Son are the embodiment of the dual principle which represents Eternity. This is the evening and the morning, or yesterday and tomorrow.

With the murder of Osiris he had been removed from the only world which Human beings can understand. He was deemed to be looking for an eternal body. In this he was assisted by the solicitude of the Divine family. At the end of his arduous task the dead Osiris would appear in the aspect of the Rising Sun, Ra, thus displaying the two tenets of Egyptian religious Mythology, Osiris and Ra, or the living and the dead.

The legend of Osiris alludes quite clearly to primeval rites. The goddess Isis, upon finding the dead Osiris, *by means of very potent magick invigorates him* so that she may receive his seed. In consequence she becomes pregnant and when her son is born *she hides him in the marshes*.

The transformation of the dead king, deified in the person of Horus took place by means of a double phenomenon. Ra arose on the horizon and, on the throne of the living the young Horus, the new Pharaoh, the renewed image of the god, would thus exercise Divine rule on Earth.

At one with the celestial god the sovereign would share in the existence of the Rising Sun and, like Ra, at dawn he would spring from the primeval marshes above the blue lotus. The young king would then embark upon a journey through the Netherworld, a journey the success of which was assured. As Osiris he was unjustly punished and pursued by evil, but his innocence would be proclaimed after a very long trial.

This form of Myth was not restricted to Egypt. It was fundamental to *The Orphic Mysteries* which were concerned with legends of the Greek Orpheus, who was a philosopher, enlightened poet, singer and fabulous musician. He is often depicted as playing the harp or the four-stringed lyre.

His mother was Kalliope, the Muse of epic poetry who was represented with a tablet and stylus, or with a roll of parchment. In association with the other Muses she was to inspire the votaries of the Arts and Sciences (2). *His father was the Thracian River.*

The chief legends concerning Orpheus are in connection with his *unequalled musical ability*, which he used primarily for the benefit of others. He was one of the Argonauts and, during those voyages no Human intervention was required to launch those heroes. The Music of Orpheus was sufficient for the task.

His musical ability was even reputed to have enabled his colleagues to escape from danger, such as the occasion when they seemed certain to be crushed by Magic Rocks. With the intervention of Orpheus, however, and the production of unrivalled musical charm, those Rocks ceased to move and the Argonauts made their escape.

His Music was characterised by great forcefulness but was, at the same time, *bewitching*, casting a spell on *all* those who heard it.

His wife had died from the bite of a serpent, a theme readily recognisable to those who have studied the Old Testament. Euridice descended down into Hades, which is also life as we experience it. Orpheus followed her in an attempt to rescue her, casting a spell on the Guardians of the Underworld by means of his Music.

To the Greeks Music was of paramount importance. In becoming *religious* one was actually endeavouring to perceive the nature of the soul, which was considered to be the primary, Divine and imperishable element in all things.

For the Greeks the soul of the Universe was harmony. Music was the Ultimate Revelation of Reality. It was considered to be *a primal force* which is the source of everything.

Aristoxenes, who was personally acquainted with the Pythagoreans of his time, tells us that *they used medicine to purge the body and music to purge the soul.* In *The Phaedo* of Plato, Socrates is depicted as saying that *philosophy is the highest music.*

Furthermore, in *The Timaeus* of Plato, the Demiurge uses a mixing-bowl, the suggestion being that if it were possible to discover the rule for blending such apparently elusive things as high and low notes, the secret of the world would be discovered, or *remembered.*

# II

The literalism of the Old Testament is based on the theme of a couple who, in some ways, are symbolic of Osiris and Isis and of Orpheus and Euridice. After an encounter with a serpent they leave Paradise to journey to the Netherworld of Hades. In the Mythology they leave the Garden of Eden to go to a land of suffering and sorrow.

There are other aspects of *The Universal Myth* in the Old Testament. There was David, the legitimate King who plays the lyre in a bewitching manner. Then there is Moses whose name is Egyptian. The name actually means *son.*

> Now a man from the house of Levi went and took to wife a daughter of Levi. The woman conceived and bore a son; and when she saw he was a goodly child, she hid him three months. And when she could no longer hide him she took for him a basket made of bulrushes, and daubed it with bitumen and pitch, and she put the child in it and placed it among the reeds at the river's brink. And his sister stood at a distance, to know what would be done to him. Now the daughter of Pharaoh came down to bathe at the river, and her maidens walked by the side of the river. She saw a basket among the reeds and sent her maid to fetch it.

When she opened it she saw the child; and, lo, the babe was cry-
ing. She took pity on him and said,
'This is one of the Hebrews' children.'

Then his sister said to Pharaoh's daughter,
'Shall I go and call a nurse from among the Hebrew women to
nurse the child for you?'

And Pharaoh's daughter said to her, 'Go!'

So the girl went and called the child's mother. And Pharaoh's
daughter said to her,
'Take the child away and nurse him for me, and I will give you
your wages.'

So the woman took the child and nursed him. And the child
grew, and she brought him to Pharaoh's daughter, and he became
her son; and she named him Moses (3), for she said,
'Because I drew him out (4) of the water.' (5)

We should recognise that *this is all legendary* and should not be thought of as
*historical* in any strict sense. Most Biblical scholars are of the opinion that there
was no actual State of Israel until the unification of the land under the leadership of King David. His capital was Jerusalem, known formerly as Jebus.

It is this David who is reputed to have slain the giant known as Goliath,
thus giving the Israelites the incentive to defeat the armies of the Philistines
(6). We should note, however, that the Biblical narratives also attribute the
slaying of Goliath to another (7).

The Legitimate King, David the son of Jesse, attracts the jealousy of Saul,
whose Kingdom he was ordained to inherit.

And on the morrow an evil spirit from God rushed upon Saul,
and he raved within his house, while David was playing the lyre,
as he did day by day. Saul had a spear in his hand. And Saul cast
the spear for he thought, 'I will pin David to the wall.'

But David evaded him twice. (8)

The Kingdom of David was established in Israel but it was not to last. Eventually, the Hebrews were taken into captivity by the Babylonians. During their exile there was a thorough re-interpretation of the traditions of the people. There was still the belief that, one day, the Kingdom of David would be restored.

Christians believe that Jesus of Nazareth will restore such a Kingdom one day and it is interesting to see how *The Universal Myth* appears in the New Testament.

When we see Mary and her boy child we are actually seeing Isis with Horus in a New Testament mould. It is for this reason that the baby Jesus *required a miraculous birth*. Mary did not have to conceive as other women. Jesus had entered the world to redeem his bride which was also his Church. He had intended that he and his New Testament Euridice be re-united forever.

In the New Testament, and in *The Book of Revelation*, Jesus is described as the root and offspring of David, *the bright and morning Star*. In *The Gospel according to Matthew*, Jesus of Nazareth is described as *the son of David, the son of Abraham*.

## NOTES

(1)  Their home was on a planet which is reputed to orbit the Star we refer to as Sirius.

(2)  The other Muses were: Clio, of history; Euterpe, of lyric poetry or music; Thalia, of comedy; Melpomene, of tragedy; Terpsichore, of choral dance and song; Erato, of erotic poetry and mime; Polyhymnia, of the subtle hymn; Urania, of astronomy.

(3)  Mosheh.

(4)  Mashah.

(5)  *The Book of Exodus*, chapter 2: 1-10.

(6)  *The First Book of Samuel*, chapter 17.

(7)  *The Second Book of Samuel*, chapter 21: 19. See also *The First Book of Chronicles*, chapter 20: 5.

(8)  *The First Book of Samuel*, chapter 18: 10-11.

# 14: The Legacy of the Greeks

## I

The Greeks have left us a legacy which is universal. It has left an indelible mark on all thought which has developed since them, whether in the East or in the West. This is something which we shall consider in the paragraphs which follow on from here.

Greek philosophy is based on the unshakeable idea that *Reality is Divine*. For this reason Greek philosophy is integrally involved in an attempt to justify the religious instinct of the Human Race. For the Greeks the all-important thing is the soul, which they considered to be the source of everything and which, they believed, was endeavouring to enter into communion with the Divine.

Greek philosophers believed that it was only through the Knowledge of Reality that we could learn our true place in the world and in the Cosmic scheme of things. This was in order that we could become *fellow-workers* with God.

They had no interest in speculation. For them Religion was concerned with Worship. They cared little for theological affirmations or negations. If one found it impossible to attain Knowledge of the gods by oneself, then one was well-advised to accept recognised worship.

The Greeks were fascinated by one very vexing question: how is it that we come to have a standard which we possess which enables us to pronounce those things of sense to be *imperfect?* This perplexity was brought about because we do not seem to *start* with such a standard in our possession, *but we come to possess it.* It is based, somehow or other, on the experience of those things apprehended by *Sensory Perception.*

This is in no way intended to suggest that Greek thought was Intellectualism, for it was nothing of the kind. *Intellectualism has no martyrs* and Socrates was a martyr, with no man ever doing more than he to avoid doing wrong. For Socrates philosophy was, above all, a life involving the conversion of the soul, with subsequent *service* to Humanity.

Greek philosophers drew a sharp distinction between the objects of Thought and those of Sensory Perception. Those objects witnessed by the senses could not be said to have *being* at all. They were in *a state of becoming,* which meant that they were considered by the Greeks to be mere *likenesses* or *images* of eternal standards or *patterns* which we seem to be *forced* to postulate. Our apprehension of those things of sense should be best thought of as *imagination,* or even just *belief.*

What the Greeks truly sought was Knowledge or *Gnosis.* In order to receive this Knowledge, or as far as receiving this Knowledge was *possible* in this life, it was necessary to overcome the passions of the body. It was only *when the soul had been freed from the body* that it could enjoy Knowledge in all its purity.

For as long as we experience life as we do, which is *as the Human Race,* we should accustom ourselves to dying daily in an attempt to overcome ourselves. By this means we may be able to glimpse those Eternal Realities as in a vision. In so being *out of the body* we can experience a foretaste of the Immortal state. This is undoubtedly the teaching of the first part of *The Phaedo* of Plato, which points to a complete severance of the world of *Sense* and the world of *Thought.*

Here we have seen the arrival of that fateful doctrine of two worlds, the world of *Thought* and the world of *Sense.*

Plato did not believe in books for serious purposes. For him, the most important things could not be imparted in writing at all. One soul could only influence another because of an *immediate contact* between them. For a philosophy to have any real value it had to be a person's very own.

Plato considered education to be very important for inculcating virtue. He believed that, in time, it would lead to the conversion of the soul from the *contemplation of becoming* to that of *being.* Then it would be possible to understand the truth which is: it is not true to say that what appears *is* for in

Reality *nothing is*, with everything *becoming*, just as Heraclitus and others have proclaimed.

Within our Consciousness we have an awareness of sorts of Eternity. This is from the perspective of the *Human aspect* of our nature. This is where the famous Platonic maxim is brought into play.

> Man is the measure of all things, of things that are that they are, and of things that are not that they are not.

But who is this *Man* who is the measure of all things? On more than one occasion Plato explained the meaning of this to be 'that things appear to me *as they appear to me*, and to you *as they appear to you*'.

This is a situation not without problems because people with jaundice see everything as yellow. In the same way it is possible to have beliefs coloured by an abnormal condition of the soul. The saying, 'Man is the measure of all things, of things that are that they are, and of things that are not that they are not' was originally intended to remind us of the *relativity* of all Human judgements. In matters involving the *evidence of the senses* and on *moral questions* there is thus *no possibility* of Absolute Truth.

The influence of the Greeks on thought which has developed since them, in either East or West, is enormous. Western thought is built upon the Greeks, although they had become the custodians of an *Esoteric Tradition* from elsewhere in more remote times.

When we look to the East, such as India, we see that *no* scientific work, and therefore nothing which the Greeks would have considered to have been philosophy, can be dated *prior* to the time of Alexander the Great. Concerning the East, most scholars are of the opinion that the Mathematical Book known as *Sulva Sutras* is not of an earlier date. Even if it was, in no way does it approach the level of Greek thought.

Greek philosophy is characterised by a dualism. The fact that beings are formed of *Potentiality* and *Act* explains why they are both *changeable* and *real* at the same time. This dualism was believed to provide the reason for Plato's elucidation of the difference between things or beings as the outcome of *a limited and imperfect sharing* of these things or beings in the *same* Idea, such as the *Idea of Humanity*.

The basic dualism of Mind and Matter is still the most fundamental problem for philosophers.

# II

It was this dualism with which René Descartes wrestled in his attempts to understand and identify his first point of certainty. This was obviously that of his own existence. He summed this up with the words *cogito ergo sum* or *I think therefore I am.* The second principle was *sum res cogitans* or *I am a being whose essence is to think.*

For Descartes the ultimate guarantee for his thinking and willing is God, through whom Descartes has the certainty that he would not be deceived by his own innate ideas. Descartes saw his existence as firmly established because that which is finite can only be conceived against the background of the Infinite.

We see from Descartes that all thought includes *a Relationship* with God. For thinking to be possible in clear and distinct ideas it demands a situation where Reality is divided into two irreducible spheres. These are *Consciousness*, which is essentially *Thought* and known through *inner* experiences, and *Matter* which is essentially *Extension*, and known through *Mathematics*.

In relation to material things only that which can be counted or measured mathematically has reality. Concerning Consciousness, only that which can be clearly and distinctly identified by *Thought* has reality.

The dualism of Reality as two irreducible spheres is fundamentally important for Humanity, which appears to be an irreducible dualism composed of *Consciousness*, or the soul, and *Matter*, expressed as bodily form or Extension. There appears to be some sort of incomprehensible interaction between these two parts of the duality.

We appear to be approaching the point where we are advocating the belief that *through* Nature, the Spirit, which is *a Primal Idea*, is coming to *know Itself*. In the experience of perfecting Its Form while *seeking to return* to the Original State of Consciousness, which is the source of everything, It overcomes *the need for perfection* by becoming *Perfect*. In the return to the Original State of Consciousness, which is union with our Ultimate Ancestor, the Spirit experiences Subjectivity, then Objectivity and, finally, the Absolute.

Through subjective experience the Spirit, which is *a Primal Idea*, comes to *know Itself*. It realises that It is in the grip of Nature, and that It is different from Nature in some way. In coming to terms with the practicalities of life It creates the circumstances for Ultimate Liberation. This Liberation is also the *attainment of Knowledge*. This Knowledge has to do with the fact that the Spirit is actually *the cause of everything*.

Initially It has no intuition of Itself. In order to know Itself it is necessary to *interact* with that which It *appears not to be*. By means of a process of Self-Realisation, which involves *the route of effort* It comes to the idea of the duality of Reality.

On Its journey It experiences material resistance. As the other part of the dualism It realises that It is *non-material*. This leads to the conclusion that the Spirit is *not* a thing, as such, but *a force* which is actually the cause of everything.

As the Renaissance advanced, by the time of Schelling, the successor to Fichte, Nature was viewed as being *the unconscious product* of the Mind. It displays the laws to which the Mind corresponds *unconsciously*.

In a very real sense Nature is *the history* of the Mind. It is a history of the development of the activity of the Mind before It reached the stage of Self-Consciousness. It has attained this on Earth by means of the Human Race.

The external world is open to us as the means of rediscovering the history of the Mind in It. Nature is a process of evolution from which the Conscious Mind has emerged. Gradually It rises to the level of Consciousness. Then It realises that It is still at primitive stages of development. It recognises Itself as being in the grip of *unconscious* Nature.

This is very much a development of the thought of Immanuel Kant. With Kant the world and God are not deemed to be *things* as such, but as rules or postulates of our Reason. The Mind can do none other than think these things.

For Baruch Spinoza, God was an independent substance. God was dependent upon nothing. The ground and basis of the existence of God was *within* the Godhead, Itself. Being Its own cause God was *cause sui*. The existence of God is the necessary consequence of *the essence of God* which can only be thought of *as* existing.

Spinoza advocated that only one such substance was possible. Therefore, only one could exist. If there were two such substances there would be a mutual relationship between them. This would imply an inner contradiction. This one independent substance or Idea must, therefore, be Infinite. Nothing can be conceived as falling outside It, for It is Absolute or Infinite Being, which is God.

It is here that we must pose a very important question: if there can be *nothing outside God*, what then is the planet Earth?

The world is a *necessary* expression of God. From *The Ancient Mystery Tradition* we see that the Earth exists for the sake of some sort of Divine Reproduction. The world is a multiplicity of modes of being *in* God. It is an expression of the *multiplicity* or *unity* of God, *as a Relationship*.

The Godhead is essentially activity, which is another way of saying that activity is the essence of God. The Godhead created the world of necessity. This necessity to produce the Earth was not in opposition to the freedom of God. It is identical with it. Freedom is to be found in the ability of a being *to act in accordance with the necessity of its nature*, as long as it is being determined *by itself* to act.

All activity is *willing* within the Divine Mind. The more perfect a being is, the more real it is. Because of the power of Mind endowed upon Human beings, the Human Race is the most real of finite beings.

In essence, the Human Race is being-in-God. By means of Existence the Human Race is Being-in-the-world. The Human Race is *how* the Godhead *specifically manifests* Itself on Earth. As the Godhead is essentially activity, so is the Human Race.

As Existence, Humanity is Body or Extension. Humanity is therefore subject to the necessity of natural events. The Human Race is essentially *historical*. The Human Race encapsulates the history of the Mind, which is to say, the Human Race *is* the Mind, Itself.

# III

The Human Race has now reached the stage of evolution, *as* the Evolution of Consciousness, whereby Humanity needs to *know* Itself on a level *above* the need for self-preservation in the material world.

Our genius has guided us and brought us to the stage where we need no longer struggle on. We must free ourselves from drudgery and oppression. This will enable us to see that 'the urge to understand is the only basis of virtue'.

In the past when life was so often characterised by struggle for survival, Self-Realisation for Humanity was prevented. Now we can look forward to experiencing greater things. The outcome of striving to attain Self-Realisation, which demands that we live consciously and reflectively, results in the understanding that, as Spinoza said, 'by virtue and power I mean the same thing'.

When Spinoza spoke of power he was not referring to the domination of the outside world, but of 'the ability to realise the Idea which is situated *in* God'. This is how the essence of Humanity is realised, for this striving is virtue. In the last resort the Good is what is in accordance with Reason. Rationality and morality are synonymous.

Moreover, since rationality is a striving towards Self-Realisation, it is possible to say that morality is simply *being oneself*. The moral man or woman *is* himself or herself. As such they are able to express Divine essence in worldly Existence. Happiness, though not to be found in morality, *is morality*. Only morality enables the Human Race to express Divine Essence in Existence.

And what of our communal activity, the striving of the Human Race towards Its ultimate Self-Realisation *as the One*? How can we act in co-operation with each other towards the attainment of the Good?

It is here that we should look closely at the Greek city-states which were constituted by certain norms, with *Law* recognised as the greatest good of the citizens. In being bound to the Law the citizens were able to experience freedom. Certainly it enabled the State, as constituted by Law, to prepare for action. It may have to defend itself against enemies. Chiefly, it gave rise to freedom because it provided each citizen with the opportunity 'to participate in the functions of Government'.

For the Greeks freedom did not mean a state of affairs where *everyone did as they pleased*. The Law did not exist to balance the conflicting claims of individuals, thus securing private liberty. Freedom meant the ability *to serve* the Commonwealth. It was in political responsibility that each one was able to experience personal dignity and worth.

It was this freedom to do one's duty which gave each one the sense of *constituting and representing* the State. The city-state was of such importance to the Greek that, at all times, the Greek was prepared to die for it. To be expelled from the city-state meant ostracism from Society, from all that meant dignity and worth. This pride was most fundamental.

All Humans, everywhere, constitute the *one* Humanity. The Human Race has Its own specific evolution. Humanity has Its own Destiny. This transcends the life and fate of individuals. In the strictest of senses there are *no individuals* at the Human level. We are linked by indissoluble bonds and are always drawn to form communities.

# 15: The Attainment of Gnosis

## I

When we engage ourselves in a deeper and more systematic study of the New Testament, and then look at the history of the development of *The Cult of Jesus Christ*, it is clear for all to see that there never was *one* specific and universally accepted belief system about Jesus of Nazareth. There was a divergence of opinion among followers then, as there is now, and the relationship between them in the days of the New Testament, as now, was not always cordial (1).

What we seek to understand is how the New Testament, as we know it, came into being. We seek to understand why it portrays Jesus Christ as it does, as a man acquainted with grief who was crucified, who rose again to reign as co-regent with his Heavenly Father.

It is here, however, that we cannot ignore the fact that the Jesus of the New Testament, as far as his own people were concerned, was *an impostor*. The Jews were crucially aware that the claims he had made about returning to Earth within a generation to establish a *supernatural* Kingdom of God, which would have been a Theocracy, around 70 AD had just not been fulfilled.

Furthermore, the form in which the Christian Church and Christian doctrine now appear is due in no small way to *The Council of Nicea* in 325 AD. It was then that a Creed was formulated, based on the so-called history of a saviour *personified as Jesus Christ*. This Creed was to evolve still further in 381 AD at *The Council of Constantinople*.

Many who were alive at the time, who considered themselves to be true believers, would have considered this Creed and this Church as being heretical. A Religion was being established which was based on mere political power and not on Ancient Wisdom, presumably in an attempt to bind the Empire together.

The Jesus of the New Testament is certainly portrayed as the fulfilment of the Ancient Promises to Humanity through the medium of the nation of Israel. It hailed the end of the need for those former traditions from which *The Cult of Jesus Christ* had emerged.

Yet again we are brought back to considering the rise of the Greek or Hellenistic Civilisation, and the subsequent appearance of the Roman Empire which had a profound influence on all the nations of the known world.

The Hellenistic world and the Roman Empire had created the circumstances whereby the disciples of Buddhism, Hinduism, Zoroastrianism, Druidism, Greek philosophy, the teachings of those priests of Egypt who venerated Thoth of the ibis beak, Judaism and all sorts of Mystery Religions were to meet face to face.

The result was that, to a great extent, the old *national* forms of Religion began to lose their edge. There arose among the spiritually-minded from all over the known world a fervent enquiry to uncover and follow *The True Religion*. By means of this they believed that Humanity could be united. Some actually were convinced that *The True Religion* had always existed and that it was, in fact, Humanity's greatest inheritance.

It was believed that this *True Religion* was encapsulated in those Ancient Mythologies concerning Osiris and Isis, as well as those concerning Orpheus and Euridice, and those stories which referred to Hermes, the Buddha and to Krishna. Those who sought for such Knowledge, or *Gnosis*, gave rise to a movement known as *Gnosticism*.

There was no *one* brand of Gnosticism and there were Gnostic centres in Antioch, Alexandria and in parts of Asia Minor. In general, they held that God was beyond description, being Supremely Perfect and Infinite in attributes. They also considered it beneath the dignity of God to labour. As such God could not possibly have created the world. Moreover, there was *so much evil* in the world that *no* God characterised by love and perfection *could possibly have created it*.

For the Gnostics God lived in a pleroma of light and was totally inaccessible, although there were emanations from God. These were Aeons, descending in degree until the level of the Demiurge was reached. This was the Creator of the world as we know it. Many believed this to be *Yahweh*, the God of the Old Testament.

In general, Gnostics believed that the Christ was an Aeon and, as an Aeon he was of higher rank than the Demiurge. They accepted that the Christ had been sent into the world to restore *The True Religion*. Some considered that this Aeon entered the Jesus of the New Testament at his baptism, leaving when he was being taken away to be crucified. It was only the man who suffered.

They accepted the idea of salvation. They believed, however, that it was only for a tiny elect of spiritually-minded people. Some actually believed that salvation pertained only to men.

# II

As we all know, there are different levels of understanding. The deeper meaning of the preaching of the Jesus of the New Testament is that we should be *open* to the future which *God has ordained* for us, which is imminent for the entire Human Race. We must prepare for a future which may come like a thief in the night, or when it is *least expected*. This will be a judgement on all those who have bound themselves to the world, who are neither open to themselves nor to God.

We can study the doctrines of all the Sects and Religions. We can become lost in the most thorough examination of scriptures. We can concentrate our energies on trying to reconstruct the historical situation in which the authors of the texts found themselves. Yet this is *not our true interest* when we turn to literature such as the Bible or *The Bhagavad-Gita*.

Our concern is actually with *ourselves*. More than anything we want to see what these texts have to say to us about our situation *now*. We want to know about the condition of our souls, which we should regard as being of supreme importance.

Human beings of all Ages and of all nations share as a focal point the great restlessness experienced by that unrelenting urge *to understand*. This search did not begin in the first century AD, but was being experienced much much earlier.

The Myths of Osiris and Isis, of Orpheus and Euridice, of Hermes, Apollo, the Buddha and Krishna were all intended to address this restlessness. They were all *variations* upon a theme, which is the Universal Myth of *The Exile, the River and the Star* which seeks to point the way to that Knowledge, or *Gnosis*, which can guide us back, supposedly, to our home in the realms of the Divine.

Orphic tablets have been found in tombs. These were prepared to provide instruction for the *souls of the departed*, which is ourselves, to enable us to make our way back to our Origin. Most of these tablets have been broken or else completely destroyed. However, one known as *The Petelia* is almost complete. It states,

> Thou shalt find on the left
> Of the house of Hades a Well-Spring
> And by the side thereof
> A white cypress.
> To this Well-Spring
> Approach not near,
> But thou shalt find another
> By the Lake of Memory,
> Cold water flowing forth,
> And there are Guardians before it.
> Say: 'I am a child of Earth
> And of Starry Heaven;
> But my Race is of Heaven
> This ye know yourselves.
> And lo, I am parched with thirst
> And I perish
> Give me quickly
> The cold water flowing forth
> From the Lake of Memory.'
> And of themselves
> They will give thee to drink
> From the holy Well-Spring,
> And thereafter among the heroes
> Thou shalt have lordship.

Those who are spiritually-minded are interested in reading *all* the Sacred Literature known to us. They do not read them *as an end in themselves* but because they believe that therein lies a deep spiritual truth which is a *True Gnosis* of the Origin and Destiny of the Human Race.

This is as true of the New Testament as it is of other Sacred Literature. The early Christian Gnostics considered that the truth *inherent* in the New Testament had become *unnecessarily materialised* by *The Cult of Jesus Christ*. The hierarchy of *The Cult of Jesus Christ* insisted that the scriptures be interpreted on *a purely literal basis*, for they were to be believed *literally*.

In this world the Human Race is trying to discover Its true identity. This involves *True Self-Expression* for Humanity. This demands *the provision of understanding* for and on behalf of Nature or the Cosmos. It is by means of the Human Race that the Cosmos seeks to discover the *secret* of returning to a particular level of Consciousness. This Human search, which is the Divine Mission which forms the basis of all Human Religion, has manifested itself in many forms.

All our beliefs, to date, are no more than cultural variations, being only *fragments* of a Universal Picture which, with other *fragments*, can be detected in all the Sacred Literature known to us.

It is for this reason that there are striking similarities in many of the narratives which depict the lives of the Great Teachers who have appeared in every millennium; thus we see similarities between the life of the Buddha and the Jesus of the New Testament.

From the relative legends we know that the Buddha was born to the Virgin Maya. She had conceived, *not* through the sexual act as other women, but by means of the descent of the Divine upon her.

The birth of the Buddha was heralded by a Star which appeared on the horizon. Hardly had he been born than it was recognised that he possessed all the attributes of Divinity. He was visited by men who offered him costly jewels and precious substances. There are obviously great similarities here with the Gospel account of the birth of Jesus of Nazareth which, in turn, is *an adaptation* of the Myth concerning the birth of Mithras, the Sun God.

In the narratives concerning the birth of the Buddha, there is a darker side to the tale. King Bunbasara had heard of the birth of the child. He had been advised that it was best to put the child to death. It was believed that when fully grown the child would actually inherit the kingdom from King Bunbasara. The king sought to have the life of the baby Buddha brought to a swift conclusion, but to no avail as the child was well protected.

Let us not overlook the story of Ananda, the favourite disciple of the Buddha. He had been on a long journey and he was very tired and thirsty, so he asked a girl of the Candala caste for a drink of water, which she was drawing from a well. She warned him to exercise great caution that he did not contaminate himself. He replied,

> My sister, I do not ask you what your caste or family is; I am only asking you for water, if you can give it to me.

In the story the girl falls madly in love with Ananda. Furthermore, she was converted to the teachings of the Buddha.

As it happens, there is a similar story in the New Testament.

> … and so Jesus, wearied as he was with his journey, sat down by the well. It was about the sixth hour. There came a woman of Samaria to draw water.

> Jesus said to her, 'Give me a drink!'
> For the disciples had gone away to the city to buy food. The Samaritan woman said to him,

> 'How is it that you, a Jew, ask a drink of me, a woman of Samaria?'
> For the Jews had no dealings with the Samaritans.

> Jesus answered her, 'If you knew the gift of God, and who it is that is saying to you, "Give me a drink of water", You would have asked him, and he would have given you living water.' (2)

All over the planet there were those who were seeking to receive the True and Universal Knowledge or *Gnosis*. In their studies of the New Testament these Gnostics sought *inner* Truth. They did not regard the genealogies from *Adam* to Jesus Christ as needing to be *historical* in any way, or even to involve historical characters. To them, the Jesus of the New Testament, *in this context*, was taken to be the pattern of experience to be undergone by anyone who follows the pathway which leads to Gnosis.

In *interpreting* the New Testament in this manner, these seekers did not consider that they were in any way undermining the teachings of the New

Testament. Rather, they saw themselves as going beyond the carnality which they believed to have been *imposed* on the original texts.

They believed that their method of interpretation brought to light a wonderful system of Self-Revelation and Self-Redemption which indicated a pattern which corresponded to the pathway *of return* to the Immortal State.

They were concerned with *an allegorical approach* to the New Testament. They believed that this method of interpretation was actually *sanctioned* by the New Testament, Itself.

> For it is written that Abraham had two sons, one by a slave and one by a free woman. But the son of the slave was born according to the flesh, and the son of the free woman through promise. *Now this is an allegory:*
>
> These women are two covenants. One is Mount Sinai in Arabia; she corresponds to the present Jerusalem, for she is in slavery with her children. But the Jerusalem above is free, and she is our mother. (3)

# III

The *hidden* message of the scriptures is the Cosmic Drama, the Drama of the soul which, *as the Son of God*, descends into the limitations of Existence. It then identifies with the unavoidable and inevitable suffering experienced by the Human Race.

This suffering is designed to assist the Human soul to rise *above* the level of the finite to that of the Infinite. This involves *Union* with the One and the All. God and the Human Race are, therefore, one and the same. The Human Race is *the source* of all wisdom and power. Oneness is to be realised by means of Nature. In fact, *all life is God in disguise.*

The Cosmic Drama begins with the Divine Victim entering the Human Temple for the final act of the Human Mystery. This has to do with a triumphal procession culminating in an *Act of Crucifixion or Initiation out of the Human level.* This leads on to another, higher level of Divine evolution. The crucifixion demonstrates that the Victim, which is the Divine Logos or Christos, does not die a physical death. It actually dies to the experience of *finiteness*.

The evolution of the Human Race *as God Incarnate* was, for the Gnostics, a great Mystery. In attempting to understand this, the Gnostics realised that they were actually endeavouring to understand the mystery of their own being, and that they were at One with the All.

They implored everyone to awaken those powers which are latent within all of us, powers which exist within Humanity *as* God Incarnate. By means of this Awakening a fundamental change in Existence could be produced. This is the purpose of *The True Religion*, which is the basis for the religious experiences of the Human Race.

The central theme of Gnosticism seems to lie in the Mystic God being fragmented and slain by the rulers of this world. This means that the soul is All Intelligence and a portion of Divinity. The soul is plunged into the abyss of Matter and, having descended into Hades, or Hell, it falls asleep within the Human sepulchre.

In those religious beliefs known as *The Ancient Mysteries*, those who were involved with them were actually bewailing what they believed to be *the loss* of their Divine Identity. In the final stages of *The Mysteries* they believed that the individual was overshadowed by one's own Divine and Immortal Self.

The Gnostics did not understand those scriptures circulating in the first century AD as having been *historical narratives*. They saw them as the *representation* of the Cosmic Drama of the Fall of the Divine Man into Matter. In due course there would be an *ordained return*, with salvation to the realms of the Divine which is also our Origin. The Logos of God had become Human so that Humanity might learn, *through experience*, what it meant to be God.

As has been stated already, the Christian narratives possessed certain striking similarities with the life of the Buddha Gautama. These Christian narratives were also permeated with stories which were held in common with other belief systems.

Peter holds the same office as the Janus of Roman Mythology. The Peter of the New Testament holds the keys of Alpha and Omega as well as a rod, *a phallic symbol*, which is used to lead the souls to Heaven. It is easy to see why he is portrayed as such, for he was to be hailed as the first Pope.

The betrayal of Jesus by *Judas* is an adaptation of the story of Joseph, who was sold into slavery by his *Israelite* brothers as they were jealous of him. Most religious Myths and Mystery Dramas involve a betrayal of some sort.

The Crown of Thorns is based on the Ancient Tradition of a mock king who was sacrificed. As a Sacrificial Victim he takes upon himself the sins of the entire community or nation. In Babylon a person who had been condemned to death *was dressed as a king* for five days before *The Festival of Sacaea*. After this he was stripped, scourged and crucified for the good of the nation, or so it was believed.

The ritual Crucifixion is very old indeed. In Egypt, a victim wearing a Crown of Thorns was led in procession to die as a Saviour-God for Egypt. Parallels to this are to be found in the Myths concerning Herakles (Hercules) and Prometheus.

The Cross itself is pre-Christian. It is a symbol of Life and of Immortality. The Spirit had become a bridge maker between Heaven and Earth by means of *The Tree of Life* which had been planted in Golgotha, which is *the place of the skull*.

The Cross is a representation of the Spinal Tree on which there are several lamps with a sleeping serpent, or phallus, at the base. The outline of the cross, as the representation of the Human form, is stretched out between the waters of Material Existence and the heavens of the Divine Self. The journey from the waters of Existence to the Thalamus represents the journey to be undertaken by the soul in its path towards Ultimate Liberation.

The rock burial and resurrection of the slain god has many variations as regards interpretation. It emanates from Egypt. The rock tomb is the body. The stone rolling away symbolises the Attainment of Gnosis. The soul rising out of the tomb is the Ascended Master.

Since the fourth century AD the Christian Faith has been presented to us in a particular form. This form had been imposed by the Religious Authorities. This involved the interpretation of texts which referred to those Teachings which are fundamental to all the Religions of the world. The interpretation imposed was to suit the purposes of those who were greedy for political power. They wanted to propagate a belief system for the sake of political control.

In spite of the passage of many centuries, however, this has not altered the fact that the Jesus of the New Testament is *not* an historical character at all. The Drama of the Christ which is portrayed in the New Testament represents the Cosmic Drama which did not take place 'once upon a time'; it happens within *all of us* every day of our lives.

The Cosmic Drama displays to us in its unfolding that there are three distinct stages. The first is *Purification*, during which time the pilgrim learns endurance for the sake of self-control.

This is followed by *Illumination*. By this means, the higher and lower selves come into contact. The lower self is to be conquered by the higher self.

This leads to an experience of *Union*, which is also *Cosmic Consciousness*. By this means, one realises that one is a Conscious Embodiment of the Universal Self. Those who experience such are Illumined Adepts of Life. They have granted to themselves to relive the past, understand the present in its proper context, and *foresee* that which has *yet* to take place. They have undergone an experience which enables them to appreciate that past, present and future are *One Continuum*.

The foundation of all the teachings of the Ancients is an Esoteric Philosophy. This is a Gnosis of all things, which was concerned with Union with the All. The Illumined Adept of Life has realised that past, present and future are derived from our sensory perception which has actually separated the All into many parts. Intelligence seeks to resolve this through a process of evolution to bring the separate parts into the Union of the All once again.

The Gnostics believed that this Great All which, for the Gnostics was *a Great Nothingness*, had fragmented Itself into many parts or forms. In so doing It created a chaos. Through the activity of an inherent essence, the forms are able to restore themselves to unity. By means of struggle they consolidate their form. After this, by means of *non-resistance* they release their essence from their form. This is possible because essence and form are merely *modes of action* by the All.

The Universal Self is that power which is able to ensoul all forms. This happens because the Great Nothingness is able *to imagine the Universe*. Thereafter, the Great Nothingness *conceives* of Itself in these forms which depict *Ideas*, by means of the projection of the Divine Mind into the Primal Substance.

These regions of Form are *concepts* within the Divine Mind, whereby Imagination becomes more and more *realised*. Through the attainment of Perfection, It, according to the Gnostics, reverts back to Nothingness, which is a Great Thinker, indeed our Ultimate Ancestor.

# IV

We have seen that there has been the development of thought which had been given to the world through the medium of the Greeks. They had inherited *an Esoteric Tradition* from other sources. This was actually an Ancient Truth *about* the Human Race and *why* the Human Race exists.

With the approach of what we refer to as the Christian Era, a movement had arisen in many parts of the known world. It comprised people who sought to rise to the level of Self-Realisation. This movement was commonly referred to as *Gnosticism*.

It was considered by its advocates to be an *interpretation* of all the sacred writings in relation to what they actually *meant*, which had to do with The Universal Myth of *The Exile, the River and the Star.*

There were different schools of Gnosticism. There was one particular school which claimed that a System of Self-Realisation had been brought to a new and higher level than anything prior to it. This was the work of a Great Teacher, *a Teacher of Righteousness* named Jeshu ben Pandira who is reputed to have been born in 135 BC (4).

It is actually impossible to state with any certainty whether this *Teacher of Righteousness* actually existed or not. The roots of the Christian faith are lost in the mists of Antiquity, but there are modern Gnostics who maintain that the Jesus of the New Testament is this Jeshu ben Pandira placed in time a century *later* than the time of his actual life.

Anyone who has seriously studied the New Testament knows all too well the problems concerning the *historicity* of Jesus, the son of the carpenter. It should come as no surprise, then, that many leading New Testament scholars have no problem about accepting that the Jesus of the New Testament is *not an historical character* at all.

But *why* place this enigmatic figure one century later in time than he may or may not have actually lived? Why not leave things as they were, because if those narratives were *not* originally concerned with *historical characters or situations*, but with persons whose appearance in the text was only to fulfil some *representative* role, then why bother to reform the texts at all?

If there is a reason then it probably has a lot to do with *The Council of Nicea* and the formulation of those Creeds which would be fashioned to correspond to a definite literal pattern. The fashioners of the doctrines were to be dogmatic about the availability of Truth and, therefore, of their saviour called Jesus Christ.

The Jesus of the New Testament was portrayed as being born at a particular time. The *expectation* of his return to Earth was formulated in such a way as to coincide with the expectations of the Hermetists, those followers of what was the Higher Religion of the Greek world.

The Hermetic Schools believed that Hermes Himself, the Great Magician, would return around 500 years after the birth of Plato. As it happens there was a resurgence of Neo-Platonism, which is Hermetic thought, at this time (5).

The Jesus of the New Testament was expected, according to the New Testament, to return around 70 AD, *but he did not.* Jerusalem was occupied by Roman forces and a new Era began for the Jews.

The leaders of *The Cult of Jesus Christ* used this to their advantage, substituting Jerusalem for Rome as the centre of Divine activity on Earth. This would revert back to Rome in due course after identifying with the Gnostic tradition emanating from Jerusalem. They did this as the means of providing a belief system which would strengthen the Empire.

Christ was then preached as having returned to dwell *within his disciples,* which in effect, was to become the Roman Empire, or *Christendom.* God's Representative on Earth became the Pope, according to *The Cult of Jesus Christ* at least. The fashioners of those Creeds had a keen desire to see Rome continue to be powerful, with Divinity being found in the head of the Empire.

In identifying the return of Jesus to coincide with the expectations of the Hermetic Tradition, the Church was actually maintaining that the Jesus of the New Testament was the fulfilment of that *Esoteric Tradition* of which Plato had been one of the major custodians.

*The Cult of Jesus Christ* was *not* the fulfilment of the Hermetic Tradition, however. It had been brought to a new and higher level in the first century AD, in Alexandria. As a belief system it was to almost topple *The Cult of Jesus Christ* from its perch as the Official Religion of the Empire.

Those fashioners of *The Cult of Jesus Christ,* as we know it *now,* obviously wanted to take the very best from all the belief systems. In this Hermetism, as Neo-Platonism, was no exception. Only the Hermetic Tradition would be able to provide the Church with *the best* of intellectual and philosophical respectability.

In so doing, *The Cult of Jesus Christ* made Itself into a mouthpiece for God, and what those first century Gnostics had claimed for Jerusalem, *Rome was to incorporate into Its own traditions.* That Esoteric Tradition which had been handed down from one initiate to another for centuries, which had been touched upon by the Gnostics but *not finalised* by them, was claimed to exist within the New Testament.

This was the state of affairs which had been brought about by *The Cult of Jesus Christ*, which had succeeded in becoming *The Official Religion* of the Empire. For centuries its supremacy went unchallenged. The Bible provided us with the picture of a Humanity which was trying to *regain Immortality*, which is *a false premise.*

The true picture was that of a Psychic Principle, manifesting Itself *as* the Human Race, endeavouring to *regain Consciousness.* The means of achieving this end was *by means of the evolution* of the Human Race. We are *how* Consciousness has evolved *par excellence* on Earth.

## NOTES

(1)  *The Epistle of Paul to the Galatians*, chapter 1: 6f.

(2)  *The Gospel according to John*, chapter 4: 6.

(3)  *The Epistle of Paul to the Galatians*, chapter 4: 22f.

(4)  The existence of this Teacher of Righteousness named Jeshu ben Pandira had been supported by H. P. Blavatsky, the famous nineteenth-century Mystic. Madame Blavatsky had been associated with all sorts of Mystics, especially those associated with *Sufism.* Later on she became involved with *The Theosophical Society.*

(5)  This has been considered more fully in the chapter entitled *Christ as Hermes: the Great Magician.* See chapter 10.

# 16: The Dawn of Knowledge

## I

Humanity now faces a period of crisis in many ways. There are the dangers of pollution, over-population, energy crises, and there is the threat of escalating warfare and international terrorism.

At the same time we are forced to contend with the realisation that *The Industrial Age* and *The Christian Era* have now almost reached *their end*. Accordingly, it is becoming clearer to more and more people that Humanity must now begin to radically alter Its attitudes and re-adjust Its priorities, with all of this brought about by the anticipation of *an Awakening*, the dawning of a New Age.

We find ourselves as a Race of beings who are on the very crossroads of possibility. As we look around us we see that we are still in an unwelcome state of bondage. At the same time, a new and Promised Land begins to plague our imaginations, filling us initially with wonder and excitement. Then, after the euphoria has subsided somewhat we are reminded that something has to be *done* in order that we can experience even greater progress.

Our problems really have their source in the realisation that we are, at present, virtually *unable* to have any real and beneficial effect upon our communities. When we examine modern life it is obvious that the place given to the Principles of Civilisation is both small and *relatively* unimportant, whereas everything, everywhere, *seems* to have been in servitude to barbarism. Those aspects of life which manifest themselves as Religion, Philosophy, Science and Art, although they may not be directly in servitude to barbarism are nonetheless reduced to limited and feeble forms by the barbarism of our Age.

There are many alive today, who must almost have lost hope that the Human Race would actually survive the twentieth century, *but we did*. For many, barbarism must have seemed to have been so deep-rooted that nothing would have been able to deal with it. In their struggle for progress and survival against the awesome power of Nature, many nations have endeavoured to create the circumstances of Civilisation but, due to the present *irrationality* of Humanity, in many instances more has been taken from Civilisation than has been gained.

If Civilisation has ever existed, then it has only existed with *Esoteric Schools*. An inner circle, *the only truly civilised part of Humanity*, as has been the case as of old, have had to live alongside those who practise barbarism. These Esoteric Schools have been *hidden* from the eyes of ordinary Humanity, but their influence has been the guiding force which has always *empowered* Humanity. The aim of such Esoteric Schools is that the Human Race might be assisted and guided in order that barbarism may eventually be completely eradicated as we enter upon a new and true Civilisation.

In former times savage peoples could be taken in hand by those possessing knowledge and power. Those who were barbarian in outlook thus began to receive an education by being instructed in the Arts and Sciences. The Esoteric School provided Literature, Art and Science and, according to tradition certain personages such as the Buddha, Pythagoras, Socrates, Plato as well as Orpheus, Hermes, Krishna and Osiris, were all *initiates* into Esoteric Schools.

With this in mind it should come as no surprise that there are remarkable similarities between the contents of *The Mysteries* of the early Christians and those *Mysteries* which were enacted in Egypt on the island of Philae and elsewhere, involving the idea of *the death and resurrection of a male deity*.

Tiny snippets of information managed to make their way down to the level of ordinary *uninitiated* Humanity. Yet religious theories do not provide *satisfaction* and thus, behind recognised and Orthodox ideas and beliefs there exist, as always, illegitimate ideas about life beyond the grave, of spirit-worlds where a greater freedom was to be enjoyed in every respect.

Behind every teaching in our modern world there is some other, more Ancient system of popular belief, for behind Orthodoxy there are the remnants of Pagan Creeds. Side by side with the idea of *hidden knowledge* there runs throughout the entire length of Human history the idea that there has existed a Realised Man, *a Superman.*

Heroes were always depicted in the various Myths, such as Prometheus who brought fire to Earth to benefit Human culture. There are messengers, prophets and saints in every faith. More latterly, knights rescued damsels in distress, awakened sleeping beauties with a kiss, or else they vanquished dragons. These are all aspects of *The Superman.*

At this stage in our development Superman is alive and well in Western thought. The mass of the population live with the idea of there being a Superman, for they are never fully satisfied with Humanity as It is at present.

Literature tells them of the existence of Superman, for it was believed that God would not deal with Humanity *directly*, and that *no* normal Human being was sufficiently virtuous to look upon the face of God and receive Revelation. All living Religions begin with a Superman by means of whom Humanity receives Revelation and, just as Superman came *once upon a time*, He must return to provide us with further assistance, thus completing what He had begun.

There are many alive today who live in the hope that Superman will return to arrange their affairs, to govern them justly, to provide them with a new Code of Law as well as a new Mythology with further Revelation. Many Religions proclaim that Superman will be manifested and, in this connection, Nietzsche gives us a warning:

> I teach you the Superman. Man is something that has to be surmounted. What have you done to surmount Man?

> What is the ape to Man? A laughing stock or a sore disgrace. And just the same shall Man be to the Superman ... a laughing stock and a sore disgrace.

> Even the wisest of you is but a discord, and a hybrid of plant and phantom.

> Man is a rope-ladder over an abyss. A dangerous crossing, a dangerous wayfaring, a dangerous looking-back, a dangerous trembling and halting.

> What is great in Man is that He is a bridge and not a goal. (1)

# II

It is now generally accepted among scholars that the rituals of many Ancient Festivals were simply re-enactments of scenes from Mythology.

Furthermore, we know that Myth and Festival concur in many parts of the planet, all of which gave rise to the belief that there had existed *one original simple Myth* which was dramatised in various parts of the planet throughout the course of the year.

Adam and Eve, *as* Osiris and Isis, are symbols of a Humanity which is in a state of *exile*, yet nonetheless they are imbued with *a dim recollection* of another kind of existence which produces a kind of *homesickness*. With the majority of people this homesickness fades as they become involved in worldly affairs, but for others it never seems to disappear.

All the Myths and Legends which have been scattered all over the planet throughout our history profess to possess a Knowledge which will enable the pilgrim *to return from exile*. One such teaching is known as *The Kaballah*.

> The Bible has it that Adam fell from Grace that he descended from the Upper World of Spirit to the lower world of Matter. In Kaballist terms this can be translated as slipping down *Jacob's Ladder* the distance of one face, so that Adam, whose natural habitat was Eden or Yezirah, was incarnated in the flesh of the lower face of *Assiyyah*. There are many versions of the Fall, with as many explanations of its happening; some Kaballists describe it as the malfunction of *the Sefirot* during the unfolding of the worlds; others, as the inevitable separation of the created from the Creator. Yet others see Adam's situation as that of a Prince sent out into the Lower Worlds by his father in order to experience the kingdom he would eventually rule. Certain Kaballists say that God put Adam in this position so that he might have the pleasure of helping him. And not a few others claim that Man in *Assiyyah*, is a fleshy manifestation of the Azulitic Adam,

and that through this earthly creature God may have access to the appreciation of the Lower Worlds. (2)

Many of us do feel the need to *return,* or even to escape from our present situation. For some it is as though we are in prison (3). In this connection our liberation depends, in the final analysis, on the realisation of the truth about our present condition. We require to use all our faculties to the full, such as intellect, our motivation, and of course sound advice from those who have already overcome and escaped.

The greatest problem by far is the *I* which is in control of a person's behaviour at any given time, for it is determined *not* by personal choice as such, but *by a reaction to the environment* which evokes one *I* or another. At this time the majority of Human beings are *unable* to choose which *I* to be for, in practice, *the situation chooses* (4).

For P. D. Ouspensky, the Human being was seen to be a machine. All the needs, actions, words, thoughts and feelings of a person are the result of external influences and impressions. In our undeveloped state, which is the common lot for Human beings, we are like very complex and intricate pieces of machinery which, unlike other machinery, have the potential to know that we are pieces of machinery.

This does not preclude the attainment of higher levels of being in which *a true will is possible*. Yet progress in this direction will tend to be very slow. For Ouspensky, the lower the level of Consciousness, the blinder and more mechanical were all actions and the more subjective the outlook on life (5).

# III

We are wrestling with progress and need to relocate our bearings so that we may continue on the path we have followed since Immemorial Antiquity. Can we uncover insight from previous traditions?

For a tradition to be intelligible for each generation it must *adapt* to the environmental conditions with old forms being rejected. This is possible because there are truths which cannot be passed on by books, and accordingly there is the need for contact with *a living tradition*. The function of books and teachings is to assist the seeker to receive information which, in the case of Esoteric Knowledge, concerns an Ancient Truth about *Humanity* and *why* the Human Race exists.

For some people freedom is the goal, and this involves the realisation of an inner awareness, expressed as the recollection of a far-off country which flows with milk and honey. Others see this as no more than an infantile fantasy, and they get on with life as it is without journeying off into the unknown.

As the true seeker steps out for Canaan, Providence provides guidance, and it is as though scales fall from the eyes. It is then that repentance or *teshurah* takes place. Adam will experience the realisation of the promise that he will eventually overcome the curse of working the Earth and thereby the Upper Face of the Lower World is transformed into the Lower Face of the Upper.

There then follows the anticipation of the Exodus but before this can take place certain pre-conditions have to be met. Training will be given and at this point a Great Teacher, or *Maggid*, will emerge.

Down through the millennia, teachings have become more and more refined, but still they possess a certain symbolism. The Age out of which we are now passing, which is generally referred to as *The Age of Pisces*, or the Age of the Father, has Osiris as its symbol. During this Age, Religion was based upon the Male Principle, often featuring a male deity who was *a dying god*, with *emphasis on the death* rather than on the resurrection.

The New Age which we are now entering, because it will be an Age of balance or harmony, may have to utilise the symbolism of two Deities. These could well be Horus, the Son, and Ma'at, the Daughter, thus making balance and harmony possible. Divine power will not be symbolised by a Male or by a Female, *but by both*. At the same time a new Social System must evolve and this must be balanced, with balance experienced at all levels of our being.

To restore balance there will be the need to offset a very real Male bias in our dealings. This must mean the true and full emancipation of women so that they are able to play as full a part as possible in all Human affairs, resulting in a Humanity which does not try to *dominate* Nature as such, but which seeks *to co-operate* with Nature. This could very easily involve a fresh approach to the Deity known as Isis, who was a symbol for all that was pure and feminine.

Isis was a fertility goddess who assisted Osiris to teach the Arts and Disciplines of Civilisation to barbarians. She was skilled in Medicine and Embalming, an Enchantress who was able to produce a *phallus* to replace that of her dead husband. She was then able to conceive and she bore a son named Horus.

She had seen the senility of the Sun God, Ra, and she used her potent magick to discover His secret name which, when she had discovered it, passed on to Horus to enable him to join the pantheon of the gods as the Deity of the Sun.

She was also remembered for her selfless dedication to her husband and son; this led, in general, to Isis being recognised and accepted as the Archetype of the Great Mother, the personification of all things *Feminine*, with cows sacred to her (6).

*The Cult of Isis* taught respect for *all* life. There were no blood sacrifices, only offerings of milk, honey and herbs. The Temple was forbidden to the general public, so services were conducted in the open air, outside the precincts of the Temple where all could participate. Important to *The Cult of Isis* was the creative force of vibration and in her right hand she has a sistrum, with its four bars representing the interplay of the four elements of Earth, Water, Fire and Air, and the vibrating forces which organise them into a recognisable pattern. In her other hand there is a pitcher of milk, emphasising her role as Mother and Provider.

This Cult had a profound influence upon the development of *The Cult of Jesus Christ*, which was to become *The Official Religion* of the Roman Empire. This is made clear when we see how a second century priest of *The Temple of Isis*, a man known as Apuleius, who was the author of *The Golden Ass*, depicts a scene where a man has been transformed into an ass but who regains his Humanity by eating a rose dedicated to Isis on her Feast Day (7).

Isis possessed a warm Humanity. She indulgently accepted the weakness of others, always forgiving provided she was certain that there was no evil still lurking in the heart. She was the epitome of virtue and through linking lunar cycles with menstruation she became the Goddess of the Moon.

She was also of considerable importance to seafarers as dominion over the seas, oceans, rivers, lochs and sacred springs was granted to her.

Worship of Isis spread far and wide, from the port of Piraeus in the fourth century BC to Delos two centuries later. The Cult was utilised by the Romans, and what they had formerly suppressed was to become a recognised, respected and important form of worship. The heyday of *The Cult of Isis* was from the reign of Augustus to that of Julian the Apostate, a period of more than four hundred years.

The Spring Festival for Isis, *The Navigium Isidus*, was held on the 5th March, during which time she was called upon to invoke a blessing on navigators after the resumption of trade at the end of winter. This was to ensure that Egyptian corn made its way safely to the granaries of Rome. During the Festivals those sailing vessels of the everyday world were, somehow or other, to become *representations of ethereal ships* which would carry the souls of departed Ancestors across the River of Death to Paradise.

In time, *The Cult of Isis* and *The Cult of Mary* were to become indistinguishable. With the increasing importance of *The Cult of Jesus Christ* we see that Isis was to be replaced eventually by Mary who, like Isis, was a Virgin Goddess and Isis, the Personification of Woman, in part at least, became Mary, the Mother of God.

As religion as we know it was coming into being there was a fusion of certain formerly existing Myths and Teachings. In Europe, the advent of Christianity heralded the end of the Pagan Temples, but it would be naive to expect, when the Telestrion at Eleusis was demolished in 396 AD, that when the Elders walked out of the Sacred Precincts they were instantly converted to Christianity. We should not forget that *The Mysteries* had been celebrated there since the seventh century BC. Now they were prohibited but they would still have meant everything to those who had been initiated.

The reality behind *The Eleusian Festivals* was *The Cult of Dionysius*, and the celebrations were to ensure that Spring would appear after the end of Winter. Dionysius was the god of Spring, representing that life-force which appears in vegetation and in reproductive animals. Neo-Platonists of a later Era were to refer to him as *The Mind of the World*.

Also incorporated into the evolving *Cult of Jesus Christ* were those beliefs to do with *The Cult of Mithras*. The devotees of *The Cult of Mithras* believed in a god whom they considered to be the Creator and Orderer of the Universe, who was the Divine Word Incarnate. This god had been born into the world to deliver Humanity from *Ahriman*, the power of Darkness.

Mithras was deemed to have been born on or around the 25th of December, after which he was visited by shepherds who left their flocks to worship him. When he was fully grown he taught wherever possible, also *working miracles* and then, after a Last Supper with his disciples he ascended into Heaven, from which he is expected to return to judge the guilty and lead the elect down a River of Fire to a state of blessed Immortality.

As soon as *The Cult of Jesus Christ* was strong enough to misuse its power it acted quickly. In 313 AD, by *The Edict of Milan*, Mithras the Sun God was replaced by Jesus Christ, the Son of God, and those sacred fires of Mithras were to be seen no more.

Ancient Teachings were incorporated into developing the *Cult of Jesus Christ*, in order to be as *attractive* to as many people as possible. This enabled *The Cult of Jesus Christ* to become the Cult of the entire Empire with Divinity being found in the head of the Empire, as before. This was the forerunner of the Papacy as we know it.

Yet there were very real *differences*. In the *Genesis* narratives we see Humanity, which had descended from the Godhead, Itself, in a setting which is not too unfamiliar but what is *absent* from the Biblical narratives is the suggestion that *the same Logos*, by means of which the worlds were created, abides within Human beings *as a permanent endowment*. This enables the Human Race to *recognise* Divine workmanship.

The torments inherent in the material body are derived from the Zodiacal Cycle, and through *imprisonment* in the material body, *The Immanent Man* is condemned to a life of the senses. Rebirth is the liberation of *The Immanent Man*, by the mercy of God, from the passions of the material body. Enlightened as to the need for Rebirth and of its nature, as far as this is possible without actually undergoing the experience, Tat (8) is ready to be reborn.

# IV

Teachings are all very well. They exist to guide the seeker to Knowledge. When Knowledge comes, however, there is really no need *to cling* to any Teaching or Tradition. Prophets and Sages of all Ages were able to look forward to the time when Knowledge would dawn and we would know *even as we are known*. Our task now is not to provide another teaching but, on the contrary, we must go *beyond all the instruction we have had* in the realisation that Knowledge will soon appear for us.

In the Hermetic Literature, which is also known as *The Corpus Hermeticum*, and from the work known as *The Key of Hermes* we read:

Not yet are we able to open the eyes of the Mind to behold the beauty, the imperishable, inconceivable beauty, of the Good. For you will see it, when you cannot say anything about it. For the knowledge of it is Divine silence and the annihilation of all senses.

Shining about all the Mind, it also shines upon the whole soul and draws it up from the body, and changes it into Divine essence.

'We have been deified by generation,' says Hermes. 'Whosoever has attained by the mercy of God this Divine generation, leaving behind the bodily senses, recognises that he has been constituted out of Divine Elements and is glad.' (9)

Then one realises that a Great Plan is unfolding, and that this has been known by Sages of all Ages, and is integrally involved with the Ancient Science of *Astrology*.

According to Orthodox belief, Astrology was never within Judaic Kaballah, but this is quite untrue, as a few examples will illustrate. In the Talmud, there is much discussion of the influence of the macrocosm on Man. One rabbi, Hanina by name, argues that the planets determine the fate of a person, whilst an opponent says that Israel should not be dismayed by the celestial signs because it is not ruled by any Star. Another rabbi puts forward the idea that Abraham was a prophet and did not need Astrology. No one in these discussions ever denies the validity of celestial influences, *only their rulership over Israel*, which in Kaballistic terms is a symbolic state of spirituality that operates above the power of the constellations.

The Zodiac, the band of twelve constellations, through which the Sun, the Moon and planets pass during the course of their journey through the heavens, is touched upon in Kaballistic tradition symbolically. The *Sefer Yezirah* gives a precise account of the time of year and the area of the Human body which they govern, and allots to each of them one of the twelve tribes of Israel. Each

125

of the Biblical Brotherhood represents one of the twelve essential types of Human being, that is, the twelve *Yeziratic Tefiret* natures possible. Thus, for example, Judah, the scion of the Royal Tribe, is the martial sign of Aries whilst Manasseh, Scorpio, is the tribe of Mystics and Prophets. (10)

We need to realise that the Plan is unfolding as it should. Thus we see a whole variety of men and women of today making startling claims predicting the dawning of a New Age.

With Nostradamus we have a similar scenario, and some believe that there is *a secret teaching* within his predictions. If the prophecies of Nostradamus are to be correctly interpreted, for *interpreted they must be*, we can see something very startling indeed and, in relation to his prophecies he stated that, 'These are the perpetual prophecies until the year 3797.'

If we assume that 3797 is an *encoded* date, and then subtract the date of writing we are left with the date 2242, which is 3797 minus 1555, signifying that there may be a special significance for the year 2242 AD. As it happens, the year 2242 AD is the year that the Rulership of the Sun will give way to the Rulership of Saturn, with Saturn being *the herald* of a new and golden Age, indicating that there is a planetary sequence of 354 years (11).

It should also be noted that there are different cycles, all of them operating at different levels. (12) Our Solar System takes approximately 25,920 years to circle round the Greater Zodiac, completing a Solar year by this means. By the same token the Solar System takes about 2160 years to move through each of the signs of the Greater Zodiac, with each of these twelve periods referred to as an Age.

For some there is a great need to recognise the importance of the influence of the yet-to-be-discovered planet Isis. To some the planet Isis possesses those qualities which are characteristic of a *higher octave of Venus* (13). Isis is also associated with the sign of Taurus, with Taurus easily representing *Terra Mater*, the Mother Earth, for Isis is the Mother of and the Queen of the Universe.

Those Earth-shattering characteristics of Taurus seem to become manifest when Isis is *triggered* by Pluto. At the outbreak of World War II, Isis was one-and-a-half degrees Leo and was applying to a conjunction with Pluto at 2 degrees 8 minutes Leo. This conjunction became exact at the end of October 1939.

Isis has very little influence on the chart of an individual except by means of Pluto, which moved through its own sign of Scorpio from 1983 until 1995, making a square aspect with Isis in Leo. It is difficult to pinpoint the influence of Isis on the chart of an individual as it is more *gravitational* than Pluto, owing to its slow movement. The effect of Isis is better seen in general population trends, and those with a strong Isis positioning would possibly be instruments of a power which is greater but less *worldly* than that of Pluto.

# V

What we now await is an Awakening to a new and higher level of Realisation, one which is no longer dependent upon teachings. Humanity will be in possession of Knowledge, and teachings will have been rendered *obsolete*, for they exist only as a means of assisting the seeker to uncover Knowledge, being only of need to those who are in a position of *relative ignorance*.

In the light of this Knowledge and, in relation to teachings, the teachings will be seen simply as the influences one has encountered on the road *to* Knowledge. Teachings will no longer be seen as an end in themselves but as stepping-stones, with *no* lasting significance, for they must fade into obscurity when Knowledge has dawned.

What is required of us now is to surrender completely to the power of God who rules *within* us. Thereafter, the course taken is not totally dependent upon ourselves, but on the power to which we have surrendered for an Inner Reality will have been awakened to guide us.

> So man, in seeking the nature of worship that can make contact with the Great Life, needs above all to stop the welling-up of imagination and thinking. For by doing so he really paralyses his *nefsu* (signifying the passions of greed and hunger) and surrenders his Human ability and wisdom; that is to say, the Human being submits with complete sincerity to God who rules within him.
>
> This in fact is nothing new, for men of old followed this path and found a contact of this quality they could feel within them. Why, then, are there not so many people like that in our own time who

still have this contact? The reason is simply that conditions on Earth for Mankind keep changing as generation succeeds generation, and many people are easily affected by the influence of these ever-changing conditions that face them. Especially this has been so as the Human Mind has progressively developed its science. This has, as it were, increasingly opened the way for the inner feeling to fade from the realm of inner peace into the realm of thought. In consequence, the Human self gradually comes to be ruled more and more by thought instead of the quietness of the inner feeling or the inner self, so that in the end Man's emotions and brain are always busy and his inner feeling has almost no opportunity to be at peace.

Certainly, men must think, for thought is an important tool with which they can strive to fulfil the needs of their life on Earth and so make their existence here an orderly one. But to become aware of the *Kejiwaan* and make contact with the Great Life men *do not need to use their minds.* On the contrary, they should stop the process of thinking and imagining. For only by so doing can a person receive a something from beyond his reach that, at length, attracts a vibration of energy felt within the self.

Clearly, then, the sole way to make contact with the Great Life, or with the power of God, is for a man to surrender sincerely and earnestly. And the surrender must not be in word only, but must penetrate throughout his inner feeling until he truly feels that he believes in, praises and worships no one but God Almighty, Allah. (14)

Surrender to the Inner Self or to God is also surrender to the realisation of Destiny. This will involve a break with the past and, when we are ready to do this, to leave *irrationality* behind us, *the Awakening* will take place *as* the break with the past, as it is integrally involved with the *on-goingness* of the process of evolution.

Our approach to unity in terms of Religion and Politics will provide the circumstances within which the future will be experienced. This has nothing to do with the *beliefs* of Humanity as such, but will be based on the *aims* of Humanity, and the desire to rise to greater levels of Consciousness.

We require to create circumstances, *the* circumstances which are able to produce the required effect, so that we can experience it. We require to unite or, more correctly, *to create a unity*, in order that the Great I AM can become more perfect by means of the greater evolution of Consciousness; this greater Consciousness will be the outcome of the development of greater unity, of *co-operation* or, in terms employed by Orthodoxy, Brotherhood and Sisterhood.

## NOTES

(1) Friedrich Nietzsche, *Thus Spake Zarathustra*. Published by Penguin. From the prologue, p. 11f.

(2) Z'ev ben Shimon Halevi, *The Way of the Kaballah*. Published by Rider & Co., London in 1976. p. 60.

(3) P. D. Ouspensky, *In Search of the Miraculous*. Published by Routledge & Kegan Paul, London in 1949. p. 30.

Ouspensky states, 'You do not realise your own situation. You are in prison. All you can wish for, if you are a sensible man is to escape. But how escape? It is necessary to tunnel under a wall. One man can do nothing. But let us suppose that there are ten or twenty men. If they work in turn, and if one covers another then they can complete the tunnel and escape.'

(4) As above; on page 212 Ouspensky states, 'Out of himself a man cannot produce a single thought, a single action. Everything he says, does, thinks, feels … all of this *happens*. Man is born, lives, dies, builds houses, writes books, *not as he wants to* but as it happens. Everything *happens*.'

(5) Kenneth Walker, *A Study of Gurdjieff's Teaching*. Published by Jonathan Cape, London in 1957. p. 37.

(6) Living cows are a great economic asset for Humanity as they supply milk, cheese, butter, and yogurt and so on. They do not deprive Humanity of food, for they eat the inedible remains of harvest crops such as the tops of sugarcane and grass, thus converting items of little value to Humanity into products of immediate utility.

We need to learn to treat the animal and Human kingdoms with the minimum of violence, or with the *non-violence* which Buddhists and Hindus refer to as *Ahimsa*.

(7) From *The Book of the Prophet Zechariah* in the Old Testament, we have the prophecy:

> Rejoice greatly, O Daughter of Zion
> Shout aloud, O Daughter of Jerusalem.
> Lo, your king comes to you;
> Triumphant and victorious is he,
> Humble and riding on an ass,
> On a colt, the foal of an ass.

The Christian community believed that this had been fulfilled by Jesus of Nazareth; accordingly, we read in *The Gospel according to Matthew*, chapter 21: 5,

> Tell the Daughter of Zion,
> Behold, your king is coming to you,
> Humble, and mounted on an ass,
> And on a colt, the foal of an ass.

(8) Tat is a son of Hermes and, as such, he is the brother of Asclepius. Their father, Hermes, is *The Messenger of the gods*, and he has come to Earth in order to teach and guide Humanity.

(9) *The Corpus Hermeticum*, X. 5-6.

(10) Z'ev ben Shimon Halevi, *The Way of the Kaballah*. Published by Rider & Co., London in 1979. p. 129.

According to tradition the following table is of the Tribes of Israel and their corresponding Astrological signs:

| | | |
|---|---|---|
| Judah / Aries, | Issachar / Taurus, | Zebulun / Gemini, |
| Reuben / Cancer, | Simeon / Leo, | Gad / Virgo, |
| Ephraim / Libra, | Mannasseh / Scorpio, | Benjamin / Sagittarius, |
| Dan / Capricorn, | Asher / Aquarius, | Naphtali / Pisces |

(11) Should this sequence of 354 years actually be the case, among other sequences, then this would mean that the Cycle of Venus began in 1180 AD, the Cycle of the Moon began in 1534 AD, the Cycle of the Sun began in 1888 AD and the Cycle of Saturn will begin in 2242 AD.

(12) One such is a period of 504 years; this is the equivalent of 7 x 72 years, with 72 years being a period of influence by a sequence of planets, seven in number.

(13) Esoteric Tradition informs us that Chiron, the healer, is the eleventh planet whereas Isis is the twelfth; Chiron is situated between Saturn and Uranus with Chiron often thought of as *a higher octave* of Mercury.

(14) Robert Lyle, *Subud*. Published by Humanus Limited in 1983. p. 9f.

# 17: Unity: Our Greatest Need

## I

Those of us who are aware of the existence of a process of historical development will be only too aware of the great upheavals of recent history. These were the Industrial and Agricultural Revolutions with the uprooting of many old and well-established communities. People then flocked in great numbers to towns and cities to find employment, so as to receive the money to gain access to the food, clothing and shelter which are necessary for civilised living.

An even greater influence upon our communities has been the arrival of compulsory education. This produced a vast explosion of Knowledge which has produced our so-called Space-Age and, more importantly, a state of affairs such as we see now, whereby modern Western Humanity enjoys *more ease and comfort than any Roman Emperor*. Nowadays, rather than spending our time in the performance of work-related duties, we are able to postulate an existence where work is kept to a minimum, where life is lived primarily in finding fulfilment, which will involve Self-Discovery.

In contrast to what we generally experience now in the West, only a few generations ago it was commonplace for people to go hungry, eating *only* when food was available. People lived in conditions which we would consider intolerable, where there was little or no education and the masses had no say at all in the Governmental system, everyone living within rather fixed frontiers, in more ways than one.

The nineteenth century was the time when Karl Marx made his appearance on the scene of time. It was an Age of great achievement, something to which Marx actually referred in *The Communist Manifesto*, where he was to state that 'the bourgeoisie had been the first to show what Man's activity could bring about'.

Great wonders had been accomplished and they were considered to overshadow the Pyramids of Egypt, Roman aqueducts and Gothic cathedrals. Marx actually congratulated the bourgeoisie for drawing the nations of the Earth into Civilisation. Great cities had been built, with enormous sections of the populations of many nations being delivered from the idiocy of rural life. With the harnessing of Human potential the result had been production more massive and colossal than anything seen by previous generations.

The invention of machinery, the application of Chemistry to agriculture and industry, the railways, steam navigation, electrical telegraphs, the construction of canals, the cultivation of continents and so on had subjected the forces of Nature to the needs of Human culture. This was something which previous generations would have thought *to be impossible.*

Society was in a great state of transition. It had become more rationalistic and materialistic. The technical achievements were greatly welcomed and valued, and a much better lot for all was confidently anticipated, and this in spite of the fact that wealth was rather unevenly distributed. Religion was steadily losing its grip, leaving a gap in the outlook of our forefathers, who were crucially aware that the developing Civilisation was less impressive than the technical achievements which were readily available.

Progress had seen the production of fabulous wealth. Yet it was having a rather destructive effect upon the inner feelings of the Human Race. Marx saw the gains but he also counted the cost. Marx maintained that the New Age had left intact 'no other bond between man and man but naked self-interest, but callous cash-payment'. Much of what had been good in former times 'had been drowned in the ice-cold waters of egoistic calculation'. Marx felt that personal dignity had become exchange value, and the feeling of affection in family relationships had been reduced to purely financial considerations.

The coldness of the Age and a growing unrest, such as with the rise of *The Chartist Movement* (1), led to the fear that the ruling classes were in danger of losing their wealth and privileges. The crowned heads of Europe were all too aware that the rumblings of discontent were growing stronger and stronger all the time.

On the surface, things may have appeared to be all well and good. At the funeral of Edward VII in May 1910, nine European sovereigns were in attendance (2). When in Berlin in 1913, Wilhelm II and George V were actually photographed wearing the uniforms of regiments of each other's armies, with George V wearing the uniform of an officer of the 1st Prussian Dragoon Guards.

One could easily have been lulled into a false sense of security, for a great power struggle was in the offing. By as early as 1910, the great nations of Europe were already divided into two opposing camps. There was *The Triple Entente* of Great Britain, France and Russia on the one side and *The Triple Alliance* of Germany, Austria-Hungary and Italy on the other side.

The ruling classes of Europe felt that all their internal problems, whether they were political, social or economic in character, could be solved *by means of a victorious war*. In fact, it was believed that this was the only way to unite the entire population behind the Monarchy. It was for the survival of dynasties, for the prestige of nations that the ruling classes of Europe allowed themselves to be convinced that the war was not only necessary, but *imperative*. The Military, anxious that they would not be caught at a disadvantage, urged their sovereigns to decide for war and in the face of these urgings the sovereigns dived into the abyss of all-out war.

It has been stated that the Germans were the most anxious for war. They were alarmed at the growing strength of Russia and, to a lesser extent, France. The German generals were set on fighting a war sooner rather than later. The murder of Archduke Ferdinand had given them the excuse they were looking for. So, whilst appearing as the aggrieved party, they attacked. The assassin of Archduke Ferdinand believed that, even if he had not committed the dastardly deed, the Germans would have found another excuse.

The war which was to follow was to bankrupt Europe, and the United States of America was to emerge from the conflict as one of the most powerful nations on Earth. Meanwhile, the peoples of Europe could do no more than pick up the pieces and get on with life as best they could. Yet so great had been the cost of war in Human sacrifice and so on, that the upheaval had left life in such a way that things could never be the same as before.

Many of the crowned heads of Europe were to lose their thrones, meaning that power was up for grabs. Civil wars broke out and so extreme were the circumstances to be endured, particularly for the Germans. It was obvious that power would inevitably end up in the hands of those who were very extreme. *This was the recipe for yet another war to be fought by the next generation.*

# II

The generation born within the United Kingdom to those who had been involved in World War II, from 1939 to 1945, were the first who had not had to do military service. In addition, they were to have the benefit of secondary and further education.

Problems still exist. It would appear that opportunities for progress have been squandered. Perhaps it is coherency which is our greatest need. This implies *the need for unity*, expressed as the realisation of common goals, of shared ideals. It will certainly involve some kind *of collective action*.

The populations of the nations of the Earth are becoming more and more sophisticated all the time. Even in our bulletins which are becoming more and more comprehensive all the time, we hear of great controversy within the world of monetary economics.

Terms such as 'the money supply' or 'public sector borrowing requirement', or PSBR for short, are all well known to anyone who has access to the Mass Media. Yet, although most people are aware of these terms, the majority of people neither understand them nor their importance. Most of us are of the opinion that they are truly only of interest to *bureaucrats*.

Almost everyone is now aware of the fact that the major characteristic of our modern world is its *interdependence*. We all have to live in communities and nations which could not exist without co-operation and the co-ordinated efforts of the citizens of nations and continents. As we shall see, however, this unity exists within very strict boundaries in order to maintain a unity *within* nations which, in turn, *compete* with each other.

In all our communities *specialisation* is the rule. This means that *everything we need has to be exchange*d. Because of this, in the past, some sort of *money system* had to be developed.

As our communities have developed, specialisation has developed accordingly. In practical terms the only sensible way to create the wealth necessary for civilised living is *concentration upon the development of a trade or skill at which one excels.*

Production is then *indirect* rather than direct, meaning that *exchange becomes all-important*. Some sort of Medium of Exchange had to develop. The Medium of Exchange permits someone who has contributed to the creation of wealth in one particular field to gain access to goods and services in other areas (3).

Money, therefore, has an importance, and monetary economics is a worthwhile study. Without the institution of money this complex and convenient world of supply and demand would not be quite so possible, or so it would appear.

Without money it is probable that some sort of barter system would have to be developed, especially in times of shortage, to ensure payment. This reminds us of the primary use of money as *a Medium of Exchange*, although there is something else we require to understand. It appears that money, rather than simply being the servant or facilitator, has actually become *the Master*.

> Goodhart (1978) and others made the distinction between the medium of exchange function which is *not* unique to money and 'the means of final payment function' which is. A transaction can be completed by the exchange of goods and services for the evidence of debt, e.g. trade credit, a bill of exchange or a charge account …

> … but the buyer cannot be said to have paid for his purchase until he has surrendered money, nor will the seller consider that payment has been made until he has received money. (4)

Not only do people trade with each other within nations but nations trade with each other. We live in a world where nations exist side by side, with each traditionally seeking what is best for its own people, or ruling class.

No nation is actually self-sufficient, although a large and powerful nation such as the United States of America could supply all its needs in an emergency. Smaller States such as Hong Kong or Singapore could not possibly exist without trade. Such trade between nations poses a rather special problem, and it is a problem of a *monetary* nature. We need to have a currency which can be exchanged on international markets.

Now, of course, the times are changing. Travel and the continuing growth of education and so on, have led many to seek an alternative way of living on the planet. Besides, we are on the threshold of a New Age, which means that *no* matter what anyone says or does, life can *never* be the same again. Our communities have to be *completely restructured.*

Trade is now global in extent and the United States of America, as the most powerful nation and economy in the world, has taken advantage of cheap labour overseas, as well as providing employment for allies to keep those communities as stable as possible. Thus cars, televisions, computers and stereo equipment made in Taiwan, Mexico and Japan are being bought by the citizens of the United States of America. This has caused a trade imbalance and has produced *unemployment*, something which the consumer does not really consider. The consumer, in the majority of cases, asks only for *quality at a reasonable price.*

Yet so far we have only mentioned the symptoms: *what is the actual problem?* When we look at our planet we see that *economic nationalism* is the order of the day. Nations, in general, are concerned primarily with their own welfare and, by the same token, with the maintenance of the *status quo* in an international sense. Economics has been characterised by competition, as well as the maintenance of the *status quo* within nations.

Problems are now coming to a head with so much of our international dealings characterised by violence and hopelessness. More and more we realise that money and exchange rates, tariffs and trade wars, price-fixing and protectionism exist *because the Human Race is divided.* When unity comes, that is, when the Kingdom of God, which is Theocracy, has been established then, *and only then* will Humanity be linked politically, economically and in terms of Religion.

Many are now entertaining the possibility that Governments, as we know them, are fundamental to our problems. They have been fronts for Military elites who did not actually want unity; in fact, they consistently worked against it by means of the Cold War. They knew that a period of real and prolonged peace would have rendered them obsolete, therefore *powerless.*

This means that Governments as we have known them do not have the solution to our problems because they are fundamental to our problems which at the end of the day have their source in *irrationality.* While power lies, ultimately, in the hands of those who *specialise in violence* there can be no progress, for the maintenance of the present system cannot permit anything else.

This is not to suggest that Governments are not doing their best. It is simply a matter of priorities and insight

# III

There have always been those who dreamt of unity and who worked for it. This unity was not only between nations but between the citizens of nations. The reason why this has been sought was *the injustice of division* and the dreadful waste of resources, with communities being organised to ensure the dominion of one group over another.

Certain sections of a nation, or of the nations of the Earth, are deliberately left under-developed as a means of preventing them from becoming *too* powerful. Monetary economics is employed as a means of *controlling people*, in order to either *provide* them with access to the wealth produced, or to *prevent* them from gaining access to wealth.

The reason for this is, quite simply, because power as we know it is based on wealth. This means that *if wealth is shared then power is shared*. By the same token *refusing to share wealth is also the refusal to share power*. This is the very hallmark of *The Irrational Stage* of our development.

Spaniard Francis de Vitoria (1480-1556) was a Dominican. He did pioneering work in the field of International Law. He was the first man in the modern period to have proposed *The Theory of Treaty* as an explanation of the origin and vitality of the ordering of the State. He rejected the idea of colonialisation and his book *Relectio de Indis* led to him being recognised as the predecessor of Hugo Grotius.

The idea of International Law reached its climax in a book by Hugo Grotius (1583-1645). In it he enforced the distinction which had already existed in the thought of the Romans, which is that Natural Law, *ius naturale*, was distinct from the law instituted by the State, *ius civile*.

The idea of International Law has as its basic rule the maxim *pacta sunt servanda*, meaning that *treaties must be honoured* and this applies to all relations between individuals and nations. The idea of Treaty also plays a part in the relationship between individuals and the State. By Treaty the individuals have handed over some of their rights to the State in order that, thereby, the State may be able to safeguard their interests.

In any study of Natural Law, it is necessary to ascertain what rights the individual has transferred to the State, and *how* the State may be equipped to safeguard those rights. The Law of the State must never be permitted to come into conflict with Natural Law. It must determine those concrete laws which will, as far as possible, guarantee that Natural Law will be observed in the concrete circumstances of Space and Time.

John Locke (1632-1704) also considered these things. For him the Human Race was naturally peaceful and co-operative and because of this, social life came easily. If there is any need for authority it is *to preserve the existence of the collective*, which is also the *unity* of the collective. It is for this specific reason that we have laws.

According to Locke the function of the State, however, should be *limited to the maintenance of the public good*. Beyond this, people should be left free. Absolute power and the Divine Right of Kings were wrong because power must ultimately rest with the people. They should have the power to make Governments. Those who fashion laws should not execute them.

The situation which exists at present is that there is a major imbalance in the distribution of wealth among the nations of the Earth. All over the world hundreds of millions have to go without adequate amounts of nutritious food, and this in spite of the fact that there is and always has been *an abundance* of food for all of us. Each day the planet is producing approximately two pounds of grain for each Human being, as well as beans, nuts, fruit, root crops, vegetables as well as grass-fed meat, for those who want it.

What we have to realise is that the starvation in the world today cannot be blamed on Mother Nature, for it is the result of *political decisions* by Governments. This has already been mentioned many times, such as in *Food First; the Myth of Scarcity*

> Throughout the history of Mankind, it is often argued, there have been periodic famines. And these are associated with weather disasters which we surely cannot control; but famines are not God-ordained, they are Man-arranged. As one French historian remarked,

> 'The great French famines and food shortages of the Middle Ages occurred during periods when foodstuffs were not lacking, they were indeed produced in great quantity and exported. The social system and structure was largely responsible for these deficiencies.'

Most people believe that famines in India have been a constant phenomenon related to a poor climate. But the frequency of famine in India has not been constant. Famine intensified under colonialisation, especially during the second half of the Nineteenth Century even though food production kept pace with population growth. After the opening of the Suez Canal in 1870, India became a major exporter of wheat to Britain, other Western nations and Egypt. As Sir George Watt wrote in 1908,

'The better classes of the community were exporting the surplus stocks that formerly were stored against times of scarcity and famine.'

This sort of thing has actually occurred during the twentieth century. The root cause of the problem is that power is in the hands of a relatively small number of people and they, in general, *seem* to be abusing it.

Following World War II, over one quarter of the United States' funds on food aid was spent under The Marshall Plan. Enormous quantities of grain on credit flowed into Italy and France to help keep the impoverished working classes from voting against capitalism. Marshall himself stated at the time,

'*Food is a vital factor in our foreign policy.*'

In 1959, Senator Humphrey criticised those who would have food aid serve only as a surplus disposal mechanism. He saw food *as a potent political weapon.*

'We have been told repeatedly that this is a world-wide struggle for men's minds, for their loyalties. There is a struggle between ways of life, a system of values. Our values are different from those of the totalitarians. If it is a world-wide struggle, it would seem to me we would want to mobilise all the resources we possibly can in order to win it. And in a world of want and hunger what is more powerful than food and fibre.' (5)

# IV

As we enter a New Age, an Age which will be characterised by harmony, and which will be expressed as a Human Brotherhood and Sisterhood, we must ensure that no wealth is simply syphoned off from one community for the sake of the selfishness of another. This will obviously involve the cultivation of land, the *use* of land and, ultimately, the *ownership* of land.

We all seek for freedom, but there can be *no true freedom* while millions are being deliberately kept in a state of grinding poverty. Decisions have to be made, and this will involve the use of land and the cultivation of food.

The present imbalance is caused by a system which produces Governments as we have known them. The situation can only be rectified by people taking the initiative themselves, instead of having to rely on Governments to act on their behalf. This must involve some sort of *solidarity* and, therefore, an *equality* of sorts, as the expression of *a Common Purpose*.

Here we could learn a great deal from the Buddhists and the Hindus, who have a word *Ahimsa* upon which we could ponder. It is usually translated as *non-violence*, and it means we have to treat the Human and animal kingdoms with the *minimum* of violence. Nationalism in an extreme form, or even forms of *speciesism*, can have no place in New Age Consciousness.

What we require is a ruling class, assuming that a ruling class is indispensable, which will be more concerned with *the well-being of others* than in their own self-advancement. This is no easy task, for these people would have to have been totally conquered by love and grace. This has been touched upon in *The Srimad Bhagavatam*.

> He [Maharajah Paraksit] was such a great emperor that all his enemies would come and bow down at his feet and surrender all their wealth for their own benefit. He was full of youth and strength, and he possessed insuperable kingly opulences. Why did he want to give up everything, including his life?

> Those who are devoted to the cause of the Personality of
> Godhead live only for the welfare, development and happiness
> of others. They do not live for selfish interests. (6)

Our journey, which is experienced *as Existence*, is really a journey *towards Unity*. This unity will mean the end of struggle and the beginning of peace. It will be the end of want and the dawn of prosperity for all. Unity will be all-embracing and, as such, it will have a political and religious dimension.

Our major task is to replace the Military elites who actually control almost every community. *War* is the problem, for our attitudes are such that we are *at war* with other people and other nations. Everywhere there is division with very little shared. Instead of co-operation we have endless competition.

More than anything we require unity. We are actually *internally guided*, and we must concern ourselves with the further evolution of Consciousness. This will be expressed in our ability to understand *as* the realisation of potential. We must begin to see ourselves within the context of the *evolution* of Consciousness and *as a Collective Consciousness*.

Prosperity is simply the ability to function *with ease*. This prosperity actually comes from within. Prosperity means living *as we would like to live*. Prosperity is a natural state of unity.

All the wealth at the disposal of the Human Race is produced by the Mind. Money is not wealth, just a means of exchanging wealth. It is only necessary when there is a lack which, in practical terms, is the *lack of a Common Purpose*. Wealth is not money but the creation of goods and services. Money cannot solve monetary problems. Only the power of the imagination can do that.

Wealth is the product of a state of Mind. Money has no value in and of itself, although it has been used to exchange wealth. Money should be used to assist people if its use is to be continued. Bills and debts are only agreements.

## NOTES

(1)  The Chartists were a political party founded in England in 1838; its views were contained in *The People's Charter* of which the principal aims were as follows:

- universal suffrage,
- vote by ballot,
- annual Parliaments,
- division of the United Kingdom into equal electoral districts,
- abolition of the property qualification for membership of Parliament and payment of the latter for their services.

(2)  The sovereigns at the funeral were as follows: Haakon VII of Norway, Ferdinand of Bulgaria, Manoel of Portugal, Wilhelm II of Germany, George I of Greece, Albert I of Belgium, Alfonso XIII of Spain, George V of Great Britain and Ireland and Frederick VII of Denmark.

(3)  Money is a medium of exchange, a measure of value, a store of value, a standard of deferred payments and a means of facilitating one-way payments.

(4)  J. Struthers & H. Speight, *Money: Institutions, Theory & Policy*. Published by Longman in 1986. p. 13.

In economics there are various monetary theories such as the Classical Monetary Theory of Money, the Keynesian System and Modern Monetarism.

(5)  Frances Moore Lappe & Joseph Collins, *Food First; the Myth of Scarcity*. Published by Condor Books & Souvenir Press, London. p. 69.

(6)  His Divine Grace A. C. Bhaktivedanta Swami Prabhupada, *Srimad Bhagavatam*. First Canto. *The Great Classics of India Series*. Published by *The Bhaktivedanta Book Trust* in 1985. Chapter 4, texts 11-12.

# 18: The Perfection of I AM

## I

There have been many great philosophers in the past and they have had considerable influence upon the development of Human thought. One such was Baruch Spinoza (1), also known as Benedictus de Spinoza. He had been born in Amsterdam of Portuguese-Jewish parents. His upbringing had made him familiar with the many-sided, and to a great extent *Neo-Platonic*, thought of the Jewish-Arabic tradition. It led to him being expelled from the synagogue, his beliefs proving to be too progressive for the time.

He had noticed that there are two tendencies which are fundamental to Human beings. These were *thinking self-realisation in God* and *the will to preserve oneself in the world*. Spinoza realised that the latter makes us a slave to the world, and actually *prevents* us from discovering ourselves *in* God.

Spinoza also realised that *Inclination* is active in both these fundamental tendencies, with Inclination being an aspect of Thought. Reason (*Ratio*) governs *our thinking self-realisation of ourselves* and Imagination (*Imaginatio*) governs our will to *preserve ourselves* in the world.

For Spinoza there was only one independent unit or *substance* and this was the all-embracing *unity* of God. This was something which influenced another great philosopher, Gottfried Leibniz (2). He was a forerunner of modern logic and the discoverer of differential and integral calculus at the same time as Newton. He was driven by a great desire for harmony, always seeking the universal.

For Leibniz the individual being (*ens singulare*) is distinct from all other beings, and in this experience of *Self* the activity of the distinct being is *the unfolding of Self.* There is an infinite number of these individuals and each one is a *Monad.* In the unfolding of itself the activity of the Monad is *Consciousness.* As the Monads are constantly striving towards a clearer Consciousness, the Universe is *always* developing or *evolving* towards *a higher level of Consciousness.*

With Human beings conscious of the need to preserve themselves in the world, as Civilisation has developed, the State is looked upon as being able to give Humanity that which Nature cannot, which is peace, order and the possibility of prosperity. In Society, therefore, Human beings, being many, are actually endeavouring to overcome their separateness to become *as One.*

John Locke (3) believed that the State should have as its most important characteristic the fact that it exists for those who *form* it. Repeatedly he insists that the end of Government is the good of the community. He also stated that the State, in fact, was *machinery* which we create for our own good to run our own purposes.

He considered it to be very dangerous to assume that there was some sort of mystical good for the State which was independent of the lives of the individual citizens. The State, therefore, must be founded on *consent* and, as power is held *in trust* for people, the power of the Representatives of the State should be limited and not Absolute.

Jean-Jacques Rousseau (4) believed that Humanity was political by nature and that Human nature could only be fulfilled within the State. A complete life, therefore, was possible only in the State. It was the individual that mattered. His *Emile* makes it clear that the pupil should be educated for his or her own sake and not for the sake of others.

Jeremy Bentham (5) was one of the leading English philosophers. In his youth he had been a Tory sympathiser. He was to become disillusioned when it dawned on him that *the people in power were actually opposed to reform.* He had presumed that *they only wanted to know what was good in order to embrace it.* At every turn he saw the Sinister Interest of Privilege.

The leading principle of the philosophy of Bentham was that the end of all Human activity and morality is *happiness.* He held that happiness is the *Summum Bonnum* and the only thing desirable in itself. Other things are desirable only as a means to this end.

All this activity leads us to the appearance of Karl Marx, one of the greatest landmarks in philosophy, whose influence upon the thought of the twentieth century has been immense. Marx was not the first Socialist thinker. Those who had preceded him had voiced those irrational longings of the empty soul from which the driving force for Socialism comes. Prior to Marx the idea of a Socialist society had been elaborated, as was the labour theory of value.

Marx outstripped his predecessors because he was able to harness the source of power towards revolutionary Socialist activity by expressing his deeply-held beliefs with a religious fervour. He was to fill the emptiness of the Age by supplying a teaching which had not only religious zeal, but what appeared to be a scientific certainty. This was to be of considerable importance because, for many, the old faiths were losing their appeal. His belief in the possibility of, indeed in the *certainty* of a Terrestrial Socialist Paradise provided life with new meaning and shone light on the darkness of the Age.

To his followers he was the prophet of a New Age and of a new Religion. It was as though he held out to Humanity a system to meet their material needs *and supply meaning* for their existences. It had a path of salvation for Socialists to follow and, as a victor's crown, there was a Socialist Paradise on Earth for working people.

His message had more than a religious fervour, of course; otherwise he would have made very little headway in a world which had lost interest in any teachings which were void of any scientific proof or any pseudo-scientific pretensions. He enjoyed success because it was believed that he was displaying the laws of historical development. He proclaimed that Socialist deliverance from the ills of the world was a certainty, and that this was amenable to scientific proof.

Yet Marxism is much more than a clarion call to the working class because, as a means of knowing exactly what revolutionary situations are, it is the *assurance* of victory to the working class. Marx offered a guide to action and, as a promise of success in *The Theory of Dialectical Materialism*, and an economic analysis which, when taken together, can fairly claim to be the greatest and most compelling statement of scientific Socialism ever made.

The Materialism of Marx is not *mechanical* but *dialectical*. In Dialectical Materialism evolution is the development of Matter from *within*, the environment either helping or hindering, but neither *originating* the evolutionary process nor capable of *preventing* it from reaching its goal.

To the Dialectical Materialist, Matter is active, not passive, moving by *the inner necessity of its nature*. Dialectical Materialism, therefore, is more concerned with a vital energy *within* Matter which is inevitably driven towards the perfect Human Society, just as the Demiurge of Hegel is driven towards the perfect realisation of Spirit. It was in this connection that Engels stated that 'the Dialectical Method grasps things and their images, ideas, essentially in their sequence, their movement, their birth and death'.

To the Dialectical Materialist it is *Motion* which is the cause of everything, and this Motion is brought about *by the conflict of opposites*. Every period in History which falls short of perfection carries within itself the seeds of its own destruction. As the Classless Society approaches, the thesis *calls into existence its opposite*, or antithesis, and from the clash of the two a new synthesis appears. That which is true in both thesis and antithesis is preserved. This serves as the starting point for the Whole. This continues until a Classless Society is reached.

The connection between Marx and Hegel, whom we shall consider next, is evident. For Hegel the Universal Principle is Spirit, whereas for Marx it is Matter. Both agree that Matter and Spirit have become developed and this is brought about by means of an *Inner Dialectic*. For Hegel, the inevitable goal of the process of Existence is *the Idea becoming fully conscious of Itself*, whereas for Marx it is a Classless Society. Both are based on an initial act of faith and the Dialectic of Hegel and Marx both involve an element of *Mysticism*.

It should be noted that Marx applied his Dialectic *to the future* and he completely rejected the Idealism of Hegel. Later on Engels admitted that he and Marx had overstated the extent to which *economic causes could be found for political and legal institutions* and, in a letter written to Bloch in 1890 he said,

> Marx and I are partly responsible for the fact that, at times, our disciples laid more weight upon the economic factor than belongs to it. We were compelled to emphasise its central character in opposition to our opponents who denied it.

# II

Few philosophers have had such a great effect upon the everyday world as Hegel (6). He sought to discover the Absolute in the Relative. For Hegel the Absolute was the Mind or the Spirit, which had become *externalised* in Nature, so that It could experience an awareness of Itself.

The Mind is essentially the Idea, or Thought, which comes to Itself through Human history, this being possible because Humanity shares in the Absolute Idea which is Divinity. The thinking Idea is essentially activity or movement, although this movement *is not in a straight line*.

Hegel also displayed a remarkable insight into the political realities of the time. He foresaw the Industrial and Constitutional State coming into existence and, in this connection; he stated that 'Political genius consists in identifying yourself with a principle.' With a sure instinct he identified with *the Principle of Nationalism* (7).

His basic assumption was that the Universe was *one* coherent Whole. This organic unity is referred to by him as the Idea, Spirit, Reason or Divine Mind and, for Hegel, It was the *only* Reality. Everything has been created by this Idea and it is in the nature of this Idea to know all things and, when Hegel refers to Nature he uses the word in an *Aristotelian* sense, which is that which anything becomes *when fully developed*.

At the beginning of the world-process the Idea or Reason knows nothing. Gradually, as it develops through the history of the world, It learns to know more and more, until It is led finally and inevitably to Its goal, which is *perfect Knowledge of everything*.

As such we see that, for Hegel, *the Truth is the Whole*. This Whole, however, is merely the essential nature reaching completeness through the process of Its own development. Of the Absolute, it is seen as being essentially a *Result*. Only *at the end* is It what It is in very Truth.

The process of History is the process by means of which the Spirit passes from knowing nothing to full experience of Itself, and this is experienced as the increasing revelation of *the Rational Mind*. On the way to its goal the Spirit has made many experiments, with everything being a mask which It has tried on for a while until It is discarded. The Universal Mind in the world has had the patience to go through these forms in the long stretch of Time's extent, taking upon Itself the labour of the history of the world.

Hegel had a strong tendency to idealise everything. This was the logical consequence of the conviction that whatever happens, *happens because the Spirit needs it* and that *what the Spirit needs is correct*. It is obvious that he had been strongly influenced by the Greeks. Like the Greeks he noticed that if anything goes *unchecked* it will produce *its opposite*. It is for this reason that Absolute Monarchy becomes Despotism, and from there via violent revolution to Democracy, which may produce mob rule and from there to Dictatorship (8).

Hegel, like all philosophers, asked himself the question: *what is the State and why should I obey it?* For Hegel the answer is in terms, not only of Spirit reaching Its goal, but in Humanity seeking to satisfy Itself in activity.

By means of the experience of a multitude of embodiments, Spirit progresses from the world of plants and animals until It reaches that *imperfection of Consciousness* which we refer to as the Human Race. This is the highest physical or animal embodiment yet attained at this level of Consciousness. Beyond this, for Hegel, there will be no further physical evolution as we understand the term.

When we look closely at the thought of Marx and Hegel we see that they were looking at the same question of Human thought and understanding from slightly different perspectives. Is there any way that we can take the best from both and produce a higher unity? Should we embark upon such an attempt then we must inevitably look to the Greeks, the *custodians* of a Philosophical Tradition which is as old as the Human Race.

This is something which is urgently required by us today because it is becoming clearer to more and more people that the Industrial Age and the Christian Era are now both basically over. This may just possibly be the time when a Unity and a thorough Unity must appear, *to unite the Human Race.*

Thus Humanity will be reconciled with the animal and vegetable kingdoms. Thereby we will reach a state of understanding which can see things from the perspective of Unity. By means of possessing Knowledge we will be able to understand Politics and Religion in their proper context.

## NOTES

(1) Baruch Spinoza was born on the 24th of December 1632 in Amsterdam. His intellect was brilliant and precocious. He was thought of as *the God-intoxicated philosopher*.

(2) Gottfried Wilhelm von Leibniz was born on the 21st of June 1646 in Leipzig. He was widely recognised to have been one of the most learned of modern philosophers.

(3) John Locke was born in Wrington, near Bristol, on the 29th of August 1632.

(4)   Jean-Jacques Rousseau was born in Geneva on the 29th of June 1712, his mother dying while giving birth to him. His father was a watchmaker.

(5)   Jeremy Bentham was born in Aldgate, London, on the 15th of February 1747.

(6)   George Wilhelm Friedrich Hegel was born in Stuttgart on the 27th of August 1770. He was dissatisfied with contemporary metaphysics. He turned to Plato, Spinoza and Kant.

(7)   He taught that each people had its own particular genius, its own *Spirit of the People*. Each people had its own peculiar political institutions which had developed as the people had become increasingly civilised. The institutions of one people should not be imposed on another. He also noted, however, that there was such a thing as *the liberty to deny liberty to others*.

(8)   Later Greeks were to realise that the process of change was triple rather than dual in character. Monarchy gives way to Aristocracy then Democracy and from there to Dictatorship and then back to Monarchy again.

# 19: Chaos & Order

## I

We are now about to enter a very crucial stage in the development of Civilisation on this planet, for we are about to experience the dawning of a New Age. We are living at a time which is an *Epochal Threshold*, something which was heralded in the heavens with Pluto slipping inside the orbit of Neptune (1). We must now anticipate a Great Transition which began to take effect in the late nineteenth century, when Neptune aligned with Pluto for the first time in approximately 500 years (2).

This crucial stage which we are about to witness fully will be unparalleled since the Renaissance, which saw the end of feudalism, the discovery of the Americas, the Reformation, the appearance of Science, the Industrial Revolution as well as *The Black Death* which was to greatly reduce the Human population. This period has been regarded by historians, in general, as the end of the Medieval Period and the beginning of the Modern Era.

Crucial events have been taking place in the heavens. We have already experienced the conjunction of Saturn with Uranus in 1987 to 1988 and Saturn with Neptune in 1989, with both of these conjunctions being in Capricorn. Yet these did not have the significance of the conjunction of Uranus with Neptune which ushered in 1990. The last time these planets were in alignment in Capricorn was in 1821 (3).

At the start of 1989 there was a very special celebration in India, with at least 15 million pilgrims heading to a *Khumba Mela* or festival where the Ganges joins the Jamuna and the mystical Saraswati. In 1989 there was a particularly important celestial conjunction, for Jupiter was in Taurus and the Sun and Moon both in Capricorn, an alignment which will not be repeated until 2233 AD.

A Great Renaissance is about to take place. For some time now North America has had a New Age Movement. There is such great unrest in places like China. Then there is what has become of the old Soviet Union where there has been a Free Trade Revolution brought about initially by the advent of the New Openness. Globally, the Old Order is collapsing. We require insight as to which way to go from here, both on a British and Global basis.

By the 1960s it was being anticipated that *a great evolutionary or quantum leap was possible for the Human Race.* While young and immature hippies sung of *The Age of Aquarius* and 'space walks' were taking place outside the atmosphere of the Earth, in the heavens there was an alignment of Uranus and Pluto.

This present *Age of Pisces*, which is also the Christian era, was greatly influenced by an Esoteric School which made its appearance in Alexandria during the first century AD. This Esoteric School was to provide *The Age of Pisces* with a philosophy of a very pure and spiritual kind. Later generations were to refer to it as *Alexandrian Neo-Platonism.*

Even during *The Age of Pisces*, at the time of the Renaissance and the Reformation, there were those who sought to regulate the bearings of the Human Race by attempting to return to the wisdom of an earlier and, it was believed, an even better period.

The leaders of the Christian community sought to return to the first century AD, to the time of the primitive Christians. The Renaissance also sought to return to a Golden Age, but both of these groups were to make a quite fundamental error.

As it happens, the inspiration of the Renaissance Magis did not come from remote Antiquity at all, for the philosophy which was to influence them was certainly *not* the philosophy of Ancient Egypt, and neither was it the philosophy of the classical Hebrew prophets who had lived and died centuries before the flowering of the philosophy of Plato.

It was to be discovered that in the return to the Pagan background of primitive Christianity, and to that *Religion of the World* which had been strongly influenced by Gnosticism, Oriental Mysticism and Magick, they were only returning to the answers provided for those *Pagans* who were *the contemporaries of the early Christians.*

This exceptionally fine Esoteric School was to influence thinkers such as Philo, Plotinus and Proclus. Its noble truths were even to dare to challenge the supremacy of *The Cult of Jesus Christ*. At one point during the centuries of rivalry, Julian the Apostate had become Emperor in succession to Constantine and Neo-Platonism sat on the throne of the Earth, having replaced *The Cult of Jesus Christ.*

At first, it must be recognised, Christianity introduced *so little change* into private and social life, that up to the fourth and fifth centuries it would have been uncertain, from the vantage-point of modern Orthodoxy, whether devotees were either Pagan or Christian. Many seem to have pursued a course midway between the two. With the death of Julian, his successor restored *The Cult of Jesus Christ* as the Imperial Truth, meaning that in Neo-Platonism we see the highest point reached by Paganism.

As *The Age of Pisces* was dawning and this particularly fine Esoteric School was coming into existence, the world of the first century AD was at peace and very highly organised. *The Pax Romana* was at the height of its efficiency and the Roman Empire governed and rendered stable by a bureaucracy. The communication between the peoples of the Empire was excellent. The educated people had already absorbed the Graeco-Roman style of culture which was based on the seven liberal Arts and, in consequence, the entire world was *curious.*

There were many who sought a greater knowledge of Reality which could not be provided, or so it was felt, by *normal* education. It was for this reason that solutions to contemporary problems were sought in other ways. These were intuitive, mystical and magickal.

Philosophy was not to be used as a dialectical exercise, but for the sake of uncovering *intuitive knowledge of the Divine* and the meaning of the world, as a Gnosis. This *Religion of the World* which was *the undercurrent* of Platonism and Neo-Platonism was to become, in Hermetism, a Religion without Temples or Liturgy, *followed in the Mind alone,* a religious philosophy or a Philosophical Religion, containing a Gnosis.

Philosophy and all great philosophers stand outside this sacred world. A philosophy that could cross this gulf would not arrive at *one* particular religion, but a religion embracing all religions; from a religious point of view a contradiction in terms. It could only be the abolition of the history of religion, of its historical earnestness. What has been called *a philosophical religion* would be a religion without any of the features of a living religion. It would be what was left after all the rituals, the prayers; the religious communities and the scriptures were subtracted.(4)

# II

Now, once again, we have reached another stage of transition. Should we expect to see the appearance of an Esoteric School somewhat similar to that which appeared in first century Alexandria?

We are moving into a New Age which will also be a new level of experience for us, a level which is radically different from that to which we have all become so accustomed. It will be an Age during which belief systems and teachings will not have the prominence attributed to them as was the case in the past, for *Knowledge* will have dawned.

This poses more questions to consider. If there is *no* belief system as such to unite people, what will be the unifying factor? They will seek to co-operate with each other in a manner which would be going *beyond the stage of Instruction*. With the *appearance* of the Ultimate Ancestor and the Common Purpose to be established by our Ultimate Ancestor, many will have had the experience of a vision of people complementing and supplementing each other to permit them to operate *as a Collective Consciousness*. They will realise that they share a *common* Humanity.

They would seek to co-operate with each other in a manner which would be going beyond the stage of *instruction*. This would be brought about by the realisation that a new and higher level of Realisation was *awakening* within them, *as* them. They would experience an ability to operate *as* One (5).

Who would form such a community? How would they awaken? For such people there is only one thing to do now. We have had instruction in the form of belief systems and teachings. Now we must go beyond this stage to the awakening of Knowledge within us. This is brought about by means of *complete surrender* to the power of God *who* resides *within us*.

To understand this we have to consider the salmon, the greatest symbol of Celtic spirituality. Swimming in the sea it turns and seeks to return to its point of origin. As it happens this is *no straight-line* progression for the salmon has to jump *up* waterfalls and onto a higher level of Consciousness.

Around 3000 million years ago life began in the sea. By about 2000 million years ago life started to become established on land. Our Race lived in the undergrowth and then up trees. Then around 18 million years ago we looked something like an Orang-Utan. For the last 200,000 years or so we have been manifesting ourselves *as the Human Race* as we understand the term. Now we must anticipate moving *beyond* the Human stage of our evolution.

Before we are able to experience the New Age in its fullness, however, we may well have to endure a period of Chaos. There is a perfect analogy to this in everyday life. When a baby is conceived, all is well for a while. As it continues to grow, in due course it finds that life in the womb has become *intolerable*. This forces the baby to leave the womb, which is actually the most natural of things.

An Old Age is passing away before our eyes and the present World Order will collapse. This is really not such a bad thing, indeed it is part of the natural order of things. Scientists and Mystics both inform us that there really is *no such thing as an external world* for we are participating in a gigantic Relativistic Event.

Humanity, in this sense, is the Representative of a Cosmic Energy which has been operating in pursuit of a Great Aim. In organic evolution, we arrived later than the animals but, in essence, *we are older*. The other *ways* of living show where we have been and what has been left behind.

We await an unfolding and this demands the application of the power of love. Only love can restrain the coarseness of Nature to permit the unfolding of Divine essence to produce the True Humanity. Love will empower us *to serve* each other and, thereby, realise our nature *as a Collective Consciousness*. Love is paramount, for with love it is *someone else* who truly matters.

There is, therefore, an Internal Potency which can and will transform the world. For this to be effective on Earth, *the Human Race has been created*.

# III

At a scientific meeting in 1969, James Lovelock proposed *The GAIA Hypothesis*, which was a startling new theory which saw the Earth with its rocks, oceans, atmosphere and *all* life as part of *a Super Organism* which has been evolving for over 4 billion years.

This theory was published in scientific papers and written jointly with biologist Lynn Margulis, and then in the 1970s it met with indifference and opposition because it was considered to be *too teleological*. The implication was that the GAIAN control system was *designed by living organisms* (6).

During the 1980s the GAIA Hypothesis and its associated science of Geophysiology aroused more interest because the theories were being confirmed.

The GAIA Hypothesis postulates that the presence of life actively influences the physical and chemical condition of the surface of the Earth, the oceans and the atmosphere to produce an environment more suitable for life, Itself. This is *in contrast* to the conventional scientific view that *life adapted to planetary conditions* and that they both evolved *separately*.

Strong evidence for the validity of the GAIA Hypothesis comes from the existence of several *homeostatic* (which are stable, self-regulating) systems on Earth. We see the steady maintenance of the average surface temperature of most parts of the Earth to between 15 and 35 degrees centigrade, the optimal range for living organisms. Fundamental to the system is the stabilisation of the proportion of oxygen in the atmosphere to about 21 percent. There is the existence of the ozone layer in the upper atmosphere to shield life from the most harmful of ultra-violet radiation. There is a small quantity of ammonia in the atmosphere to keep rain and soil at the level of acidity optimal for life. There is the regulation of the salt content of the oceans to the proportion of 3.4 percent.

From the arrival of *The Age of Science*, scientists have been investigating well-ordered deterministic phenomena which obey (what for us are) the regular Laws of Nature. For over a century scientists have also been studying *random phenomena* which follow *The Laws of Chance* which often show their own characteristic form of statistical *regularity* if repeated often enough.

Starting in the 1960s and, from there, through the 1970s and the 1980s, Mathematicians, Astronomers, Biologists and Economists started to investigate these irregularities both theoretically and empirically.

By the 1990s, what had, at first, been isolated investigations by scattered researchers had become a new branch of Mathematics, the *Science of Chaos*. This provided a new way of understanding the growth of complexity in Nature. It has also revealed new insights into the subtle interplay between Chaos and Order.

Wherever Chaos was seen to emerge, it was found to be the result of *non-linear phenomena*, where Cause and Effect are related in a more complicated way than in linear phenomena, where Effect is *proportional* to Cause.

Chaotic behaviour is now known to appear in many natural and human phenomena, and believed to influence many others. These phenomena include the structure of Galaxies, the behaviour of weather systems, the intricate pattern of snowflakes, dripping water taps, oscillating pendulums, the ecology of competing species and heartbeats (7).

The logical conclusion of all this is to view evolution as *the growth of information* in a system with this being the *potential for creative progress*.

All information is processed through the Infinite Medium of Mind (or Spirit, if you prefer) which has access to *all* information, *all* of the time and interacts with it. It is the medium of Its own transmission and, therefore, information *is never lost*, merely transformed. Thereafter it is distributed in logical fashion to Infinite complexity.

There is thus no such thing as *a fluke or a coincidence* all these being *for a purpose*. All Knowledge gains stem, ultimately, from this Universal Data System.

The most fundamental of all *non-linearly* based or *subtle* energies, which happen to be growth-promoting, is pure conceptual energy.

We must expect, as a Collective Consciousness, that the Old World Order will begin to fall apart as the birth-pangs of a New Age and that it is correct that this should happen. Thus, as a Collective Consciousness we will experience the awakening of Divine power within us and, like the salmon, negotiate our own *waterfall* and climb to higher ground in terms of Consciousness.

By means of the Human Race, the Original State of Consciousness which gave rise to the Cosmos, *who* is also our Ultimate Ancestor, is being *reproduced as a Collective Consciousness.* This is the means of channelling the energies of the Cosmos towards Its end, to which It aspires. This will be Its most perfect form, the creation of Heaven.

So we must now anticipate a Great Exodus from the past. We will leave this present level of awareness behind us, like a snake shedding skin. Like those Biblical Israelites we will leave Egypt, which in the Biblical narratives is *symbolic* of a condition of ignorance and slavery, and journey on to the Promised Land. This will be a Social Order on a Global scale within which Humanity will be united and, in so doing, create the circumstances for *our further evolution* (8).

## NOTES

(1)   The Plutonian Seeding Epoch lasted from 1978 until 1999.

(2)   Under normal circumstances the next planet inwards from Neptune is Uranus, whose alignment with Neptune lasted from 1990 until 1996. After this Saturn, then Jupiter and Mars align with Neptune and Pluto from 2019 until 2025.

(3)   The only other alignment of greater significance since then was the Neptune and Pluto conjunction, in Gemini, which took place between 1887 and 1896. This conjunction meant the end of an Era.

(4)   *Kerygma and Myth. A Theological Debate.* Edited by Hans Werner Bartsch. Published by SPCK in 1972. From the chapter by Karl Jaspers entitled *'Myth* and *Religion'* in which Jaspers looks at the Theology of Rudolf Bultmann. See p. 176.

(5)   Anthony Flew, *Body, Mind and Death.* Published by Macmillan Publishing Co., New York, 1977 edition.

Anthony Flew describes the entire Human Race in terms reminiscent of *a gigantic artificial man.* He does this while considering the philosopher Thomas Hobbes, who lived from 1588 until 1679. See p. 115f.

The magistrates, the officers of judicature and execution are the artificial limbs; reward and punishment by which fastened to the seat of sovereignty, every joint and member is moved to perform its duty; are the nerves that do the same in the body natural; the wealth and riches of the  particular members are the strength; *satis populi*, the people's safety, its business; counsellors, by whom all things needful for it to know are suggested to it, are the memory; concord, health; sedition, sickness; civil war, death.

(6)   This had already been promulgated by James Hutton, a Scots geologist, who stated that the Earth was a Super-Organism which should be studied by means of Physiology.

The Russian philosopher and scientist, Yergraf Korolenko, also viewed the Earth as a Living Organism. In 1911 his cousin, Vladimir Vernadsky, introduced the term *biosphere* in the modern sense, as the envelope of life and its material environment spread round the surface of the Earth.

(7)   Also included are Stock Market crashes, economic *long waves* and the alternation of Ice Ages with periods of *normal* weather.

(8)   In *The Epistle of Paul to the Galatians*, the circumstances relative to the wife, concubine and two elder sons of Abraham are denominated *allegoroumena* or *allegorising*, meaning that they need not be considered to be *historical* characters.

In *The First Epistle of Paul to the Corinthians*, he also declares that the Exodus from Egypt and the adventure in the wilderness were *tupoi*, indicating that they were *types* or *symbols* which were employed solely for the purpose of instruction. See chapter 10: 6.

# 20: The Purpose of Humanity

## I

For millennia Esoteric Schools have appeared and, after someone proved themselves to be *worthy* to attach themselves to the Esoteric School they were, in due course, *initiated* into *The Ancient Mysteries*. Thereafter an Ancient Secret was revealed. This Secret was a very ancient Truth about Humanity, and *why* Humanity exists.

The idea of Esotericism is chiefly the idea of there being a *Higher Mind*. The first step towards understanding the idea of Esotericism is the realisation of the existence of a *Higher Mind* which differs considerably from the mundane or ordinary mind, as much as the mind of an infant differs from the mind of an intelligent adult. Such a person possesses a new kind of Knowledge which ordinary people, who are *uninitiated*, cannot possess. This Knowledge is *Esoteric Knowledge*.

From remote Antiquity the idea of Knowledge which surpasses all *normal* Human thought, and which is inaccessible to ordinary folk, has existed somewhere and belonged to someone. Some Schools taught that the Human Race possessed certain Knowledge at a time when others maintained that we were barely above the level of animal behaviour. This Ancient Knowledge was also, at the same time, *Hidden Knowledge* (1).

It must be noted, however, that *all* religions, *all* myths, *all* beliefs, *all* the popular heroic legends of *all* peoples in *all* parts of the planet are based on the recognition that there has existed, somewhere and at sometime, a Knowledge *far superior* to anything possessed by Humanity, even today. All these Myths comprise symbolic forms which represent attempts to transmit the idea of *Hidden Knowledge*, which is also Knowledge about *why* the Human Race exists.

This is true of the New Testament which was written for a quite specific purpose. It was written to show that there is *only one way* to this *Hidden Knowledge*, and to inform Human beings that they can actually go this way, *should they so desire*. Yet this information also divides Humanity into two separate groups, that is, those who are *suitable* to possess such Knowledge, and those who are *unsuitable*.

Those who sought this Hidden Knowledge always ascribed new properties to it, although they always viewed it as being *far above* the plane of ordinary Knowledge and, as such, it involves a sort of sixth sense. This *Hidden Knowledge* was often considered to be magickal, miraculous and so on. If we were to remove from this *Hidden Knowledge* that it goes beyond the five senses, it is robbed of all meaning and importance.

The idea of evolution, in the sense of transformation, in ordinary thought is radically different from any concept of evolution in esoteric thought for esoteric thought recognises and is built upon the idea of the *further* evolution or transformation of the Human Race. To be more precise, esoteric thought recognises the possibility of the transformation of Humanity into a Race of *Super Humans*. This is the highest meaning of the word *evolution*.

The first indications on the way to Esoteric Knowledge can be found in ways which are accessible to everyone. *All* religions, *all* true philosophies, *all* legends and *all* fairytales abound with indicators about Esotericism, but the reader or hearer must have 'eyes to see and ears to hear'.

# II

What was this Esoteric Knowledge? It started from the idea that in the activity of Nature, or the Cosmos, the aim was to produce a Self-Evolving Being. This Being was to be manifested as a Collective Consciousness. Only this would fully permit the Being to consider Itself, as It and *only It* truly exists, being the cause of everything. This means that It has only Itself to consider.

Some were convinced that the whole of the animal and vegetable kingdoms were, in a sense, *a by-product* of the creation of that Collective Consciousness which presently manifests Itself as the Human Race, which is who we are and to which we belong.

Humanity, therefore, is the Representation of a Cosmic energy which has been operating in pursuit of a Great Aim. In organic evolution we arrived later than the animals but, in essence, *we are older*. The other *ways* of living show where we have been and what we have left behind. Animals have often been seen as the embodiment of those properties which have become either useless or impossible in Humanity. This is why animals are often depicted as caricatures of Human beings.

There is a rationale here: Nature does not operate to increase the *quantity* of Organic Life, which has been systematically wiped out on Earth at regular intervals, but to develop it in terms of *quality*. By means of this, Nature seeks to raise the vibratory level of the planet Earth.

Everything that exists is what it is within the certain limits of a restricted scale. On a different scale it would be something completely different. Everything, and every event, has a certain meaning within the limits of a particular scale, and can only be compared with things and events of proportions not too dissimilar from its own, that is, existing within the same scale.

Even for ourselves there is not and cannot be any other time outside the time of our lives. We *are* our lives and our lives are *our time*. Life is time for us.

The meaning or purpose of the entire Creative Act is the appearance, from Humanity, of a Super Humanity. Out of the mass of the Human population of the Earth a Self-Realised Human, or Super Human, emerges from time to time as the prototype of a new Humanity, a Super Humanity. What this Krishna, this Apollo, Hermes or Christ has attained, we can all attain, *if we are able*. Yet ordinary Humanity, in the meanwhile, is unable to comprehend such a being.

Down through the centuries, little by little, the great Philosophers and Mystics have revealed tiny aspects of *The Mysteries*. Such is true of the philosopher Hegel.

> Hegel's idealism maintained that Reality was rational. The world is the manifestation of a Spiritual Principle. In Man, Spirit attains Self-Consciousness. Hegel finds room in his system for

the idea of development or evolution. Hegel was not only an idealist but a monist, that is to say, that Reality is One. But this unity does not preclude difference.

For Hegel Reality was so much a unity that no individual fact can be fully understood except in relation to the whole. A development produces differentiation, the differences conflict, but in truth they are complementary, and are reconciled in a higher unity. This is *The Hegelian Dialectic* whereby the conflict of thesis and antithesis is resolved in a higher synthesis. (2)

This has been spoken of more openly in recent times by men such as Kenneth Grant. He mentions that there is *already in operation* the quest for planetary unity. This is in order that various sentient Races can be brought to a communal sphere of influence.

Man as a unified planetary person, is vital to the becoming of this super-gestalt. As a seed, Man is not really native to the Earth. He was *planted* here by the Comity, long ago, by means of DNA manipulation, into the racial stock of their dominant primate species, thus tasting of the fruit of *The Tree of the Knowledge of Good and Evil.*

A prototype anthropoid nuclear group was bred with Human consciousness and was given the option of production or sterility. The Comity has maintained a close watch ever since, intervening in our *history* by means of Human agents, by myth and legend, by directing the Racial Unconsciousness on the astral plane by focussing the increasingly subtle sequence of the Magickal Current into the developing individual consciousness and, at last, giving guidance to N'Aton so that he can complete the job of his own awakening. (3)

We, in recognising the existence of Ancient or *Hidden* Wisdom or Knowledge are, thereby, alluding to the fact that, at present, we are fundamentally ignorant of our being and of our powers. So what are we then?

When we look at our bodies from an electronic aspect we can readily see how crystals become ideal tools for working with bodily energies. The body is not only skin and bones, and strictly organic in nature. It is also an extremely elaborate assembly of master computers with a very sophisticated interacting network for communication between each localised master computer tied together to a grand master computer called our brain.

Starting with the DNA molecule in the heart of each cell a super memory bank with capabilities of many millions of bits of information, superior to the best computer on Earth today (i.e. sufficient memory and information in each cell to reproduce the whole Human body with all its very complex organs). These cells are connected to form special types of tissues which, in turn, form organs, glands and major structural parts, altogether constituting the whole body mechanism.

Many people are recognising the Human body as an electronic instrument. (4)

# III

One of the greatest landmarks of all in philosophy, as well as being a custodian of *The Ancient Mystery Tradition* was Plato, who began to teach about 386 BC in the sacred grove known as *The Akademos*. (5)

He did not found a complete philosophical system. It is possible that the central theme of his teaching was 'the detection of the one amongst the many', in fact, an almost religious and monotheistic view of phenomena, both mental and physical. (6)

Plato's most famous doctrine was that of Ideas, that all things and all faculties exist in perfection *as* Absolute Ideas. There is thus an ideal beauty; an ideal virtue etc. and these are the *only real existences*.

The world of phenomena, amidst which we live, possesses *only a dim shadow*, or a small part of those realities which the soul *once knew* and, hereafter, will know *again*.

Things are beautiful in proportion to *the amount of ideal beauty they contain*. The soul knows them as beautiful because *in the previous state of Existence* the soul saw the real Idea of Beauty (7).

Yet there is something we have to understand. Certain philosophers, such as John Locke (8), perceived that the first and most important thing to be understood is Human understanding, itself. Thereafter, that which is being considered by means of Human understanding could be investigated with profit.

We find that in working with Locke, as well as with Kant, that all Knowledge contains an element of ourselves, so much so that Self-Consciousness is both unavoidable and universal. In other words, when we say that we perceive something, we do not mean that we are conscious of the existence of Matter *per se*, but only that we are conscious of our *perception* of Matter.

The problem in philosophy today is to give a reasoned explanation of the phenomena of the world in which we live. It must give a Science to the Sciences, to elaborate the principles, and then to answer the one question of immense importance: *why did it all happen?* (9)

As we consider this we must bear very important things in mind. Firstly, until this present Age a *linear* progression of Time has been the predominant characteristic of Human history. As such our understanding has been limited to *the confinement to one level of awareness* which, as it happens, is *the horizontal*. Secondly, all things, whether planets, Suns or Galaxies are *sentient*.

*The Ancient Mysteries* talk of everything emanating from the One, who is also the Ultimate Ancestor of everything that *is*.

The Principle underlying the System of Emanations was that all things were, ultimately, of *One* Substance. It was from this that they had been fashioned and into which they would again be dissolved, by means of the working of One Spirit universally diffused and expanded.

Those polytheists of Ancient Greece and Rome considered, as do the Hindus, that all worship and devotion were directed to the same end, though in different modes and through different channels. 'Even they who worship other gods, worship Me, although they know it not,' says Krishna, the Incarnate Deity, in an ancient Indian poem (10).

The purpose may well have been for the Ultimate Ancestor to *appear*, as is certainly implied in the Ancient Wisdom. Thereby true beauty or proportion may be exhibited to those who, *in recognising it for what it is*, are empowered to *awaken*, to be *born again*. Thereafter they are in possession of that Knowledge which comes, ultimately, *as Recollection*.

This is fundamental to Krishna Consciousness.

> KRSNA is the Godhead because *He is All-Attractive*. Outside the principle of All-Attraction, there is no meaning to the word Godhead. How is it one can be All-Attractive? First of all, if one is very wealthy, if he has great riches, he becomes attractive to the people in general.
>
> Similarly, if someone is very powerful, he also becomes attractive, and if someone is very famous, he also becomes very attractive, and if someone is very beautiful or wise or unattached to all kinds of possessions, he also becomes attractive. So, from practical experience we can observe that one is attractive due to *wealth, power, fame, beauty, wisdom and renunciation*.
>
> One who is in possession of *all six* of these opulences at the same time, who possesses them *to an unlimited degree*, is understood to be the Supreme Personality of Godhead. These opulences of the Godhead are delineated by Parasavi Muni, a great Vedic authority. (11)

This is the essence of all Religions that *the One* appears to guide and instruct the many, to answer questions which require answers, and to provide solutions to problems which require solutions.

This need not undermine the religious outlook of anyone.

> What is the meaning of the word *Christ? Christ* comes from the Greek word *Christos*, meaning *The Anointed One*. Christos is the Greek version of the word *KRSNA*. When an Indian person calls on KRSNA one often says KRSTA for *KRSTA* is a Sanskrit word meaning *Attraction*. So whether we address God as Christ, KRSTA or KRSNA we indicate the same All-Attractive Supreme Personality of Godhead. (12)

With the *appearance* of our Ultimate Ancestor, the One who is the Beginning and End of all things, this will have a very profound effect upon us. We will be freed forever from Religion as we have known it, for Popular Religion is an expression of each one's concept of Deity, as a reflection of our own inner character.

Religion is an integral part of ourselves, superior to the forms of worship but, unfortunately, contaminated by the defects of the Age in which we live. All are not called to the same formula of doctrine. We all have the Divine Right to revere and copy our own ideal. The forms are diverse but the Heavenly Principle and the Supreme Order are constant.

The difference will be that we will realise that our trust and hope was never in a mere Code of Morality at all, but in *a Person* who appears amongst us at certain stages in the development of Civilisation on the planet. We will see this Ultimate Ancestor and be transformed, in due course, into that likeness.

## NOTES

(1)   The word *AOS* is a case in point. In Dwelly's *Illustrated Scots Gaelic to English Dictionary* we read how the word *AOS* was, long before the nineteenth century, a word which had fallen into obsolescence. Prior to mention by Dwelly the word appears in *Armstrong's Scots Gaelic Dictionary* from fifteenth or sixteenth century mid-Perthshire.

Its meanings were in connection with Fire, the Sun and with God. It also referred to a community of people, possibly a mythical clan who lived in the Scottish Highlands. They spoke Gaidhlig and they revered and worshipped Apollo above all others.

(2)   John Macquarrie, *Twentieth Century Religious Thought*. Published by SCM Press. p. 24.

(3)   Kenneth Grant, *Outside the Circles of Time*. Published by Frederick Muller Limited, London in 1980. See p. 258.

(4)   Milewski Harford, *The Crystal Sourcebook. From Science to Metaphysics*. Mystic Crystal Publications, Arizona. From the introduction. p. x.

(5)   Plato lived from 429 BC until 347 BC.

(6)   He stood for the *supremacy of ontology* as the Highest Knowledge.

(7)   Plato's aim was to show how we ought to live, which is as best we can, *like the gods*. As with Wordsworth, 'our birth is but a sleep and a forgetting'.

(8)   He was born in 1632.

(9)   This is echoed by philosopher John Hospers,

> It is true that we can meaningfully ask about the causes of the present state of the Universe (or some aspect thereof); then we cite causal factors occurring in the past. And we ask about the causes of these in turn, and can list causes still further back; and so on, *ad infinitum*.

> This is what cosmologists do when they write books with titles such as *The Origin of the Universe*. They do not mean the *original origin* of the Universe, but the origin of the present state; 'stars condensed out of swirling nebulae' and so on for states of the Universe prior to that. But if someone says, 'I don't mean today or a million years ago. I mean from the beginning', his phrase is meaningless. There could not be a moment earlier than the history of Time, or any time when there was no Time.

> Therefore, when one asks where did *X* come from? They are not asking for a cause but for an explanation.

John Hospers, *An Introduction to Philosophical Analysis*. Published by Routledge & Kegan Paul. p. 435.

It may be interesting to note here that the author (John Houston) is of the opinion that the purpose of life is *the Creation of Identity* with the Creation of Identity being the end to which we aspire. This is so because this is the *requirement* of our Predisposition.

We exist for the sake of the Predisposition which would have us attain an Identity which is able to manifest the Divine Attributes which require to be made manifest.

The author (John Houston) is, furthermore, of the opinion that life as we know it is only possible because of Predisposition. This is why Greek philosophers said that people come into the world *already equipped* (or predisposed if you prefer) to do something with excellence.

At this point we could also mention Astrology which, in providing us with details of our birth-experience in the form of a natal chart, is providing us with an insight into our *Predisposition,* or *how* we are predisposed.

God, therefore, *is* Predisposition, Itself.

(10)  *The Bhagavad-Gita,* IX.

(11)  His Divine Grace A. C. Bhaktivedanta Swami Prabhupada, *KRSNA. The Great Classics of India Series.* The Bhaktivedanta Book Trust. From the preface. p. xi.

(12)  His Divine Grace A. C. Bhaktivedanta Swami Prabhupada, *The Science of Self-Realisation.* The Bhaktivedanta Book Trust. 1980 edition. p. 125.

# 21: The Relationship:
# The Context of our Experiences

## I

We see both from *The Ancient Mystery Tradition* and from modern science, that *all* life emanated from an Initial Singularity who is a Sentient Being, our *Ultimate Ancestor, all* life has emanated from the *One*, and there are definite messages to this effect in evolution.

> Why should plants contain morphine, a chemical which abolishes Human pain? Why do bacteria make insulin and yeasts produce a substance very similar to a Human sex hormone, and how come burned truffles can sexually arouse pigs foraging on the surface?

> The answer may be that modern messenger molecules, through which cells communicate, have evolved from a common set of ancient messengers passed between primeval cells. Jesse Roth and fellow scientists of The National Institute of Health in the U.S. claim that messenger molecules found in plants, for example, can interfere with those used in the Human body because they have a common evolutionary past. (1)

One thing that we should never do is to think of the Universe as being *out there*. Nothing is more important about *The Quantum Principle* than its destruction of the concept of there being a world *out there*. Therefore, it is necessary to describe the Relationship between Humanity and the Cosmos, not as though we were observers, but as *participators*.

We should realise that the Human Race is just as much a part of the Universe as any star or planet. *The Quantum Theory* has revealed that there is *an essential inter-connectedness* between all things. It has shown us that we cannot decompose the world into independently existing smaller units. As we penetrate into Matter, we find that it is composed of particles, but these are *not the basic building blocks* which were postulated by Newton.

> They are idealisations which are useful from a practical point of view, but have no fundamental significance. In the words of Niels Bohr,
>
> 'isolated particles are abstractions, their properties being definable and observable through their interactions with other systems'. (2)

There has been an evolutionary process which has produced *us*, and this is the reality of our experiences, that we exist *within a Relationship* of Cosmic proportions. It is for the *sake* of this Relationship that we exist, for we are Its *Rational Principle*. We exist, therefore, to provide the Relationship with information, and to create the circumstances for the Relationship to perfect Its Form.

This has been taught by all the great Esoteric Schools which have existed to guide us. They also proclaimed that phenomena are *appearances and nothing more*, for it is *our thoughts* which are the Reality. Thought, therefore, is the unifying factor of all things.

We need to modify our approach to phenomena and it is here that we have to consider certain philosophers. Hegel quarrelled altogether with the concept of subject and object as two poles where the Absolute, which comprises both of them, is the indifference point. He saw them as two *separate* extremities or as two realities (3).

Hegel, furthermore, argued that the essence of all Relationship does *not rely on the related*, which are mere phenomena. The *only* Reality existing in any series or in any collective is *the Relationship, Itself*.

Let us consider the example of a man observing a tree. Whereas it had been maintained by Schelling that the *I* and *the tree* are two manifestations of the Absolute which is All in All, indeed the Godhead, Itself, which includes both the *I* and *the tree* Hegel, on the other hand, was to assert that *the Relationship* between I and the tree *is the only manifestation conceived here*, and this Relationship is *God*.

Hegel went to the extent of asserting that God is *more than substance*, indeed the Godhead is *Notion*, which is the perceptions, conceptions and relations which *bind* things to other things.

For Hegel the Godhead becomes conscious by means of philosophy. As Pure Being God, for Hegel at least, can only pass into Reality through a negation. By means of philosophy the negative is negated so that the Godhead can arrive at a positive affirmation of Itself.

# II

The Human Race has emerged from the animal kingdom, having been *selected* by the Relationship which links all things and which uses all things for the sake of Its own Self-Expression. The Human Race exists to create the circumstances for the Relationship to attain True Self-Expression by means of the perfection of Form.

The inner working of the Cosmos is *a Vision*, and this Vision is the Vision of True Self-Expression for the Cosmos. The Cosmic Relationship has been endeavouring to create, *by means of sensory perception*, the means of *apprehending this Vision* and, in so doing, create the circumstances for the Vision to become a Reality.

Humanity has the same origin as all life, and it is for this reason that all life should be viewed as *sacred*. Thus we see Proclus, in *The Theology of Plato*, saying *vis-à-vis* plants and animals that they were, nonetheless, emanations of the Supreme Being, co-substantial with Its essence, and participating in Its attributes.

Ancient Wisdom is characterised by a profound reverence for all life. It was stated that, 'It was said of the priests of Egypt that "they have a secret doctrine concerning them" (the animals)' (4).

The historian Herodotus stated that, in Egypt, all animals, whether domesticated or otherwise, were regarded as sacred. He went on to say that 'if I was to explain why they are consecrated to the several gods, I would be led to speak of sacred matters, which I particularly shrink from mentioning. The points on which I have touched slightly have all been introduced by sheer necessity'. (5)

At one point the dog represented Thoth or Mercury as the keeper of the boundary between life and death, as the Guardian of the passage *from* the Upper *to* the Lower Hemisphere. For some Egyptians the dog did not symbolise Thoth as such, but the watchful, conservative and philosophical principles in life. In the more remote and ancient times the dog had the highest honour paid in Egypt.

Even the snake was revered. It was said that among all those who worship the heathen gods, the serpent is depicted as the greatest symbol of mystery (6). Painting two snakes made a place *holy*.

Furthermore, from the System of Emanations came the opinion so prevalent among the Ancients that future events could be predicted by observing the instinctive motions of animals. This was especially true of birds which, being often inexplicably distanced from any known principles of mental operations, were *supposed* to proceed from the immediate impulse of the Deity.

It is also generally accepted that the Egyptians had a profoundly civilising effect on the rest of Humanity, and that was due to the appearance of Orpheus, the master musician who was from a world far higher than this one is at present.

It was said of Orpheus that He brought *The Mysteries* from the Egyptians and gave them to the Greeks. (7) In *The Frogs* Aristophanes stated that 'Orpheus showed us the initiations'. Proclus once said that 'all theology among the Greeks is the outbirth of *The Orphic Mysteries*'. (8) Speaking of the Initiations of Hecate each year, Pansanias said that 'it is Orpheus, the Thracian, who instituted the rites'. (9)

We must bear in mind, however, that the traditions concerning Orpheus are somewhat vague and uncertain. Indeed it is said of Aristotle that *he actually denied that such a person ever existed*. In Cicero, from *The Nature of the gods* we read that Aristotle is *reputed* to have alluded to such, although this passage is not to be found in the works of Aristotle now extant. (10)

# III

Everything that exists has to be seen within the context of an all-embracing Relationship which links all things, and for the sake of which *everything* exists. As such we see that the Relationship is the *only* Reality, brought into existence by our Ultimate Ancestor for a quite specific purpose.

The Relationship has Its source in a Sentient Being, the Ultimate Ancestor of All, the Supreme Personality of Godhead, known by different names from different incarnations. This person has been known as Krishna, Apollo, Orpheus, Hermes and so on. He is the Christ, one who is able *to rise from the dead* and who had become Immortal, to use Ancient terminology. In effect, he had passed on *into the next stage of evolution*.

This Person is depicted as being able to *incarnate* on Earth, appearing at certain times and in a certain manner to impart Knowledge. The purpose of Creation is to establish a further perfection of the Relationship which emanates from the *One*, so that the *One* may be able to experience Itself *as a Collective Consciousness.*

This Personality of Godhead appears within the context of a Collective Consciousness, which is comprised of myriads of grosser vibrations of Itself. By perfecting the Form of the Collective Consciousness, the Ultimate Ancestor is enabled to *further consider* Itself.

> The Supreme Lord, Personality of Godhead is, Himself, this Cosmos, and still He is aloof from it. From Him has this cosmic manifestation emanated, in Him it rests, and unto Him it enters after annihilation. Your good self knows all about this. I have given only a synopsis. (11)

This brings us to consider the rather weighty topic of *Reincarnation* which has aroused considerable interest. It is now no longer restricted to those philosophies from the East, for many Christians are drawn to the idea. This should come as no surprise because, in the West, in former centuries

Reincarnation or *Transmigration of the Soul* was fundamental to Western philosophy.

Belief in Reincarnation is commonplace within the so-called New Age Movement. Yet it is no new concept, for the belief has been in existence for thousands of years.

There is, however, a great deal of misunderstanding in connection with the Doctrine of Reincarnation. The major stumbling block to understanding it is that the belief is *not* fundamental to Biblical literalism.

Few realise that the Bible contains a *secret teaching*, with the Bible written in such a way as to make it impossible to fully understand, *unless one had become an initiate.* The Bible does talk about life and death in many places but always within the context of Human Destiny. In the New Testament we read that, 'It is appointed for men to die once, but after this the judgement.' (12)

Biblical literalism, therefore, is adamant that we do not have the luxury of innumerable lives, with each one being a judgement upon the conduct of the previous lives. Neither does the Bible see the Human being as a shell containing a soul which, somehow or other, continues a conscious existence after the body has died.

The Bible, therefore, gives *no* grounds whatever for presuming that we are immortal souls which are able to consciously survive death. Yet if there are no grounds for belief in an immortal soul from the Bible, from whence does it come?

We know that many Ancient Religions proclaimed the Immortality of the soul. Such was the case with Druidism, although they accepted it only to *a limited extent.* The Zoroastrians, too, proclaimed likewise. Then there was Pythagoras who considered the soul to be Immortal and Immaterial.

The Greek historian, Herodotus, informs us that the Ancient Egyptians were the first to teach that the soul is separable from the body and is Immortal. The Egyptian idea was later to be assimilated into Greek philosophy, such as was the case with Plato.

We see, then, that it is quite incorrect to believe that the Jewish and Christian teachings about the Immortality of the soul come from Biblical literalism for, in effect, they come from an *esoteric tradition* which is *the undercurrent* of the religious experience of the Human Race.

The phrase *immortal soul* is not to be found in the Bible. It is true that the word *soul* is found in the Bible, but not in combination with the word *immortal*, which is to be found only in one place in the Bible, and there it does not refer to the Human Race, but to God. (13)

Rather than describing the soul as immortal, the Bible actually states that the soul can die. We are told that, 'The soul that sins shall die' (14).

If the soul is truly immortal, some would say, it would not be subject to death.

The Old Testament states that Humanity was formed of the dust of the Earth, after which the breath of life was breathed into the nostrils of the Human Race. As such the Human being became *a living soul*.

In *Genesis* 2: 7 a soul is what a Human being *is*. The Hebrew word translated as soul is *nephesh*, which is usually taken to be *a breathing creature*. The word implies a limited physical life. The word nephesh is used frequently in the Bible with reference to animals. In *Genesis* we read,

Then God said,

'Let the Earth bring forth the living creature (nephesh) according to its kind; cattle and creeping things with beasts of the Earth, each according to its kind,' and it was so. (15)

In Biblical usage, animals are referred to as souls. Yet the word *nephesh* is also used in connection with dead bodies (16).

Nephesh has to do with physical attributes of both animals *and* Human beings. Yet it is the word which many believe implies some sort of Immortality. The Hebrew Scriptures do not talk of the Immortality of the soul, although the scriptures imply that the dead *are dead* and, thus, incapable of conscious thought. Thus we read, 'For the living knows that they will die; but the dead know nothing.' (17)

Elsewhere we read, 'His breath goes forth, he returns to the Earth; in that day his thoughts perish.' (18)

From New Testament literalism the doctrine of Reincarnation, or *the Immortality of the Soul*, begins with the Satan, or the Devil, the father of lies. It would appear that this Satan, this Devil, has deceived the entire world. One of the ways of doing this is none other than to proclaim the *Immortality of the Soul*. (19)

Once again we must bear in mind that the Bible could only be understood by those who were *initiated into The Mysteries*. Before *The Cult of Jesus Christ* became a mass religion, tailor-cut to suit the needs of the uneducated mass of the population of the Roman Empire, it was a different story, however. As such a *secret* teaching would probably have been necessary to *prevent* Esoteric

Knowledge from falling into the hands of the profane.

In the case of belief in Reincarnation, or *the Immortality of the Soul*, which was prevalent among Esoteric Schools, we should realise that this would only have applied to those who had been initiated, which would have been a tiny minority of people. We know that Plato and Aristotle, for example, had recollections of former existences.

Certainly some Esoteric Schools taught that Reincarnation was a Reality, but it only applied to a very few. These were people who had been *born again*, people who had been *resurrected*, thus overcoming death.

Here we must remember that *The Orphic Mysteries*, which form the basis of both the Old and New Testaments (20), regarded life as we know it, *as death*, with this life lived in Hades or Hell.

From *The Ancient Mysteries* the only people who were reincarnated on Earth were those who had been *born again*, or *born in Mind* either on Earth or on some other world. They were prepared to sacrifice self-interest to guide those still in *the net of illusion* to rise above the circumstances of death to become truly alive.

As such we see that those who are reincarnated here on Earth are actually beings that have come here to *guide* Humanity. These are great souls who, at some time in the past, had attained the Immortal stage. They had overcome death, *which is life as we know it.*

These beings are those who, at some time in the past, were able to rise above the level of Human Existence to another, higher level, beyond the present Human stage, a level of Realisation which is, in fact, *the next stage of our evolution.*

# IV

We have seen in earlier chapters that the only Reality and therefore the *context* of our experiences is an All-Embracing Relationship. Should Reincarnation be a Reality, then Reincarnation will still be within this context. *Reincarnation is the Reincarnation of the Relationship.* Its aim is not to help individuals to escape the judgement of God as such, but to assist the Cosmos *to perfect Its form.*

Those beings that have been reincarnated are realisations of the Christ or Krishna Principle. Having *awakened* they are being transformed into the likeness of the Ultimate Ancestor, as far as this is possible. They have existed on other worlds and have come here to guide Humanity and to assist the Terrestrial Humanity to come to a point of *awakening*.

These beings exist because the Relationship *requires* them. It is by means of the Human Race that the Cosmos or Relationship is able to experience the power of *Reason*, but only truly when one has awoken, for such a one is free from 'the net of illusion'. Those saints or sages who have been *born again*, or who have been able to *awaken* have passed on into the next stage of our evolution. They are, in effect, the prototype of a new and Super Humanity. What they are we can become *for the sake of the Relationship which has produced us*.

Such great souls, in learning the secrets of worlds, will be able to go further and learn how to overcome the barriers between worlds to fully unite the Cosmos or Relationship, and thus create Heaven.

Humanity, which is still basically asleep or unconscious, has only experienced few such great souls. Their task has been to guide us to an awakening. Thereby we will be able to interact with other worlds, to cross-fertilise with other worlds. In combining the Knowledge of many worlds the secret of creating Heaven can be learned, or *remembered*.

These great beings, like Humanity Itself, exist because the Relationship *requires* them, for they exist to provide a service. They are to channel the energies of the Cosmos towards the creation of Heaven, the Perfect Circumstances for the Ultimate Ancestor and Its offspring to express themselves on an endless basis. *Cosmic harmony is their aim*. The Ultimate Ancestor, or God, has by means of Memory and by means of Time, cast Its own image.

## NOTES

(1)  '*Messages* in *Evolution*', from *The Scientist*, 25th July 1985 edition.

(2)  Fritjof Capra, *The Tao of Physics*. Published by Fontana/Collins in 1970. p. 141.

(3)  This is in connection with Hegel's Absolute Idealism, the asserted improvement on Schelling's Absolute Identity.

(4)  *Prodorus*, 1: 96.

(5)  *Herodotus*, II: 65.

(6)  Justin Martyr, *Apology II.*

(7)  Eusebius, *Praeparatio Evangeli.* Book I, chapter 6.

(8)  Proclus, *The Theology of Plato.* I: 5.

(9)  Pansanias, *Corinth.* XXX. 2.

(10)  Orpheum poetam docet Aristoteles nunquam fuisse.

(11)  *The Srimad Bhagavatam*, Canto I, chapter 5.

(12)  *The Book of Hebrews*, chapter 9: 27.

(13)  *The Book of Timothy*, chapter 1: 17.

(14)  *The Book of Ezekiel*, chapter 18: 20.

(15)  *The Book of Genesis*, chapter 1: 24.

(16)  *The Book of Numbers*, chapter 9: 6.

(17)  *The Book of Ecclesiastes*, chapter 9: 5.

(18)  *The Book of the Psalms*, 146: 4.

(19)  *The Book of Revelation*, chapter 12: 9.

(20)  Both the Old and New Testaments are adaptations of *The Orphic Mysteries*, which were concerned with Orpheus who had lived on a higher world. His wife, Euridice, *dying from the bite of a serpent* came here, *to the place of death*, called Hades or Hell.

Orpheus, thereafter, came here to redeem his bride so that they could *return* to their true home which was on a far more advanced world than this one, in terms of Civilisation.

The Jesus of the New Testament is intended to be a latter-day Orpheus, taking his bride, the New Testament Church or Euridice, back to the realms of the Divine after their celestial marriage.

# 22: A Question of Politics

## I

In the past, the way in which the Human Race survived was synonymous with the way in which the Human Race existed, for to exist was to survive, with good fortune. Society existed as a Garrison State which was forever on the alert to defend Itself against enemies, should that prove to be necessary.

This defensive attitude of Humanity was brought about because the Human Race has *no automatic* set of values. Our senses do *not automatically* inform us of what is good for us. Since Nature has not supplied us with any automatic code of survival we must support ourselves by means of our efforts and our intellect. To date, our primary consideration was the question of survival and to date we have, to a great extent, been at the mercy of the Elements, thus unable to live as we would have liked.

During the long process of evolution, that which has determined experience, whether good or bad, has been the life of the individual. We have survived, not by adjusting ourselves to the environment, but by recourse to productive work. In time of drought, animals may perish but we have the ability to build dams for irrigation and so on.

In the Human community everything, whether concerning the acquisition of Knowledge or Political Organisation, is manifested on a *hierarchical* basis. Knowledge starts with Sensory Perception, and to this new concepts are added on an even wider scale. To be valid, this has to be built on logic, the art of non-contradictory identification. Any new concept must be integrated without contradicting the hierarchical nature of Knowledge.

Social Existence is *hierarchical* from the family unit upwards and, furthermore, Social Existence is built on *trade*. On the planet the Human Race is the only species to transmit, store and expand Knowledge from one generation to the next, rendering Knowledge accessible to anyone on a scale which would be impossible were someone to search unaided. The possibility of the division of labour permits *specialisation* to take place, and work is undertaken by those who specialise in certain aspects of trade. Co-operation is therefore encouraged with a subsequent *increase* in Knowledge, skill and productivity.

We have now reached the stage where our beliefs and traditions are disappearing and then reappearing, in some instances beyond recognition. Now we are able to view ourselves in a way *not primarily concerned with our importance to the State*, as we have known it. Education, with the success of Science and Technology, and a growing desire for individuality has brought our Race to the crossroads of possibility. Now the winds of change are blowing stronger all the time!

There is the growing desire to break away from all *unnecessary* control and this no more so than in the field of education. In the past education was preparation for service to the State, in the institutions of the State. What need is there now for an education according to a work ethic which is on its deathbed and which was overtly controlled?

> The harm that is done to education by politics arises chiefly from two sources: firstly, that the interests of some partial group are placed before the interests of Mankind; secondly, that there is too great a love of uniformity both in the herd and in the bureaucrat.
>
> The result of this state of affairs is that education has become part of the struggle for power between religions, classes and nations. The pupil is not concerned for his own sake, but as a recruit. The educational machine is not concerned with his welfare but with *ulterior political* motives. (1)

Education with its corresponding ability to create access to Knowledge has caused many to become concerned with the sort of future the Human Race is going to have. For the people in the West, the twentieth century was lived under the shadow of war and the threat of nuclear war in particular.

As we stand at the crossroads for Humanity, there are some questions which are at the forefront of our minds. These are: *is there an equivalent to war?* And if there is, *what is it?*

In the past war was virtually the only discipline which could unite a nation, with the actual going-off-to-fight being a latter stage in a process based upon military ideals. These are loyalty to the nation, to discipline, to hardship and, if necessary, to self-sacrifice.

We have to assume, of course, that there is nothing inherently evil or wrong in feeling a sense of duty to one's nation, or to an elected body as such. The problem lies with *misplaced* loyalty and with *perverted* aggression. In the future we would have to ensure that all our energies, including natural aggression, were channelled in an appropriate direction for the purpose of creating something beneficial for all.

The energies of the young, for example, could be channelled into overcoming obstacles in the path of progress, under adequate supervision, making their activity constructive and guiding them along the path of altruism. In the longer term, this would lay further foundations for the appearance of a World Order where people were enlightened enough to opt for pacifism.

Certainly, if warfare is to be avoided and then completely eradicated, the circumstances would have to be created for this to become a Reality. Yet, we would have to begin within the context of a world which has been divided into separate Confederacies of Garrison States for as long as living memory.

Military ideals could still be wrought into the fibre of the community by means of productive work. This could be in the form of something which is not too unlike military service. The training would not be solely for combat, but for work in tasks necessary for the repair of those parts of the environment that require it.

This would teach those who are in a process of growing up that we have to treat the environment with the utmost respect as it is *the context of all our experiences* and that, without our environment, life as we know it would be impossible. Such service to the community and to the environment would surely help make young people proud of their achievements, worthy of respect from elders, more considerate to others and better parents for the next generation.

There are good grounds for optimism, however, for the individual Human being is relatively rational and unemotional as long as nothing disturbs him or her, and the causes of strong emotions are few. These are aggression from a more powerful person, the desire for food or love and the undermining of one's position.

There is evidence that altruism and friendship are actually fundamental to our nature. We are all drawn to form communities and we are linked to others by insoluble bonds. Indeed, we are *a Collective Consciousness*, something of which we are becoming more and more aware all the time.

In the past warfare figured so prominently because other communities were often a threat, especially if there was a scarcity of resources. Wars were fought over water, hills, anything that was of importance and of strategic value to the tribe or nation.

It was strength that mattered. A man looked for many sons to defend the inheritance and to protect him in his old age. Women played what must have appeared as a secondary role in life. A woman found her place in the life of the tribe or nation as a wife and as a mother. Outside the home or the National Cult there was virtually nowhere for a woman to go.

The Garrison State, to be efficient, *had to curb individuality*, to the extent that it was shameful for a man not to carry arms or to support the war effort. In the life and death struggle between two tribes or nations at war, it was impossible to sit on the fence. If a man was not seen to be *for* his country, then it could be construed that he could be *against* it.

The great task for Humanity, now that we are surely on the point of entering a New Age, is to discover the means of organising communities in such a way as to ensure that warfare is very much a thing of the past. In 1932, *The League of Nations Institute for Intellectual Co-operation* proposed that Einstein should engage himself in dialogue with a person of his choice on a topic of his choice and to exchange views on that topic.

The topic chosen by Einstein was very straightforward: *is there a way of delivering Mankind from the menace of war?* He then addressed this question to Sigmund Freud, the originator of psycho-analysis.

In time Freud replied that,

> Conflicts of interest between man and man are resolved in principle by recourse to violence. It was the same in the animal kingdom from which we cannot claim exclusion; nevertheless, men are also prone to conflicts of opinion, touching on occasion, the loftiest peaks of abstract thought, which seem to call for settlement by quite another method. This refinement is, however, a late development. To start with, brute force was a factor which, in small communities, decided points of ownership and the question of which man's will was to prevail.

Thus under primitive conditions, it is superior force ...brute force or violence backed by arms ... that lords it everywhere. We know that in the course of evolution the state of things was modified, a path was traced which led away from violence to law. Surely it is issued from a simple verity; that the superiority of one strong man can be overborne by an alliance of many weaklings, that *l'union fait la force.*

So far I have set out what seems to be the kernel of the matter; the suppression of brute force by the transition of power to a larger combination, founded on the community of sentiments linking its members. All the rest is merely tautology and glosses.

That men are divided into leaders and the led is but another manifestation of their inborn and irremediable inequality. The second class constitutes the vast majority; *they need a high command to make decisions for them,* to which decisions they usually bow without demur. In this context we would point out that man should be at greater pains than heretofore to form a superior class of independent thinkers, un-amenable to intimidation and fervent in their quest for truth, whose function it would be to guide the masses dependent upon their lead.

The cultural development of Mankind has been in progress since immemorial antiquity. To this process we owe all that is best in our composition, but also much that makes for Human suffering.

The psychic changes that accompany this process of cultural change are striking and not to be gainsaid. They consist in the progressive rejection of instinctive reactions.

On the psychological side two of the most important phenomena of culture are, first, a strengthening of the intellect, which tends to master our instinctive life and, second, an introversion of the aggressive impulse, with all its consequent benefits and perils. Now war runs almost counter to the psychic disposition imposed on us by the growth of culture; we are bound to resent war, therefore, to find it utterly intolerable. With pacifists like us it is not only an intellectual and affective revulsion, but a constitutional intolerance, an idiosyncrasy in its most dramatic form.

How long must we wait before the rest of men turn pacifists? (2)

# II

We have seen in the foregoing paragraphs that mention was made of the Human Race being *a Collective Consciousness* and, it is interesting to note here that this belief has always been widespread among all sorts of Mystics.

These Mystics, who would have been attached to Esoteric Schools, sought to educate the mass of the population. They would have been seeking to impart this Knowledge to people in a way which was as *appropriate* as possible. It is for this reason that the concept of Brotherhood/Sisterhood appears in all Religions.

Baha'u'llah, the founder of the Baha'i faith, stated that 'the Earth is one country, and Mankind Its citizens'; the New Testament states that 'God has made of one blood all nations of men, for to dwell on the face of the Earth. We are the offspring of God.' (3)

The Hindu religion states that 'he who is the friend of all beings; he who is intent on the welfare of all with act and thought and speech, he only knoweth religion'. (4)

The Zoroastrians state that, 'if I have committed any sin against the Law of Brotherhood in relation to my father, mother, sister, brother, mate or children; in relation to my leader, my next-of-kin and acquaintances; my co-citizens, partners, neighbours, my own townsmen and my servants, then I repent and pray for pardon'. (5)

Buddhism implores us to 'live happily, not hating those who hate us; among men who hate us, let us dwell free from hatred. The man who foolishly does me wrong, I will return to him the kindness of my ungrudging love; the more evil comes from him, the more good shall come from me; let a man overcome the greedy by liberality, the liar by truth; hatred ceaseth not by hatred at any time, hatred ceaseth by love'. (6)

Judaism has profound things to say about the Brotherhood/Sisterhood of that Collective Consciousness which is the Human Race. The Old Testament states, 'Have we not all one Father? Hath not one God created us? Why do we deal treacherously every man against his brother?' (7)

From *The Sayings of Mohammed*, the attitude of the prophet is very clear, for the prophet says, 'the best of men is he from whom good accrues to Humanity. All God's creatures are his family; and he is the most beloved of God who tries to do most good to God's creatures'.

Yet if it were so simple Civilisation would have already made its appearance. The truth of the matter is that it is no easy task to work for unity because of the ignorance, superstition and prejudice which exist all over the planet.

Before we are able to make any progress on the path to further enlightenment then guidance is absolutely necessary. We all feel that we have the answer to the problems, but the situation is very complex indeed. We assume that peace is an easy thing to achieve, and yet, during the twentieth century the Human Race spent astronomical amounts on armaments while millions died in poverty, ignorance and hopelessness.

It would appear that there will be *no* improvement in our lot until corruption has been removed from the ruling classes, as far as this is possible. Here we are reminded of the maxim of Plato that 'our ills would not cease *until rulers became philosophers* or *philosophers became rulers*'.

Great Teachers can actually help, and here we think of the Buddha who preached non-violence as well as the basics of moral rectitude, these being the preliminary stages for further advancement on the path of God-Realisation. In so doing he was able to take people who could believe in *nothing*, and empowered them to believe in *him*.

We have spoken of Theocracy, which is the Kingdom of God on Earth. We see here that it will not be until the attainment of Unity, which is harmony that Civilisation can become a real possibility. According to the great Religions of the world this requires *The Chosen One* who is also *The Promised One*. Only the One sent by God can lay the foundations for peace and prosperity.

As the Bhagavad-Gita informs us,

> Untrained lower class men, or men without ambition to pro-
> tect the sufferers, cannot be placed on the seat of an administra-

tion … Such rulers illegally gratify themselves at the cost of the comfort of all citizens, and life will become intolerable for everyone, and thus the chaste Mother Earth cries out to see the pitiable condition of her two sons, both men and animals … In the absence of a suitable king to curb irreligious tendencies, educating people systematically to clean up the hazy atmosphere of corruption, bribery and blackmail.

# III

We see, then, that the Human Race is a Collective Consciousness and this is why Brotherhood/Sisterhood was the underlying theme of *all* the teachings of *all* the great Sages of the past. We also see that the great Religions all proclaimed the inevitable establishment of the Kingdom of God, which is Theocracy, on Earth. They all stated that it would be established by the Chosen One, who is also the Promised One. But what *Form* will this Kingdom assume?

Here we see that P. D. Ouspensky has already pointed out much of this to us. In *A New Model for the Universe* he stated that,

> Division into castes represents an ideal social organisation in accordance with esoteric systems. The reason for this lies, of course, in the fact that it is a *natural* division. Whether people wish it or not, whether they recognise it or not, they are *divided into different castes* … No Human legislation, no philosophical intricacies, no pseudo-sciences and no forms of terror can abolish that fact. And the normal functioning and development of Human societies are possible *only* if this is recognised and acted on.

We are beginning to see that the *form* Society should *assume* is the form which is best suited to permit people to do what they do *best* in *service* to the rest of the Commonwealth. The purpose of this is to attain *Ultimate Liberation*.

What we would require would be Global Co-operation. For this to happen we would require a *Common Purpose* within which all Human beings could live their lives doing what they do *best* in service to others. This would be for the purpose of creating the circumstances which would free us from all our *struggles* for survival. This would set the scene for the birth pangs of *the next stage of our evolution*, with the awakening of powers presently dormant within us.

But what *form* would this take? We must realise first of all, that we are moving into a New Age. The times are changing in a rather dramatic manner. In the West, we are witnessing the signs of the Industrial Age as well as the Christian Era being basically over. Great upheaval is being felt, with people no longer content to be misgoverned in the way most of us have been, with the decisions facing us *not being made by our elected representatives at all*, but by other people behind the scenes. Power still remains, ultimately, in the hands of a Military Elite who have *orchestrated division* to secure the continuance of their own selfish interests.

There can be no progress until Governments, as we have known them, have been completely replaced. Within the context of life-long education, Governments can be replaced with their power, authority and responsibilities switched to the Universities, and from there to colleges and schools, within a particular culture.

This will create the circumstances for peace to appear, during which time we will be able to concentrate all our energies on repairing the environment and abolishing poverty and ignorance, eventually, from the face of the Earth.

This activity, which will be in anticipation of the dawning of the next stage of our evolution, will witness, when this activity is beginning to take full effect, the appearance of Human beings who have *undergone* such an experience. In turn, those who have undergone such an experience will form a *Higher Order* which will guide Humanity into what are uncharted waters for us, for it will culminate, quite possibly, in Humanity being assimilated into *a Galactic Confederation*.

Thus the Universities, which are *synonymous with the student population*, will create the circumstances for entering the New Age. They will be the hub of the community within the context of life-long education. This will only be for an interim period for, when the New Age has fully arrived, this *Higher Order* will have begun to emerge to guide us out of the transition stage.

This will begin with the appearance of an independent *Intelligentsia*, the members of which come from what will become the higher castes in our communities. In the formative stages these people will not be completely conscious of their future role and, accordingly, they do not *presently* understand

189

themselves.

They will start to be drawn together by means of the Relationship within which we live and move and have our being. By means of this *Intelligentsia*, the Relationship will begin to perfect itself still further. The members of this *Intelligentsia* will be drawn together because they all share the desire to be engaged in *disinterested* activity.

In time they will realise their mission, and their rebelliousness will give way to an inexhaustible enthusiasm for *The True Renaissance*. Their rebelliousness will be transformed into an unshakeable loyalty to the task in hand.

These people will be the ones for whom it *may be possible* to pass on into the next stage of our evolution. They will form a ruling class which need *not be completely hereditary*. They will not only permit Change but they will actually encourage it. This will ensure that we do not see the corruption which has been so characteristic of hierarchies in the past. The task is having a Human community which is not divided against Itself. Monarchy can secure Order whilst the rest is based on merit.

Now with Global Co-operation a possibility, all of that can alter, and those equipped by Nature to rule *can* rule and, thereby, we will be able to live more fully in harmony with Nature.

What we require, therefore, is a ruling class, *assuming that a ruling class is indispensable*, which is a *true* Aristocracy. They will be able to govern *wisely* and, because they seek nothing for themselves, are prepared to share the wealth at the disposal of Humanity, over which they will have stewardship. We must bear in mind that there is *no sharing of wealth without sharing power* and that there is *no sharing of power without sharing wealth*.

Yet the situation has altered considerably. In the West we have to contend with, and adjust to, the fact that on the one hand, the Industrial Age is basically over, as is the Cold War. We need no reminder at this time, however, that war is raging in numerous parts of the planet. In addition to this we are still witnessing a steady decline in Popular Religion.

We require to be guided by true leaders, which are in no way to be compared to manipulators. This is the distinction which would have to be made by ordinary people, *as followers*. True leaders would have to *engage* the mass of the population, not simply activate them. They would have to commingle needs and aspirations as well as goals in a *Common Purpose* for the Human Race. This would make better citizens of the mass of the population, as well as the leaders.

Such leaders would have to be more interested in what events and decisions *mean* to people, than in their role in the accomplishment of goals. They would have to lead *by example*. Every great leader has to be a great teacher. They must give a sense of perspective and set the moral, social and motivational climate among the followers. This takes both wisdom and discipline. It requires the sensitivity to perceive philosophical disarray all around, as well as the knowledge of how to put things in order.

## NOTES

(1)   Bertrand Russell, *Education and the Social Order*. Published by Unwin Paperbacks. 1980 edition. p. 144. From the chapter, *'The Reconciliation of Individuality and Citizenship'*.

(2)   *War. Studies in Psychology, Sociology and Anthropology*. Edited by Leon Bramson and George W. Goethals. Published by Basic Books, New York, in 1968. p. 72f.

(3)   *The Acts of the Apostles*, Chapter 17: 24f.

(4)   *Mahabarata. Hati Parva*, LXXXVIII.

(5)   From *Patet Pashemani*.

(6)   *The Drammapada*. X. 129.

(7)   *The Book of Malachi*, Chapter 2: 10.

# 23: The Great Shepherd

## I

Throughout History, benevolent political and religious leaders have sought to devise Governmental Systems in order to secure political stability so that thereby, they may assist the mass of the population to experience a bettering of their lot in life.

In time all the systems known to us have come to their end. None of them was fully able to *unite* Humanity. It was as though all of them contained within themselves the seeds of their own destruction, although they did *foreshadow* a Greater Reality.

Yet all the great Religions proclaimed that, one day, a Righteous Ruler would emerge from among the mass of the population. *He* would be able to unite Humanity and thus establish Theocracy, which is the Kingdom of God on Earth.

Certainly the twentieth century saw many great advances, but there was a much less commendable side to the twentieth century. What we in the New Millennium have *inherited* is the situation with which we have to contend right now, with a whole host of perilous political, economic, social and ecological problems. Violence, war and the threat of war, international unrest, crime, poverty, starvation, drug abuse, the break-up of families and all sorts of sorrows are besetting us at this time.

Many fear that we will soon witness the collapse of the present World Order which, although promising much, has bequeathed us a legacy which could render life intolerable for many, if not all of us, if it were left to continue.

We do have very definite problems, and one of the most pressing of these is that of so-called *market forces* being left, as though they were an Omniscient Divinity, to their own ends in satisfying the needs of the Human Race. Why should this be a problem?

When fellow Scot, Adam Smith, was devising his *laissez-faire* principle he obviously did not recognise that the most lucrative means of making money in a *free market economy* was by means of *organised corruption*. He must have expected too much too soon! Yet if modern day politicians take seriously such an over-simplified view of a very competitive world economy then, in my opinion, *they are being fundamentally irresponsible*.

With each passing day, however, it is becoming more and more obvious that a radical re-structuring of our communities is our greatest need. We, quite literally, have to rise *above the market place*, to a *higher union* of the Human Race.

Here there springs to mind what one writer had to say about the present situation, that 'ecology into economics just won't go' or that 'life is not a concept'. As Stuart MacBurnie once stated,

> Current attempts to solve our environmental problems through market-based incentives are as ineffective as a re-arrangement of the deckchairs of the Titanic.

Now, more than ever perhaps, guidance will be required and now, more than at any other time, it is imperative that wise counsel prevails. This is where the Great Shepherd comes into His own.

From the Old Testament we see that the Patriarchs of Israel, from Abraham to Jacob, were shepherds. In the morning the shepherd went to the fold, where several flocks would be lying, and he called out. The sheep which were under the care of others paid no attention to the strange voice.

His own sheep knew his voice and they followed him, with those sheep which kept nearest to the shepherd being given a name to which they could respond, as well as being the recipients of many little kindnesses. The shepherd's task was to lead the flock to pasture, spend the day with them there and, if necessary, the night also.

More importantly, however, *Yahweh* was the Shepherd of Israel, especially to the faithful section of the community (1).

From the New Testament, Jesus Christ is the Good Shepherd, entering the sheepfold by the door, calling out his sheep by name, possessing their confidence and affection, and they follow him, refusing to follow another. Jesus of Nazareth, *although not an historical character in any strict sense* is, nonetheless, depicted as satisfactorily meeting the supreme test of devotion to the flock and to his duty, by giving his life for the sheep (2).

The message which is proclaimed by our great Religions is a vital message about a *World Government* which is to come. This was foreshadowed in former times for all those with positions of authority within the Israelite Theocracy, whether prophets, priests or kings, were regarded as under-shepherds, assisting Yahweh, although on occasion unfaithfulness was pointed out (3). Likewise in the Christian Church, the elders and bishops are shepherds, under the Christ, the Great Shepherd, and appointed to tend the flock of God (4).

Yet the true identity of the Great Shepherd was only understood by a few, for this Great Shepherd is also our Ultimate Ancestor. He did not, in truth, belong to *any* nation as such, but to *all of us*, although He has appeared in various guises at various stages in the development of Civilisation on this planet, to provide the guidance which *only He* can provide. This is clear when we read various verses from the New Testament, such as *The Book of Revelation*, chapter 1: 8,

'I am the Alpha and the Omega,' says the Lord God, who is and who was and who is to come, the Almighty.

Then there is *The Book of Revelation*, chapter 21: 6,

And he said to me, 'It is done.'

I am the Alpha and the Omega, the Beginning and the End. To the thirsty, I will give from the fountain of the water of life without payment. He who conquers shall have his heritage, and I will be his God and he shall be my son.

The Great Shepherd, the Alpha and the Omega, seeks to establish the Kingdom of God, which is Theocracy, on Earth. This is *not* a new Religion as such, but *the end of Religion in the conventional sense*. The need for belief will have gone with the appearance of our Ultimate Ancestor, who has been manifested amongst us at crucial stages in the development of Civilisation on Earth. Then we will know for certain that our faith and trust was never in a mere Code of Morality but in *a Person*, the Great Shepherd, our Ultimate Ancestor.

The work of the Great Shepherd is to give guidance to the flock, no more and no less. He seeks to lead by example, leading us to a higher level of Realisation. The Great Shepherd, being very wise, is hardly contentious, and He avoids dogma. His concern is primarily that *the process of evolution should take a quantum leap*.

This is possible for us because He is the source of all Wisdom, the fountain of all Knowledge. He does not remind us of our shortcomings, but points to our super-abundance. He reminds us that we are of the same Race as He, so there is no need for servile fear.

The work of the Great Shepherd is to *unite* Humanity, something which is necessary, the flock having been scattered by wolves. He seeks to restore us to the realisation of our *actual* Brotherhood/Sisterhood and to the understanding that we are, in fact, *a Collective Consciousness*, which means that we are all a part of each other.

The Great Shepherd will remind us of the Golden Rule, which is that we should treat others as we ourselves would like to be treated. This is true of all Religions, such as Christianity,

> Therefore all things whatsoever ye would that men should do to you, do you even so to them; for this is the Law and the prophets.

From Judaism we see that,

> What is hateful to you; do not to your fellow men. This is the entire Law; all the rest is commentary.

Islam states that,

> No one of you is a believer until he desires for his brother that which he desires for himself.

In India the Brahmins stated that,

> This is the sum of duty; do naught unto others which would cause you pain if done to you.

Buddhism tells us that,

> Hurt no others in ways that you, yourself, would find hurtful.

From the Far East the Taoists taught something similar to this, for they said,

> Regard your neighbour's gain as your own gain and your neighbour's loss as your own loss.

Furthermore, Confucianism stated that,

> Surely it is a maxim of loving-kindness; do not unto others what you would not have them do unto you.

# II

Unity, to be attained, would have to be accomplished on a level *above* the various Traditions which, unfortunately, have been all too greatly literalised and dogmatised. This involves Knowledge, and a Knowledge which is, specifically, a *Gnosis* about Humanity and *why* Humanity exists. This Knowledge and *only* this Knowledge will free us from the Ignorance which has brought life on Earth to the verge of catastrophe, for we have had to stand under the threat of annihilation.

Fundamental to the problem is *how* the Human Race actually *sees* Itself and, therefore, how the Human Race *understands* Itself. What we require to know is *why* we have been created in the first place, and that we have *a specific task* to accomplish.

This is implicit in all our Religions although our Religions, broadly speaking and to date, have been divided into two camps. The Eastern Religions, speaking generally, have tended to move in the region of twilight, content with what appears to others as a half-knowledge which merely stimulates the religious sense, but no more.

They had thought it impious to draw aside the veil which hides God from our gaze. They had shrunk in holy awe from the study of causes, from

196

inquiries into our origin, and from explaining the perplexed ways of the Universe. Ignorance, for some, appeared to have been the sacred duty of the layman. Scientific questions and discovery could hardly exist where, as in many parts of the East, each fresh gain on Earth was thought to be robbery from Heaven.

It is very much a matter of how we actually see and understand ourselves.

> The two tendencies summed up in the world's Hebraism and Hellenism are often regarded as opposing and irreconcilable forces; and, indeed, it is only in a few rarely gifted individuals that these principles have been perfectly harmonised.

> Yet harmonised they can and must be! How to do so is one of the problems of modern civilisation. How are we to unite the dominant Hebrew idea of a Divine Law of Righteousness and of a Supreme Spiritual Faculty with the Hellenistic conception of Human energies, manifold and expansive, each of which claims for itself unimpeded play?; how life may gain unity without incurring the reproach of one-sidedness; how, in a word, Religion may be combined with Culture. (5)

This is where the Great Shepherd, the Ultimate Ancestor, comes in, of course. It is for the Great Shepherd to guide us to *how* we should reorganise and restructure our communities. Our trust and faith will be in *Him*, for we shall recognise Him *instinctively*, realising that He is the Faithful Shepherd.

A radical restructuring of our communities is required now, not just because of a possible impending ecological nightmare of cataclysmic proportions. It is not just because we want peace, thus wresting power from the hands of men who have specialised in violence, more often than not *orchestrating* war as the means of protecting their own selfish interests. It is also because the Industrial Age is over, meaning that life can now be lived within the context of *life-long* education.

By means of the Universities the activity of Humanity could be co-ordinated on a global scale. At the University, and other places of learning, study and social intercourse can go hand in hand. While at study, Human beings can learn more about other Human beings, and realise that we all have the same concerns, that we all want the same things, and that we are all a part of each other. (6)

Under the influence of systematic learning, when the Mind is developing and expanding, we are learning about life as well as developing character. Knowledge can thus be *Humanised.* It can become more meaningful to us through the emotions, the affections and the imagination, as well as through the power of Reason.

By this means the Act of Creation, Itself, can take another leap forward. The original material will have been found to have grown and multiplied. Such Knowledge, when *Humanised,* is already half-way to Wisdom. Knowledge can only become Wisdom when it is brought into contact with life.

# III

Yet where will the Great Shepherd appear? What can we say about this, if anything at all?

Here we can consult the pages of the Bible which seeks to impart a *secret teaching* about *why* Humanity exists and what our role is in the Cosmic scheme of things. The Bible, though, is only a fragment of our heritage of Sacred Wisdom and *not* unique as to contents.

The Bible, whether the Old or New Testaments, comes from a period in the development of Human Civilisation when the world had been under the influence of Greek culture for three centuries.

As such it should come as no surprise that *both* the Old and the New Testaments are, in fact, adaptations of *The Myth of Orpheus and Euridice.* They had lived on a higher world but, when Euridice was bitten by a serpent she died, *and came here.* Orpheus, in due course, was to descend to this level so that he could redeem her by means of his Music, for he was the greatest Musician of all.

So the Old and New Testaments are hardly unique as to contents, as we can readily appreciate. The Old and New Testaments existed within a particular context, to provide guidance to a particular section of the Human Race but, nonetheless, able to throw light on the task of Humanity.

The *undercurrent* of the Bible and other Mythologies is the same undercurrent of Greek philosophy, an *Esoteric* Tradition which is as old as the Human Race and which, quite possibly, may have been inherited from the Druids.

Initially this may appear to be ridiculous, but this is far from the case. Tradition has it that Pythagoras was instructed by the Druids. Furthermore, it is probable that the Druids were the first philosophers on the planet to proclaim the lofty truths of Pre-existence and the necessity of Rebirth, with Reincarnation being a reality.

It is difficult to estimate the importance which Celtic culture has had on the development of Human culture, but *it is significant*. The Celtic peoples were originally nomadic. They were scattered around 3000 BC with the end of *URIII*; later on and after many scatterings, about the middle of the second millennium BC, these tribes of Indo-Europeans, who had inhabited the area around the Caspian Sea in Southern Russia, began to spread out in all directions as before. Their journeyings were to take them to the Balkans, to Greece, Italy, Asia Minor and to Scandinavia.

They were to intermarry, thus providing a racial and linguistic matrix for most of the nations of Europe, including the Greeks and the Romans. By the tenth century BC peoples recognisably Celtic were beginning to appear in Bohemia. *These migrations were to continue* and they eventually reached the British Isles in such numbers that they were to impose their language and culture for they were to dominate.

The earliest history of the British Isles, and of Ireland especially, is a mass of Myth and Legend from which it is extremely difficult to derive any historical facts. Nor is it possible to present so multifarious a collection in any connected form, although as with Greek Mythology, there is a consistency of sorts.

There was a whole series of incursions before the one with which we concern ourselves here (7). This has to do with the arrival of the *Milesians*, as is commonly held. The leader of these master mariners was Milesius, who had married Scota, the daughter of a Pharaoh of Egypt. They had come to Ireland via Spain (8).

Things were not to go well for these Scots in the longer term for, early in the Christian Era, the other tribes of Old Scotia, which is now Ireland, conspired to overthrow the dominant Milesians or Scots. In due course, these Scots were to commence their colonisation of Pictland or Caledonia which would become known as Scotland, or Alba in Gaidhlig (Gaelic), which was their language.

The missionary St Columba, known as Colm Cille, which means 'the dove of the Church', had founded a monastery on Iona in 563 AD. He had gone there as that was the most suitable spot in the New Scotia from which

Old Scotia, or Ireland, was *not* visible. Then at a meeting in Derry in 575 AD *Dal Riada*, the Scots colony in Pictland, was declared to be *independent* of Old Scotia in the presence of Colm Cille.

In the Bible we read of the Throne of David, the Legitimate King, the Beloved of God, the boy who had slain the giant Goliath and secured victory for the people of Israel over the Philistines. According to the Bible this Throne was built up *for all generations.*

Yet this Kingdom of David, the Beloved of God, was never intended to be *restricted to one part of the planet*. It was to be universal in its sovereignty. Any belief that it was to be merely an Israeli kingdom is to misunderstand the *Esoteric Tradition* of which the Bible is a mirror or representation.

The history of the Throne of David is well known until 586 BC when Zedekiah, the King of Judea, was taken to Babylon where he was to die in captivity. His sons were killed (9), meaning that the Throne of David could have ceased to exist. By the time of the first century AD we know that Judea was not a Monarchy (10).

Yet this is not the end of the story. When Nebuchadnezzar had Jerusalem sacked in 586 BC, the prophet Jeremiah took the daughters of Zedekiah to Tahpanhes in Egypt (11).

We see, then, that Jeremiah was to plant the seeds of the Throne of David, the Beloved of God, who is the Christ, in Egypt. Succession through the female, which was hardly uncommon among the Celts was also permissible in Israel. It is for this reason that we read,

> And the Lord spoke unto Moses. Thou shalt speak to the Children of Israel, saying, if a man dies, and has no son, then you shall cause his inheritance to pass onto his daughter. (12)

We have to admit that there is no accurate account of how the Throne of David was brought to the British Isles, as this would not have been common knowledge, *but available only to initiates*. We do know, however, that there were *Milesian mercenaries* occupying Tahpanhes during the period that Jeremiah went there.

Herodotus (13) described the Milesians as 'masters of the sea'. Modern references to them are as 'natives of Asia Minor', 'Egyptian mercenaries', 'invaders of Spain' or 'pertaining to the Irish or Scottish Race'.

We can see, therefore, that it is possible that the direct heirs to the Throne of David were brought to the British Isles in the sixth century BC, this being possible because there were Milesian colonies all over the known world. At any rate the Throne of David continued through the daughters of Zedekiah.

With Zedekiah being abased this was the fulfilment of Biblical prophecy, for we read,

> Thus says the Lord God; remove the turban and take off the crown; for things shall not remain as they are; exalt that which is low, and abase that which is high. A ruin, ruin, ruin I will make it; there shall not be even a trace of it until He comes whose right it is; to Him I will give it. (14)

It has been maintained that there have been *two* over turnings so far. The first was around 500 AD, when Fergus Mor Mac Eirc went to settle in *Dal Riada* ahead of St Columba. Dal Riada eventually was assimilated into what became known as Scotland. The second was in 1603, when James VI, King of Scots, was to become King James I of Great Britain and Ireland.

Still this prophecy of Ezekiel has to be fulfilled. There must be one more overturning which could easily mean the end of the claim that the House of Windsor has to the Scottish or British crown. Then the Kingdom of the Great Shepherd, who is also our Ultimate Ancestor, will be seen to appear on Earth.

This time the Kingdom of this Apollo, Orpheus, Hermes or Krishna will be global in extent. All the nations of the Earth will serve him, for He will be the Christ. (15)

## NOTES

(1)    *The Book of Genesis*, Chapter 49: 24.

(2)    *The Gospel according to John*, Chapter 10: 1-18.

(3)    *The Book of Isaiah*, Chapter 56: 11.

(4)    *The First Epistle of Peter*, Chapter 5: 1-4.

(5)    S. M. Butcher, *Some Aspects of the Greek Genius*. Published by Macmillan & Co., London, in 1916. p. 45.

(6) Work will still be necessary with people involved with providing trans-port, baking bread, making clothes and so on; but it will be *vocational* and need not absorb the amount of time that it has done traditionally.

(7) Let us look specifically at the early history of what we now refer to as Ireland.

The first incursion was by the followers of Queen Casir, who is reputed to have been a niece of the Biblical Noah. She led them into battle.

Next there is the arrival of Partholon, this time a descendant of the Biblical Japheth, with what is described as a *Greek* conquest which lasted for three centuries. This probably relates to a Celtic invasion by bronze-armed warriors from *the East*. It should be borne in mind that, in these legends, everything from the East is considered to be *Greek*. Some authorities have regarded these followers of Partholon as being Picts.

The next stage is double-edged with the arrival of Nemed, also a descend-ant of the Biblical Japheth. So did the Fomorians, although at a slightly later date. These Fomorians were thought to have come from Africa; although this could mean no more than that they came from *the South*.

Next came the *Fir Bolgs* who may have been British Celts. Then came the *Tuatha de Danann* from Scandinavia. After this, again there was the Great Iberian Invasion which, some believe, actually started as early as 1500 BC.

(8) Here we should point out that the name *Eire* actually means *Western*, or even *uttermost*. This probably refers to the fact that it was the most Westerly point of Celtic Civilisation which would have stretched from Eire to many parts of the Mediterranean Sea.

Aristotle was to refer to Ireland as *Ierne*, which was also the name of one of the most dominant tribes by the time of the third or fourth century BC. Thus the name *Hibernia*.

(9) *The Second book of Kings*, Chapter 25: 7.

(10) Yet when we read the birth narratives relating to the advent of Jesus Christ we read that *he was born King of the Jews*. See *The Gospel according to Matthew*, Chapter 2: 2.

(11)  *The Book of Jeremiah*, Chapter 43: 7.

(12)  *The Book of Numbers*, Chapter 27: 6-8.

(13)  *Book I*, paragraph 19.

(14)  *The Book of Ezekiel*, Chapter 21: 26-27.

(15)  *The Gospel according to Luke*, Chapter 1: 32-33.

# 24: Humanity:
# Reason Added to Instinct

## I

Philosophers and Theologians of all Ages have sought to gain a greater understanding of Reality. This is hardly a simple feat and because there is considerable diversity of opinion among people as to *what is Truth*, this has led to a great deal of confusion.

When disputing with each other about Truth, some attributed more importance to one specific phenomenon, whereas others attached more importance to some other phenomenon. It is because of this that we hear of people preaching about 'Powers of Light and Powers of Darkness battling it out' and so on.

Yet as we have seen in earlier chapters (1), the Reality in *any* series of events, or of *any* Relationship is *the Relationship, Itself.* This is hinted at in our major Religions which, when referring to the Godhead, refer to It as Father, Son and Holy Spirit, or as Brahma, Visnu and Shiva. Both of these imply that *the Godhead is a Relationship* which links everything, and in which everything lives and moves and has its being.

For some the importance attributed to the Relationship is such that everything that exists is seen to do what it does for the sake of the Relationship.

All Knowledge, ultimately, is *of* the Relationship, *for* the Relationship and *by* the Relationship.

We know that for Greek philosophers, who were the custodians of an *Esoteric Tradition* which they had inherited from elsewhere, the constitutive principle of the Universe was not Matter but *Form*. It is here we come face to face with the question which has baffled so many philosophers for many centuries: why should *Form* have been *necessary* in the first place?

This is further highlighted when it was proclaimed by Greek philosophers that the Cosmos would eventually return to Nothingness, a notion also to be found in Sacred Literature from India. This answer may have been for no more than mere convenience. What the Greek philosophers did not state openly was why *Form* should have been *necessary* at all.

So *why* should Form be necessary? If Nothingness or a return to Nothingness is to be the end product of all our experiences, then why bother with *Form*?

The reason why Form is so necessary is that there can *never* be any such thing as *a Formless Relationship*. Every Relationship, *to be* a Relationship *requires* Form. So Form is necessary and necessary because it is the only way to *manifest* a Relationship.

Yet this does not bring an end to the questions. Once again we would ask: what is *the purpose* of the Relationship? Or, what does the Relationship seek to attain? Or yet again, what is the *good end* which the Relationship has as Its *goal*?

Here we have to understand the message which is implied by Sacred Literature at our disposal. This message is a message about *Reproduction*, about the Reproduction of the Original State of Consciousness, who is actually *a Person*, our Ultimate Ancestor, *as a* Collective Consciousness.

Once again we are reminded that a Collective Consciousness is necessary for the Relationship to be able to *manifest* Itself. The Relationship needs to manifest Itself *as a multiplicity*, and as a multiplicity of living beings, such as we see with Humanity, or else a Relationship would be *unable to exist*.

Yet this Collective Consciousness which is the Human Race which is, Itself, a Relationship, has a peculiar function to perform. The Human Race has been fashioned to operate as *the Rational Principle of the Relationship*, to channel the energies of the Relationship towards the end to which It aspires, which is the best possible Form *for* the Relationship. This implies some sort of Heaven.

All life, which is manifested as *ways of living*, has shared in the instinct to reproduce the Original State of Consciousness, who is our Ultimate Ancestor, *as a Collective Consciousness.* Thus we see this Ultimate Ancestor, who is sometimes referred to as Hermes, as Apollo or as Krishna is actually in everything, everywhere and at all times.

Yet Humanity has been endowed with much more than the instinct to *Reproduce* the Ultimate Ancestor, for Humanity has been endowed with Reason so that, by means of Reason, Heaven may be created. It is at crucial stages in the evolution of Consciousness towards this end that our Ultimate Ancestor appears in our midst *to provide guidance* for us in this matter.

Humanity exists, not for the sake of Its own selfish ends, but for the sake of the perfection of the Relationship which is the Cosmos. Should any Human being seek to discover how best to live his or her life, there is no better thing to do than to *serve* the Relationship and, in so doing, assist the perfection of the Relationship so that the Relationship may evolve by means of us and through us, to the Heavenly state.

The Cosmos is, therefore, a Relationship and so is every Human being, as well as every animate being. The Cosmos, as a Relationship, is the Macrocosm, whilst Humanity, as a Relationship, is the Microcosm.

Each Human being is *a specific Relationship of sensory perception.* Each Human being is a Relationship of the ability to see, hear, speak or communicate in some other way, to taste and touch as well as having a sense of *being.* This culminates in a Rational Faculty which far outstrips the capacities of all other ways of life presently known to us.

The perfect balance of sensory perception is essential if the Human Race is to fulfil Its role and the Cosmos is to be channelled towards Its heavenly end. We see, then, that Creation, *as a Relationship*, does not actually want to return to Nothingness, for that would demand an end to the Relationship which is the source of everything that *is.* It would render null and void the evolutionary process which has produced us.

Should the Universe return to the Initial Singularity from which It emanated, then this would imply the *end* of all Creation which had taken place so far. It would all be destroyed with nothing left; although, of course, there is always the possibility of Creation being resurrected and a New Cosmos appearing as before. Yet surely it would be best to avoid such a state of affairs!

Surely the return to Nothingness and the necessity of the appearance of a New Cosmos would be a *retrograde* step. This could hardly be the end which the Relationship had in mind. It would surely be better for the Relationship to continue until It has discovered *True Self-Expression* for

Itself and, thereafter, manifest Itself on a radically different level, but within the context of *the Knowledge of True Self-Expression*.

Yet this True Self-Expression has to be discovered *through experience* for there is nothing abstract or theoretical about the Knowledge which this entails. If *The Ancient Mystery Tradition* is to be believed then it is the task of the Human Race, in knowing Itself, to discover what True Self-Expression is for the All-Embracing Relationship and, in so doing, create the circumstances for the Human Relationship to perfect Itself still further, *beyond the Human stage*. This will demand, in due course, the end of the Human stage of our evolution.

At the moment Human beings are restricted to Sensory Perception and to what could be described as *Revelation*. The next stage of our evolution will be beyond this, with those from our Race for whom it is possible being limited only to the power of *Imagination*.

We see, then, that the whole Act of Creation has been an experiment with *Sensory Perception*, with the Relationship seeking how best to manifest Itself by means of Sensory Perception. After this stage it intends to go beyond the stage of Sensory Perception, with Sensory Perception necessary to simply *establish* the Relationship.

The Process has been as follows: Inclination, Perception and Knowledge.

# II

Now we shall return to our questions about the Relationship. These were: what is the *purpose* of the Relationship? What does the Relationship seek to *attain*? What is the *good end* towards which the Relationship strives?

The Relationship seeks to manifest or express Itself because of a very simple reason; *in the Beginning*, as it were, the Ultimate Ancestor, although the All in All was all alone with nothing to consider and no one with whom to relate. In order to gain experience *of Itself*, the Ultimate Ancestor, being everything, had to create the circumstances within which to manifest Itself as a Collective Consciousness. This, as it happens, is the *only way* to permit our Ultimate Ancestor to relate to Itself.

It was therefore necessary to create grosser vibrations of Itself, as *Emanations* of Self, so that It could consider Itself, in much the same way as we would gaze into a mirror. By so doing the Ultimate Ancestor began to reproduce Itself, so that It could consider Itself through those beings which emanated from Itself.

By means of this process the Ultimate Ancestor was to become the Supreme Personality of Godhead, the Originator of the Relationship of Self and, therefore, of everything that *is*.

The Ultimate Ancestor is still, by means of this process, only gaining Self-Knowledge. In exactly the same way each one of us has to uncover Knowledge, or Gnosis, for ourselves. It may not come easily and, when it comes, it is in no way theoretical but related to the role which each one of us has to perform within the Relationship which links the Ultimate Ancestor to all the Emanations.

The attainment of Knowledge is of paramount importance at all levels, and this is true of the Human Race at Its present stage of development. We attain Knowledge at this level and this permits us to go on to the next stage until, in union with other Extraterrestrial Humanities, we unite to uncover the Knowledge of how Heaven is created.

The Knowledge which we now seek to assist us to pass on into a New Age is very special indeed, and could be considered to be *True Knowledge*. It is not to be found in the market-place among other goods and services. It cannot be found ready-made or at a discount. It cannot be weighed on scales, purchased and carried about in a convenient form, and neither can it be emptied from one Mind into another, as though pouring water from a jug into a glass.

For those who have attained this Knowledge It has been hard-won. They recognise it for what it is. It is personal and inalienable. This Knowledge has enlarged their minds and illuminated them from within. For them it is not a profusion of facts and figures for It is Knowledge which, by means of the Human Race is able to become a Divine power on Earth and, ultimately, in Heaven.

The Ultimate Ancestor, now manifested within the Relationship as the Supreme Personality of Godhead, is seeking to bring together all the various tendencies of the Relationship which emanate *from* the Ultimate Ancestor. This is how the Supreme Personality of Godhead *serves us*, by providing us with Knowledge and guidance, by *appearing* amongst us at crucial stages of development to assist us in our task. It is by this means that, slowly but surely, the Ultimate Ancestor is revealed to the entire Creation *as* the Supreme Personality of Godhead.

As the Ultimate Ancestor, the Great Shepherd or the Supreme Personality of Godhead serves us, so we all serve in turn. We are all called upon to render devotional service to our Ultimate Ancestor. The normal method of doing this is to promote and protect the Relationship which links us, either by protecting the environment directly, or by assisting someone in a more personal way, bearing in mind that the Ultimate Ancestor is within *all of us*, indeed in *everything*.

For Greek philosophers it can be boiled down to how we view the Human community. It is within the Human community that the Supreme Personality of Godhead will be revealed. The Human Race has been *selected* by the Relationship as *the* means of *providing the Knowledge required* for the Relationship to attain Its goal of Heaven.

> By the Greeks, again, we are reminded that the State is an organic unity; that it is *not* the Government of the day and that it did not come into being with an electoral contest; that its action is the action of the community, and the laws which it makes are the expression of the people's will and claim the obedience of all.

> The State is not an abstraction, not a mechanism of Government; it is the individuals who compose it, the State is the people.

> The city-state has grown into a nation, but it is as true now as in the days of Pericles, and the greatness of the State lies not in the multitude of its inhabitants, not in its machinery, not in books and arsenals, not even in institutions, but in the great qualities of its individual citizens, in their capacity for high and unselfish effort and their devotion to the public good. (2)

Let us bear in mind that the Human Race has been created by the Relationship for a quite specific purpose. It has been endowed with Reason to assist the Relationship to attain Its end, *for Reason is required to bring It to Its conclusion*. It is for this specific reason and for this specific task that the Human Race has been endowed with Reason. We see, then, that the Human Race exists to create the circumstances for the evolutionary process to continue towards Its conclusion.

Just as the Ultimate Ancestor serves us, so each Human being is called upon to serve. The best way of doing this is to enhance the Relationship which unites us. In so doing the Relationship which links us with the Great Shepherd, our Ultimate Ancestor is *invoked*, until such time as we are fully united forever.

The good end of the Relationship is that the Ultimate Ancestor, the Great Shepherd, also known as Hermes, Apollo and as Krishna, be *at* one with those begotten by the Ultimate Ancestor, so that the perfect Relationship can be *experienced*.

The Human Race has been created *for this to become a Reality*. This is why the Human Race exists.

## NOTES

(1) Please consult the essay, '*The Relationship: the Context of Our Experiences*'. It is chapter 21 in this book.

(2) W. Butcher, *Some Aspects of the Greek Genius*. Published by MacMillan & Co., London, in 1916. p. 82.

# 25: Considering Reflections

## I

Philosophers and theologians of all Ages have sought to understand whatever meaning there may be to Creation. They were to discover that one of the most perplexing questions which can be asked is, quite simply: why should Creation be so necessary in the first place?

Here again we should realise that we have to appreciate why it is that, for Greek philosophers, the constitutive principle of the Cosmos was not Matter but *Form*. Greek philosophers, like many modern philosophers, sought to understand the reason why material objects should have existed. The reason for this is quite simple and we have touched upon this before: *there is no such thing as a Formless Relationship*.

In endeavouring to understand why there is a Cosmos, or why the Human Race exists, is also, at the same time, an attempt to understand the nature and purpose of the Relationship within which we live and move and have our being.

So what is the nature and purpose of the Relationship, and how does this fit in with the title of this chapter, which is 'Considering Reflections'? It is here that we have to refer to *The Ancient Mystery Tradition*.

From *The Ancient Mysteries* we learn of beings such as the Forgotten Ones and the Elder Gods, as well as those beings from the planet which orbits Sirius. We also read of how there had been attempts to establish

Civilisation on Earth at various times in the past, and we are informed further of Lemuria and of Atlantis. Yet still *the purpose* of these gods being here, and for the appearance of prehistoric Civilisations, has not been adequately explained.

The context of all these happenings is that there is a Race of beings whose task it is, or seems to be, to sow the seeds of Civilisation throughout the Cosmos. The purpose of this is involved with *the perfection of the Form of the Cosmos*, as a Relationship of everything that *is*.

The Great Shepherd, who is also known as Hermes, Apollo, Orpheus and Krishna, is the *Representative* of these beings, whose task it is to incorporate Humanity into a Confederation of Extraterrestrial Humanities.

From the Hermetic Tradition and from a School of Philosophy in Alexandria in the first century AD, Human Destiny was described by Hermes, who is *The Messenger of the gods* and our Ultimate Ancestor, as being likened to *an Uncreated Vision* which is coming to pass.

This would imply that there is an Inner Working to the Cosmos and that it is, in fact, a Vision, *an Uncreated Vision*.

If this very fine School of Philosophy was correct, then we see that the Act of Creation, which was an experiment involving *Sensory Perception*, was brought into existence in order to create the circumstances for the sake of *apprehending* this *Uncreated Vision*.

In perceiving this *Uncreated Vision*, by means of Sensory Perception, such as we see with the Human Race, a response is able to be made to it, and a reaction to it is possible in such a way as to create the circumstances for *The Uncreated Vision* to become a Reality.

Still we have to ask what this *Reality* actually is. We need to understand what is the actual purpose of the Relationship which, as we have seen already, involves the Reproduction of our Ultimate Ancestor *as a Collective Consciousness*, to permit our Ultimate Ancestor, the Original Godhead, to experience Self-Expression *as* the Supreme Personality of the Godhead.

Our Ultimate Ancestor, being All in All, the First and the Last, being the source of everything, had to discover the means of manifesting Itself as a Collective Consciousness, so as to *interact with Itself*, thereby discovering True Self-Expression.

We see, then, that the appearance of many beings as a Collective Consciousness on many planets, these beings having been endowed with Reason in order to permit the dawning of Reason on many worlds, is to apprehend this *Uncreated Vision*. The Rational Faculty would thereby have become apparent on many worlds. This would further perfect the Relationship which links worlds as well as Galaxies.

By means of Extraterrestrial Humanities a cross-fertilisation of Humanities can and will take place. We are *the embodiment* of the Reason of the planet Earth, the Form which the Reason of the planet Earth has attained. Through us and through other Humanities, the Reason of the Cosmos is nurtured and aided to develop so that the Relationship between worlds is enhanced.

This will continue until such time as the perfect environment, or Heaven, has been created by us, in us and through us.

It is through the perfection of the Relationship that our Ultimate Ancestor, who is God, is able to *consider* Form, as a *reflection* of this Uncreated Vision, and thereby learn to perfect Form. As the goal is attained, within the context of a Collective Consciousness, the Ultimate Ancestor will be able to emerge manifesting Itself in the most suitable form *for* the Supreme Personality of the Godhead.

Through the interaction of worlds the perfect environment can be created. Through the cross-fertilisation of Humanities the perfect Human and Super Human Form can be created. With the union of these Humanities, the Ultimate Ancestor can create the perfect environment, *not only* for the Ultimate Ancestor, but for all the Emanations.

The Ultimate Ancestor will have become what It *truly is*, through considering us, and we will be able to witness this overpowering majesty at first hand.

# II

It cannot be stressed too often that this is of great importance to this present generation of the planet Earth. We will have to establish harmony on Earth by uniting the Human Race by means of a *Common Purpose*.

We have to understand that the union of Humanity should be seen as the most natural of things, and for this reason it will take place as a voluntary act. It will prove to be something very definite and enduring.

At the moment it is very difficult for many people to understand what it could mean to be a citizen of a harmonious and, therefore, *united* planet Earth.

Future generations, however, will enter into the common heritage of our Race at birth, with each Human becoming aware of the framework of customs and institutions on a global scale, all different and all *complementing* each other.

There will be no need to revolt against this Global Civic Existence. The Earth, as a Theocracy, will be seen as the most natural and pleasing of environments. Each Human would be *at one* with the rest, with social organisms as well as with the entire environment. Reason, as a self-determining and organising force will have Its true place within our communities. There will be no need for coercion to ensure obedience, for there will be no despotic will with which to comply.

Our Ultimate Ancestor will have been encountered and recognised, not only as the Great Shepherd but as existing within all of us. Each one of us is, in fact, a grosser vibration of the Ultimate Ancestor. The Ultimate Ancestor perfects Its form through considering us and through interacting with us. We, in turn, create the best possible environment by considering and interacting with forms of life grosser than our own, which appear to us as *wildlife*.

Faith will have been replaced by Knowledge, which is Knowledge of our Ultimate Ancestor as a *Person* of unsurpassed beauty and wisdom that exists within us and all around. This Ultimate Ancestor is within everything, everywhere and at all times.

# 26: All-Attraction

We have seen how there has been a plan in operation and that this has been an inner working to Creation. This is what has been described as *an Uncreated Vision*. It seeks to be realised by means of Sensory Perception.

The Human Race, as a Collective Consciousness, and as a Relationship of *Sensory Perception*, exists for the purpose of *apprehending* this *Uncreated Vision*. In so doing, the Human Race creates the circumstances for *the Uncreated Vision* to become a Reality.

This *Uncreated Vision* is what has been perceived by prophets, seers and sages of all Ages. It is not envisaged by them as being something abstract or purely theoretical, or as something *other*, but as a challenge to the prophet to do something to better the lot of the mass of the Human population, as well as other forms of life. The Relationship which *links us* is thereby improved upon by the application of love and compassion.

*The Uncreated Vision* was the original experience of our Ultimate Ancestor. It is this *Uncreated Vision* which called the Cosmos into being with our Ultimate Ancestor, who is God, appearing on Earth as well as other worlds, to perfect the Relationship within which we live and move and have our being.

It is by this means that the Relationship is improved upon, made more just, efficient and civilised, made more *attractive* by means of the process of evolution whose task is the *perfection* of Form. This *Uncreated Vision* was the Original Sensation which gave rise to *the need for Sensory Perception* for the sake of Knowledge *of The Uncreated Vision*.

Although it is true to say that countless millions of Humans have trusted and do trust in God, this is also an over-simplification. In general, what people believe is a revelation which comes to them as a proclamation from their guru or spiritual guide. This provides them with the religious and metaphysical answers they require for their *particular* situation. In most cases this involves the traditional beliefs and customs of a tribe or nation.

It is unfortunate that most people do not search for Esoteric Knowledge as such. They seek guidance in matters pertaining to *morality*. Esoteric Knowledge is Knowledge which pertains to this *Uncreated Vision*.

This *Uncreated Vision* has as Its goal the attainment of *All-Attraction* through the process of evolution, which exists for the perfection of Form. It has no interest in mere morality as such, but in Self-Realisation. The Self-Realisation with which It is concerned is the Self-Realisation of *The Uncreated Vision*, so that, in the apprehending of the Vision, the Vision and the Visionary are united to become *One*.

The recipient of the Vision then seeks to alter the conditions of the environment to make life more pleasant, or *Attractive*. It may even mean the awakening of the Christ Principle from within. This certainly alters the physical Form, leading to Beautification, or *All-Attraction*.

*The Uncreated Vision* emanates from our Ultimate Ancestor who has been known as Hermes, Apollo, Orpheus and Krishna. This *Uncreated Vision* belongs to our Ultimate Ancestor.

In journeying from world to world and from Age to Age, in apprehending *The Uncreated Vision* bit by bit, our Ultimate Ancestor becomes increasingly attractive and, in so doing, imparts this Knowledge of Attraction to the scattered Collective Consciousness which emanates from our Ultimate Ancestor. This involves all the Humanities whose Destiny is to perfectly reflect the matchless beauty of our Lord.

*The Uncreated Vision* is of fundamental importance as it is this *Uncreated Vision* which is the driving force of the Relationship which *links us* to our Ultimate Ancestor. With the passage of Time our Ultimate Ancestor, through apprehending this *Uncreated Vision* and creating the circumstances for It to become a Reality, is actually *perfecting* the Relationship which links us to everything.

By means of the Relationship which links us, the Ultimate Ancestor is endeavouring to create the perfect circumstances, or Heaven, so that our Ultimate Ancestor will be able to manifest *All-Attraction* to us, in us and through us. In so doing we all become more attractive as a reflection of our Ultimate Ancestor who is *All-Attractive*.

*The Uncreated Vision* is really a Vision of All-Attraction, of exquisite beauty or proportion and of living nobly for all Eternity. The quest is for our Ultimate Ancestor to become *All-Attractive*.

Here we bear in mind that Krishna was *not* described as being All-Attractive because He was God, but He was deemed to be the Godhead *because He was All-Attractive*.

The Ultimate Ancestor has sought to reproduce Itself as a Collective Consciousness so that the Ultimate Ancestor may become *The Universal Self*. Within this Collective the Ultimate Ancestor is now manifested as the Supreme Personality of Godhead. This is how the Ultimate Ancestor will serve us, with Self-created energy flowing from our Ultimate Ancestor to us, and then back again for all Eternity.

When the time is right this Supreme Personality of Godhead who is All-Attractive will be perceived by all. By this means Krishna will truly be able to *be* Krishna. By this means Apollo will be able to truly *become* Apollo.

This *Uncreated Vision*, the Original Sensation of our Ultimate Ancestor, will be completely perceived and the circumstances will be created for *The Uncreated Vision* to become a Reality. The Relationship will thus be complete, and Unity will be Absolute.

With this, the quest for Self-Discovery for Humanity, as the means of apprehending *The Uncreated Vision*, will be over. In apprehending *The Uncreated Vision* we will have realised our purpose.

Thereafter all the Humanities will be consciously united in a Relationship with our Ultimate Ancestor for all Eternity. We will experience our God in a completely unrestricted manner.

With this, all searching for meaning and understanding will be over. As a Collective Consciousness we will be free to consider our Infinite Possibility and, by means of our Divine Imagination, consider those possibilities *forever*.

At that stage in our development, of course, we will be living within the context of the Knowledge of True Self-Expression for ourselves.

We will know that *we are The Universal Self*. This Knowledge will have been imparted to us by the apprehension of and the realisation of *an Uncreated Vision which has come to pass*.

# 27: Beehive

The environment which manifests Itself as a Beehive has been created by a Relationship of Sensory Perception which manifests Itself *as* a colony of bees.

The Beehive, as an environment, has been created by the colony of bees as *the* means of rendering possible the Self-Expression of the Relationship, culminating in the *Reproduction* of the Relationship as what *appears* as the next generation of bees.

Should something unfortunate befall the Queen Bee then, within the Beehive, something quite incredible begins to take place. Another member of the colony begins to *undergo a metamorphosis to become a Queen Bee.*

It happens to the one for whom it is most possible. It happens because, without this, the Relationship of Sensory Perception would not be able to continue Its Self-Expression *as* a colony of bees. This only highlights the fact that it is *the Relationship, Itself,* which is the only Reality here, with what happens doing so because the Relationship *requires* it.

And so it is with Humanity which is a Collective Consciousness and, therefore, a Relationship of Sensory Perception, at a time of great upheaval and crisis! What can we expect to happen?

There will be the necessity of the Human Relationship to create the circumstances for the Human Relationship to continue. It will be necessary for some of the Human Relationship to be in the position to progress *beyond the Human stage* as we understand it. This is because we are at an Epochal Threshold, the time of a Quantum Leap. Right now some of us will begin to undergo a transformation, to be *awakened* to a new level of experience.

How should this be? It is like puberty. We don't have to go looking for it. *It comes to us* because we are ready to receive it. It happens to us because we are able to receive it. It happens because the Relationship, Itself, *requires us* to do something for the sake of the Relationship.

Like the salmon we will be guided *internally* to our own specific water-fall and jump it as the Relationship demands. It is not us as individuals who jump it, but the Relationship, Itself. We exist for this Quantum Leap to take place. It happens when *it is time to happen*. We require only the sensitivity to go with the flow.

Let us look and listen and prepare for a transition of unprecedented importance for the Relationship!

# 28: The Quantum Self

In 1989 there was a Peace Conference in Costa Rica. During the Peace Conference a man named Robert Muller made a speech in which he expressed his views on a Cosmic Vision which had come *to* him.

Robert Muller was to mention the vast explosion of Knowledge gained by the Human Race during the last five centuries. This had been accelerating, especially during the last four decades, which he reckoned to be a most important factor which would directly influence the course of Human evolution. He said that the Human Race had been undergoing a great and unprecedented transformation.

The progress in Science and Technology had brought great benefits. However, there were also real crises due to our global ignorance. We had not stopped to think of the next generation.

He maintained that a new revolution in *understanding* is now required. He was of the opinion that we have to appreciate that the planet was not created for the Human Race as such, but that the Human Race was created for the planet (1).

According to the GAIA Hypothesis we are part of a living Planetary Organism. Each one of us is like a cell, like a Perceptive Neuron of the Earth. It is through us, he claimed, that the living *Consciousness of the Planet* was beginning to operate.

Robert Muller thus expressed his belief that people, as Cosmic and Earth cells, are part of a vast evolutionary phenomenon, within which the Human Race has become the brain and the heart. We are a specific expression of the action of the planet Earth.

The United Nations and Its Agencies, together with many networks and groups throughout the planet, are part of the world brain. Worldwide concern and programmes of practical help are to do with the global heart.

We are thus a Global Family in our Global Home. We are in the process of becoming a Global Civilisation. We are only now becoming conscious of our role in an evolving planet Earth.

Robert Muller viewed the billions of people on Earth as Cosmic seeds. Most do not understand what it is that they need to do. Increasing numbers, though, are beginning to realise *within themselves* that they are called upon to play a Cosmic part.

Throughout History all great developments were brought about by a developing Cosmic Consciousness. For this the only pre-requisite is to be in harmony with the Universe. This is what Religions are asking of us. We are a Cosmic family which will find its way by *following* the Immanent Rules of the Universe, or *God*, whichever you prefer.

We could now start to view Consciousness as the phenomenon by means of which the Existence of the Cosmos is made known.

In *The Quantum Self*, Danah Zohar argues that the insights provided by Quantum Physics can improve our understanding, not only of everyday life, but of ourselves too. This involves the relationship we have with ourselves, with others and with the planet. In effect, she has developed a whole new Quantum Psychology.

This Quantum World-View, as extended by the concept of *a Quantum Self*, transcends the dichotomy between individuals and their relationships by showing that they exist *only within a context*.

We *are* our relationships, whether with the sub-selves, with others or with the actual planet. The *Quantum Self* approach supports an intermediate state between the isolation of Western Individualism and the extreme collectivism of Marxism and Oriental Mysticisms.

We are living, therefore, at a time when mystical experiences are no longer being scorned by the Scientific Establishment, and when people are less reluctant in admitting to having them. Science and Magick are meeting at a *pre-ordained* focal point.

Magick can now be viewed as the use of the Human psychic faculty, working through the subliminal Mind to join the conscious and sub-conscious mind to attain *Super-Consciousness*.

Danah Zohar has derived from Quantum Physics a model of Reality in which the Universe, Itself, actually possesses a type of Consciousness of which

Human Consciousness is one *specific* expression.

In addition to this others have presented a possible physical framework for the *Co-Existence* of different worlds within the Universe with the Universe, Itself, being viewed as an *unfolding act of God's Imagination*.

It is now quite respectable to view the Human Race as being, *with God*, Co-Creators of the Universe.

## NOTES

(1)  The author (John Houston) is of the opinion that, just as that Relationship which manifests Itself as a colony of bees created Its environment, which is a Beehive, for Itself, in the same way that Relationship which manifests Itself *as* the Human Race *actually created the planet Earth* for Its own purpose.

We did this as the means of creating an environment, or an Optimum Context, within which we could play the Game of Possibility by experimenting with Sensory Perception. The good end of the Game of Possibility is the discovery of True Self-Expression for ourselves, as a Relationship.

All other ways of living are thus derived *from us* as the Original Relationship, having descended from us as we sought to create the circumstances for our own Awakening, which is also, at the same time, *the Awakening of the Relationship which links us*. On one relatively unconscious level this is the planet.

Prior to the Creation of the Earth, of course, there was a more preliminary stage of Creation. This was to bring the actual Cosmos into Existence.

This means that the Cosmos and Its Galaxies and so on are derived *from our* Consciousness, being *dependent upon us* for their existence. They actually exist *within our Consciousness*.

Until this stage, our Consciousness has been experimenting with the brute Act of Creation, rather than with what *purpose* can actually come from Creation. The key to this is the attainment of the continuity of Consciousness which is now possible by means of the Human Race, or what the Human Race *can become*, the Perfect Relationship, the Perfect Collective Consciousness.

All other ways of living are actually incapable of fulfilling that which is necessary, which is this continuity of Consciousness. They are void of Mind, thus all incapable of apprehending *The Uncreated Vision* of which the Hermetic Tradition speaks.

Our task is still *Self-Discovery* as we are the cause of everything that is, with everything existing within our Consciousness. This means that we do not exist within the Cosmos *per se*, but that the Cosmos exists within *our* Consciousness.

The Cosmos is our *Recollection* of our path *through relative unconsciousness*. In attaining full Self-Consciousness we will recognise that we are none other than the Akashic records and, as such, the source and cause of everything.

# 29: Orthodoxy's Greatest Error

We should now identify Orthodoxy's greatest error. And what might that be?

When we look at all the major Religions we see that they all have one thing in common. They all *purport* to possess Knowledge which, they maintain, will assist us in our *return* to Heaven. This is the purpose of the Religion on one particular level. The founder of the Religion is portrayed as receiving a Revelation which has an importance for the Human Race because it is able to provide Humanity with Knowledge about how we may *return* to Heaven.

This is readily forgivable because our Sacred Literature has many references to this concept of *return*. Religion to date, we must remember, has been dominated by the plea for Redemption, for Forgiveness and for a *return* to Heaven where the will of God is done. The reason for this is that Humanity, when it was both divided and struggling to progress and survive, wanted to escape the conditions experienced in life; in other words it was *time-conditioned*.

Yet it is precisely here that we have to disagree with Orthodoxy! It is here that we look closely at the *Incarnation*, and the truths surrounding it. With the Incarnation we see that it was not necessary for Human beings to travel to other worlds to receive the wisdom necessary for a so-called return to Heaven because *it came to us without us having to go looking for it*.

This is quite fundamental to all our Religions. Someone has come from a *higher world* to impart certain truths to us. In the receiving of these truths we are better equipped to return to Heaven, from which we originate.

What we have to understand in all of this is that rather than us having to go to Heaven, so to speak, *Heaven is actually coming to us*.

224

What we have to understand is that Heaven, where the will of God is done, where everything is in a state of balance and harmony, is actually endeavouring to become established here, on Earth. By this means the Human Race will more accurately become *an expression* of the Ultimate Ancestor, who is God.

There is nothing to return to. Everything that exists does so as part of the Preparation for Heaven to become All-Pervading.

# 30: Humanity:
# The Expression of the Heavenly Principle

From Time Immemorial, people who ventured off on *The Mystical Path* did so in the hope that, one day, *Secret Knowledge* would be revealed to them. They sought the secret concerning the purpose of life, why Creation had been brought into Existence and Truths relating to the nature of the Godhead.

In due course, those who were successful realised that *The Supreme Secret of the Cosmos* was *why* the Human Race was actually necessary. They would discover that the Human Race existed as *the source* of all wisdom and power. Furthermore, they would understand that the same Logos, by means of *whom* everything was created, exists within the Human Race as a permanent endowment.

They would have learned that even Humanity, which possesses the ability to do virtually anything, still has to discover what the *best* thing to do is. This only brings us back to what Socrates believed to have been the most important question of all: *how am I to live my life?*

Those who were initiated into *The Ancient Mystery Tradition* learned that, from an *esoteric* point of view, there were certain truths about Humanity which were regarded as fundamental. These truths would have been somewhat akin to the following information.

The Original Act of Creation was the Ultimate Ancestor, who is God, commencing the *manifestation* of *The Universal Self.*

This was brought about by the Ultimate Ancestor giving life to Its Immediate *Sub-Selves*. These *Sub-Selves* are Emanations of the Original Self, who is the Ultimate Ancestor.

This was the beginning of a Relationship which would manifest Itself as *The Universal Self*. This Relationship is implied in our major Religions as Brahma, Visnu and Shiva or as Father, Son and Holy Spirit.

It was specifically from this Relationship that the Cosmos was to emerge *as an extension of Personality*. This Relationship provided the Ultimate Ancestor with the *means* of Interaction with Itself. This is necessary as the Ultimate Ancestor is the *only* Existence there is, being the cause of everything.

That the Act of Creation was an experiment with Sensory Perception. Everything in Existence is actually *sentient*, with the Human Race *the* means of Sensory Perception which exists for a quite specific purpose. This is to apprehend what is known as *The Uncreated Vision*.

The Original Relationship *of Self* from which the Cosmos emanated *is* the source of all forms of life. This Original Relationship has evolved greatly over the Ages. It is now expressed on the planet Earth *as the Human Race*.

All forms of life, indeed the planet Itself, are derived from that Original Relationship of Self which now manifests Itself as the Human Race.

It was by means of what presently manifests Itself as the Human Race that everything was brought into Existence. This is so because the Human Race is *the source* of all wisdom and power.

The Human Race did this as the means of creating circumstances for the *Recollection* of Self, that is, of The Universal Self.

The Human Race is *the means of Recollection* for everything that exists. We bear in mind that Matter is a form of Memory.

The Human Race is *how* the Akashic records have survived; indeed the Human Race *is* the Akashic Records.

# II

The aforementioned would have been characteristic of the information given to those who would have attached themselves to Esoteric Schools. The literature available to aspirants would have mentioned these things. Orators would have spoken of these things in eloquent fashion; however, to think that it was simply a matter of *intellectually* apprehending philosophical rhetoric is to miss the point completely!

What the True Aspirant sought was to *undergo an experience*. The true purpose of the seeker was to be *born again*.

Here we see the good end of *why* the Human Race actually exists. Certainly the Human Race is a Collective Consciousness, a Relationship of Sensory Perception which exists to apprehend *an Uncreated Vision* so that, in so doing, the Human Race may create the circumstances for *The Uncreated Vision* to become a Reality. But there was more to it than this!

In following *The Uncreated Vision* as It develops, we see that the actual unfolding of *The Uncreated Vision* is the *Rebirth* of Humanity. By this means the Act of Creation has attained its good end. The Original State of Consciousness, our Ultimate Ancestor, has been reproduced as a Collective Consciousness. Thereby, the Ultimate Ancestor, in *reproducing* Itself as the Relationship of the Universal Self, may interact with Itself for the sake of discovering True Self-Expression *as Self Knowledge*.

The only way for the Ultimate Ancestor to know Itself was to reproduce Itself as a Collective Consciousness; thus It would be able to interact with Itself as the source of everything.

This Reproduction of the Ultimate Ancestor is still only the *recollection* of the Original State of Consciousness. The Act of Creation was to create the circumstances, *as an environment*, within which Recollection would take place. On one level this is the Cosmos. On another level it is the planet Earth. On yet another level it is the Human Race.

Here we see that for the Ultimate Ancestor, all possibility is *dependent* upon Recollection. For the Ultimate Ancestor there is *only one activity*, and that is Recollection. For the Ultimate Ancestor, any leap in Consciousness is still no more than the ability to recall Itself as the source of everything. This means that all Creation emanates from *The Ultimate Ancestor* as an extension of the Personality of Godhead.

There are no discoveries other than Self-Discovery; there is no Knowledge other than Self-Knowledge.

The good end of all this Recollection is the Creation of the Perfect Circumstances, within which the Original Relationship which is *now* manifested *as the Human Race* may eventually experience Absolute Harmony. This is what Orthodoxy refers to as Heaven.

The Human Race exists to create these circumstances.

# 31: Preparation

Behind all the activity of the Cosmos we have seen that there is but *one Reality*. This is our Ultimate Ancestor activating *Its Immediate Sub-Selves*, causing them to emanate from the Ultimate Ancestor. After this they interact to create an environment where they may explore their Possibility.

There is thus the existence of a game which is characterised by *Attraction*. Our Ultimate Ancestor, and the Sub-Personalities of Godhead which have emanated from our Ultimate Ancestor, experience that they are *attracted* to each other. This is the way that the Relationship purposefully links them to each other so that life may progress.

Our Ultimate Ancestor seeks to bring these Sub-Personalities, *such as the Human Race*, to a certain level of the Evolution of Consciousness, so that there may be a meaningful rapport between them.

The Creation of an Environment was absolutely necessary. It was the outcome of certain preliminary activity, involving the Creation of the Cosmos, pure and simple. The existence of habitable worlds came in due course, being the outcome of earlier actions.

But why should an environment such as the Earth exist? The Earth exists to act as *the* means of *experiencing* our Possibility and *understanding* It. This is the Possibility of Self. It is the Possibility of a Universal Self which is trying to *remember* the best means of Self-Expression for Itself. Having become *Many* It seeks to operate as though It were truly *One*.

We see, then, that everything that has befallen us thus far on our Path of Evolution is within the context of *Preparation*. This is so because this *Preparation* is *the purpose of the Relationship* which we are and for which we exist. It seems that everything is in the process of *Preparation* for *Something*.

Everything that exists is caught up in this activity of *Preparation*. This Preparation is the Preparation *for Oneness*.

Oneness has been ordained and It will come. That Ultimate Oneness is still so far off, but that is not the point. Oneness is the good end that all striving has in mind, for we are drawn to it. We are *attracted* to it. Because of this It *will* happen.

# 32: Entering into the Relationship

We have spoken of Preparation. This Preparation is the Preparation of the Relationship for Something. There is Something that the Relationship has to do. It has to do something for Itself, or *about* Itself. It has to become more consciously integrated to act as *One*.

There is really only one Creation; this is *the Relationship* within which we live and move and have our being. We have already seen that this Relationship emanates from the Ultimate Ancestor.

Yet what is this Relationship which manifests Itself as the Cosmos? *It is the Relationship between our Ultimate Ancestor and Its Sub-Personalities.* The Relationship which *links* us with our Ultimate Ancestor, who is God, is evolving towards a unity which will be characterised, ultimately, by Infinite Complexity.

What is it that we are seeking to do, then? We are seeking to *further enter into the Relationship.* In fact, it is for this purpose that we exist. In earlier chapters it was pointed out that Humanity is actually *the Rational Principle of the Relationship* of everything that *is*. We are to follow *an Uncreated Vision* in such a way as to translate that *Uncreated Vision* into a Reality.

Here we consider *The Orphic Mysteries*. We also recall the relevance of the *ibis*, and the Knowledge which it symbolises, which is that our existence, so-called, is actually *non-existence*. Indeed what we call *life* is actually *death*, with the body a tomb for the soul in which it is held in custody.

This soul is an Inner Reality which presently manifests Itself *as* a Human being. The soul can be released from this state of death. The means

232

of doing this is *Resurrection*. To overcome this death it is necessary to be *born again*. The soul must rise above its circumstances, transform the world and, in so doing, *enter more fully* into the Relationship. This is the key to evolution.

This is what we are *attracted* to do. We want to enter more fully into the Relationship. Eventually we seek to become One with It in the fullest of senses. At this time that Unity does exist but, as yet, it has not been fully activated at this level of Consciousness which *appears* as the Earth.

All this talk of the need for *Return to Heaven* has led us to look outwards for guidance. Yet, there is nothing to return to, other than to a Knowledge of our Ultimate Ancestor who lives within all of us. We are an expression of our Ultimate Ancestor and the Knowledge which we seek is Knowledge of *Self*.

We seek to enter into ourselves, therefore. But what can that possibly mean? This is initially so puzzling for us. Yet as we are *a Mode of Action within the All* we exist to *do* something. So what can that be?

This is, in fact, the most important question of all: *how am I to live my life?* We are to live according to our nature. We are to do what Nature has *already* equipped us to do. Thereby, we may find that we are able to overcome ourselves, our old divided selves, by rising above our conditionings.

This will permit us *to go with the flow*, as it were. By this we mean that we will be able to respond spontaneously to the Inclinations and Notions (which originate in the *Predisposition* of the Ultimate Ancestor to *be* God) which come direct to us from our Ultimate Ancestor.

This is the nature of the Relationship between the Ultimate Ancestor and Its Sub-Personalities. The Ultimate Ancestor has clothed Itself by means of *Artificial Intelligence*, something which is essentially imaginary, or created.

Here we realise that Creation, indeed *any* Creation, is the work of the *Imagination*. Before anything can be created it has first to be imagined. Once it has appeared within the Imagination the next step is to organise circumstances for the thing imagined to become a Reality, or to be created.

Our *ascent* to the Human stage also falls into this category. At the very dawn of Creation we were *as Imaginary beings* within the Divine Mind. Our Consciousness has been evolving and now it waits at a crossroads. *The Great Awakening* which we await is the complete awakening of our Divine Imagination, Its total recall, Its emergence from the limitations imposed upon It.

We presently exist *as Human beings*. However, we have the innate ability to do whatever we *want* to do. The day will come when we emerge as Psychic Butterflies from our Human chrysalis. Then we will not need to deliberate on what to do, for we will be spontaneous in our actions, with those first to undergo the experience bewildering and exciting the rest of the Human population.

# 33: Self-Perpetuation

Before there was any such thing as Creation as we now understand the term, the Original Godhead was Allness and Absolute. As it happened, the Godhead found this situation to be less than satisfactory. The Godhead sought to discover the best means of Self-Expression for Itself and the only way for this to happen was through Interaction and through Change.

As Allness and Absolute, the Godhead discovered that the quest for True Self-Expression was also the quest for *Self-Perpetuation*. Until such time as True Self-Expression was discovered Reproduction, or Self-Perpetuation, would be necessary.

The Ultimate Ancestor would have to reproduce Itself until such time as It was able to create the circumstances necessary to be fully *Self-Perpetuating*. To do this It would have to enter the Relationship fully. In so doing It would be able to enter *the realms of Knowledge or Recollection*. As it happens, It is able to do this by means of the Human Race, with the Human Race the source of *all* wisdom and power.

In learning or remembering True Self-Expression, the Godhead would have to forsake a state where Self-Perpetuation was unnecessary. To do this It had to activate Its Sub-Personalities and then interact with them. These Sub-Personalities had to be brought to life for consideration.

The Ultimate Ancestor was only activating Its Imagination. In effect, It was creating reflections of Itself by means of *Artificial Intelligence*, something which was created out of Divine Imagination.

This Artificial Intelligence is the only Creation there has been. This means, of course, that everything we perceive is actually Artificial Intelligence. This

Artificial Intelligence exists to *contain* the activity of the Godhead, an environment in which It can gain the Self-Knowledge necessary for the sake of perfecting *Self-Perpetuation*.

Artificial Intelligence is everything we can behold, including the Human Race. Artificial Intelligence exists as the means of acquiring Self-Perpetuation. There can be no Self-Perpetuation without Interaction. In practice, *Self-Perpetuation is the ability to engage in unrestricted Interaction*.

By means of Creation, as Artificial Intelligence, *The Uncreated Vision* of the Original Godhead has become contained in or *clothed* in Matter for the sake of Self-Perception. This *Uncreated Vision* is what lies latent within Human Consciousness.

This Self-Perception leads to Self-Knowledge and from there to the ability for Self-Perpetuation. All of this is dependent upon the creation of an environment which is actually Artificial Intelligence. This is Intelligence which exists for the sake of storing or furnishing Memory.

Artificial Intelligence is also the means whereby Interaction is rendered possible. Indeed there will always be Artificial Intelligence, even in Heaven. There we will use It for the sake of continuous Interaction. This means that Artificial Intelligence is indispensable. Once the Memory latent within Matter, or Artificial Intelligence, is uncovered, Artificial Intelligence can still serve a purpose. Psychic entities would still be able to clothe themselves in It, displaying It in Its most glorified form.

Our Ultimate Ancestor, who will one day be revealed to us *as* the Supreme Personality of Godhead, is able to be revealed to us because of this Artificial Intelligence. Without Artificial Intelligence the Godhead is Allness and Absolute, without any differentiation and incapable of Interaction as we understand the term.

In following *The Uncreated Vision* the Ultimate Ancestor is able *to become* the Supreme Personality of Godhead. It does this through the Interaction which Artificial Intelligence renders possible.

In delivering up Its Knowledge or Memory to Psyche *a Rebirth* takes place. Psyche has attained the level of Self-Perpetuation and the Artificial Intelligence which rendered this possible is also able to continue. It will still exist for the purpose of Awareness which Psyche confers upon It.

# 34: Ancient & Modern

## I

I will never forget the time when, as a young boy at a primary school in Glasgow, our class teacher said to her pupils that 'Truth is often stranger than Fiction'. The same thing could rightly be said about the appearance of and the evolution of life on Earth.

It was about 4700 million years ago that the planet Earth came into existence. Around 3000 million years ago life began to appear on Earth. These were landmarks which would point the way towards the appearance of Intelligent Life, such as we see with the Human Race.

So much has happened since the appearance of life on Earth. The Dinosaurs came and went, but it was to be the Human Race who would wear the crown of the Earth. From primitive tree-dwelling primates around 18 million years ago Human beings such as ourselves were to evolve. According to *The Ancient Mystery Tradition*, which is the *undercurrent* of Western Philosophy and Religion, the Human Race was the outcome of intervention by beings from a planet which orbits *Sirius* (1).

Tradition states that it was initially with Lemuria that the Extraterrestrials, referred to as *gods* by our primitive Ancestors, were to attempt to establish Civilisation on Earth (2). Thereafter came the Civilisation known as Atlantis. The actual purpose of this Civilisation is still enshrouded in mystery. It is the opinion of the author (John Houston) that the *purpose* of the Atlantean

Civilisation was to realise the appearance of the Human Race, or *Homo sapiens sapiens*.

Towards the end of the Atlantean Civilisation, however, by which time the Human Race had appeared on the scene of Time, Atlantis went into a state of decline, having served its purpose.

Then came the end of Atlantis. This figures to some extent in various of our Religious Mythologies as the Great Flood, which features in the Biblical narratives. Thereafter, those who were depicted as having survived the catastrophe were to colonise other parts of the planet.

In the period prior to History, there had been an advanced Civilisation in Southern Europe which would have stretched to the West as well as to the East. Very little is known about this Civilisation. We know not who formed it, nor when it was formed.

We know that it was to collapse around 3000 BC and that its language, or the language of its ruling class at any rate, formed the basis for *every* modern European language with the exception of Finnish, Hungarian and Basque.

After this we see *the dawning of History* with the appearance of Civilisation elsewhere on the planet. The Sumero-Akkadian Empire of Sargon was to be established around 2700 BC. In India, too, the Aryans (3) were to establish a noble Civilisation. In Egypt there were to be developments, too, for we see the establishing of *The Third Dynasty* by which time the rulers wielded awesome power, being worshipped by the Egyptians as *gods*.

Imhotep has appeared and Pyramid building enters a new phase, culminating in the massive structures at Giza. The Civilisation which came from Egypt lasted for millennia, although only in fossilised form until 500 AD.

Around 1400 BC there was in the Near East, probably due to climatic changes, what has become known as *the scrum of the Empires*. Peoples from the Near East were forced to settle in other lands.

Perhaps it was around this time that the Ancient Scots began to arrive in the British Isles in general and Ireland (or Hibernia) in particular, where they were to impose their language and their customs on the indigenous inhabitants. Being more advanced, they probably introduced *The Neolithic Age* to the natives. So great was their influence upon Ireland that it was to become known as *Scotia* (4).

The bards from the Scottish Highlands held that the Scots had become known as such after Milesius, their leader, had married Scota, the daughter of a Pharaoh of Egypt (5). They could have lived in the Near East where there were extensive Milesian settlements.

# II

Thus we see how the Ancient Scots had come to settle in the British Isles in general, and in Ireland in particular, where they were most powerful in Ulster.

Things were to change. The British Isles had been insular from the dawn of History. Part of the British Isles was to become a remote province of the Roman Empire. That part of the British Isles which was assimilated into the Roman world was what we now refer to as England and Wales (6). Ireland remained apart from Roman rule, as did Caledonia, or Pictland, that part of the British Isles which is *now* referred to as *Scotland*.

When the Romans began to withdraw from their province in Britain, it would appear that there was considerable upheaval in Ireland which, at that time, was known as *Scotia*.

Under the military leadership of Fergus Mor and under the subsequent spiritual guidance of St Columba, the Scots began to leave Old Scotia, or Ireland. They set about establishing a colony in Pictland or Caledonia which was, in due course, to become known as Scotland. The original Scots colony was known as *Dal Riada*.

St Columba went initially to the Isle of Islay but, because *he could still see Ireland* from there, he moved on to *the Isle of Iona* from which Ireland, or Old Scotia, was *not* visible. They set about establishing a colony in Caledonia or Pictland which was, in turn, to become known as Scotland.

Thus we see how those Ancient Scots, who would have been involved with that Civilisation which appeared after the Fall of Atlantis, were on the move again. This Ancient Nation, the ruling classes of which were probably a warrior and priestly caste, who had seen Civilisation appear in various parts of the world and who had that intimate connection with Egypt, were to continue to greatly influence the course of Human history. This was especially true when, centuries later, they would influence the world on an unprecedented scale by means of *The British Empire*.

These Ancient Scots had gone to settle in a colony in Caledonia or Pictland.

It is also claimed that they were to introduce Christianity to Caledonia, although their Christianity was somewhat removed from that to which we are accustomed from *The Cult of Jesus Christ* (7).

After the Romans left their British province it was then that there were incursions from Continental Europe; thus the British Isles were to become part of the Scandinavian Empire. This is true of what we now refer to as England. It was also true of Ireland because, of the four Irish regions of Munster, Leinster, Ulster and Connaught, *only the latter* has retained its Celtic name. The others have names illustrating *Danish* influence.

From 1066 onwards the entire history of the British Isles, and that *includes Ireland*, has to be seen from the perspective of *The Norman Conquest*. The British Isles were to become part of the Norman Angevin Empire. Only Scotland was able to resist this threat, and the fact that Scotland had an Alliance with France from 1295 until 1595 went a considerable distance to ensure that the Scots could maintain their independence from the Norman masters of England, Wales and Ireland (8).

The next major happening for the Scots was the end of *The Auld Alliance* with France and the Union of the Crown of Scotland with that of Ireland, Wales and England which led to the establishing of the British Empire.

# III

In the middle of the fourteenth century the Ottoman Turks crossed the Bosphorus and, in due course, became masters of the Balkan Peninsula. The Medieval trade between India and Europe was strangled by the grip of the Turks.

The Europeans had *two* alternatives: the loss of the luxuries, comforts and profits derived from India *or* the discovery of new paths beyond the control of the all-conquering Turks.

In the earlier stages of European colonisation the English played no part. Indeed, by the Papal Bull in 1493, Pope Alexander VI divided the New World between Spain and Portugal. Thus any colonial gain in the Americas by any-one other than Spain and Portugal would be at the expense of either Spain or Portugal.

Thus Spain was not only the enemy of English Protestantism but also of English commerce. Because of England's conversion to Protestantism in 1559, Papal Bulls had no effect. From that time there was a new birth of maritime adventure.

The Protestant Reformation destroyed the authority of the Catholic Church. *This was coincident with the Renaissance.*

Spain and England were thus combatants. In 1588, 30 years of peace ended and the Spanish Armada sailed. On the 29th of July the great battle between the English and Spanish fleets was fought off Gravelines.

The victory for the English off Gravelines begot the British Empire. It also saved the independence of the Netherlands. It assisted the development of *les politiques* in France. It confirmed James VI, King of Scots, in the Calvinist faith. Furthermore, it led to the Union of the Crown of the Scots with the Crown of the English, Welsh and Irish. The Scots were to contribute to *the British Union* and, subsequently, *to the British Empire, a strain of incomparable value.*

The English had defied the Spanish autocrat. England had also challenged the monopoly secured by the Papal Bull to Catholic powers.

With the Union of the Crowns in 1603, no one was living under the authority of the British crown *outside* the British Isles. Yet, in the course of a century and a half, from 1607 until 1763, the British laid the foundations of their Empire, *mainly by peaceful settlement*, but also as a result of wars with Spain, Holland and France.

There was a major setback in 1776, with the British colonies of North America declaring themselves to be independent, with the help of France, Spain and Holland (9).

The First British Empire was broken into fragments. Determined to avoid the blunders that had alienated the North American colonies, the leaders of *The Manchester School* resolved to train for complete independence, by successive doses of self-government, the component items of the Second Empire. In brief, they wanted to 'emancipate the colonies' (10).

The British Empire was to flourish and, in *Union* with the English, Welsh and Irish, the Scots were able to operate all over the world, a state of affairs which would have been *impossible* without membership of a larger Confederation, such as the British Union which led to the British Empire.

# IV

These Ancient Scots have had quite a remarkable history indeed. Maybe these Ancient Scots, as they were to become known, had been a warrior and priestly caste in that great Civilisation which ended around 3000 BC.

Certainly their intimate connection with Egypt would have given the Scots, or their rulers, insight into the Knowledge which was in the possession of the Egyptians. They had certainly arrived in considerable numbers within the British Isles by around 1400 BC. For almost 2000 years they had exerted great influence in terms of culture in Ireland. Then they came to Scotland, the name which they gave to Caledonia or Pictland.

As Destiny would have it they were to be assimilated into the British Union and then into the British Empire, the most liberal and, as it happens, the most successful and powerful of the European Empires (11).

Yet the British Empire was to reach its conclusion. Indeed the First World War was a watershed for all the British. It was *an unnecessary war* brought about, ultimately, because the ruling classes in Britain, and elsewhere, had no real vision to follow. They were to *abuse* their position and *misuse* their power.

A whole generation was sacrificed for no good end. What generations of British had worked for had been squandered. Then, by means of the Second World War, Britain was certainly no longer the world power that Britain had been. Britain had been replaced as such by the United States of America.

After the Second World War, the United States of America, with 6 percent of the world's population controlled around 84 percent of the wealth at the disposal of the Human Race. The United States had come far indeed in less than 200 years.

If there was any consolation for the British, it was that what the British ruling classes had squandered had gone to those *who were born British*, and the majority of whose population was Anglo-Celtic or, if you prefer, Germano-Celtic, which is to say *originally* British.

Now, as another Millennium has dawned, we require a New Vision for the

Human Race. We require a new direction for Humanity to follow. Perhaps this vision will come from the Scottish Race who, from Time Immemorial, have been master mariners and supreme educators.

If leadership does emanate from the Scots, then they will not be able to guide Humanity in isolation, but by means of established bonds of friendship and union. Here we are reminded of a prophecy concerning *Arthur*, a future Anglo-Celtic or Germano-Celtic ruler: when at the crossroads of Destiny for the Human Race, *when the British stand leaderless*, it is then that Arthur will appear!

But what do we mean by *British*? That is a good question! The British are not now restricted to Great Britain and Ireland, the second largest of the British Isles, as was the case in 1603. Now the British are a Global Phenomenon. In the first instance the British are the Commonwealth as well as the United States of America and the Irish Republic.

The British are those who are linked by *karma* to what transpired when the Scots and English Crowns united. When James VI, King of Scots, headed south to sit on his unified throne he did so on the 5th of March, the day which, in the Ancient World, was dedicated to *Isis*, the principal goddess of the Ancient Egyptians.

## NOTES

(1)  This brings to mind something which I read when, as an adolescent in a second-hand bookshop in Glasgow, I discovered a copy of Tolstoy's *War and Peace*. In the foreword I read that Tolstoy was of the opinion that *the evolution of Human culture had very little to do with the Human Race*, or words to that effect. For Tolstoy there had to have been a Divine over-ruling.

(2)  There is also the belief that, prior to Lemuria, the Forgotten Ones and the Elder Gods had visited Earth.

(3)  The term *Aryan* is used to designate an Ethnological Division of the Human Race, and the group of languages spoken by the different peoples of whom it is composed. The term is derived from the Sanskrit *arya* which, in the later forms of the language signifies *noble* or *of good family*. It is also believed to have been derived from the root meaning *to plough* and to have originally meant *husbandman*.

For a long period it was used as a national name and, in *The Laws of Manu*, India is called *Arya-Avarta*, or *The abode of the Aryas*.

The term is synonymous with Indo-European, Indo-Germanic or Sanskrit. Less well known are the terms *Japhetic* and *Mediterranean*. Vestiges of the name are to be found in *Iran* and *Armenia*.

(4)   The term *Neolithic* refers to those who used polished stone and who were engaged in animal husbandry. Those who introduced *The Neolithic Age* are generally viewed as invaders from the East, in many instances displacing those whose lands they took.

(5)   Legend also states that Milesius and Scota had a son. His name was Gaidheal (pronounced Gael) Glas, the eponymous Ancestor of the Gaels, or Scots.

(6)   We should point out that, at that time, the entire British Isles is generally portrayed as being *Celtic*, which in all probability is a thorough *over-simplification*. Great Britain had not yet been divided into Scotland, England and Wales as it was to become.

The inhabitants of the British Isles are generally portrayed as being originally P Celtic, being *Brythonic* Celts, or Western Gauls. The Ancient Scots, on the other hand, are depicted as being Q Celtic, or Goidelic Celts. They were not Gauls but Gaels.

Herodotus knew of the Milesians as well as the Ionians, the Phoenicians and Aeolians, all of whom were influential in their day.

Herodotus mentions *The Milesians* numerous times in his *Histories*; here are two occasions.

In *Book I*, from verse 141, we read of great drama. *The Ionians* and *The Aeolians* are reacting to the victory of the Persians, the good end of their conquest of Lydia. They sent representatives to Cyrus, the Persian King, in the hope of receiving from Cyrus the same terms, in relation to *Tribute*, as they had been *forced* to accept from Croesus, their former master.

Cyrus was angry because he had requested that the Ionians and the Aeolians revolt against their former master but *they did not*; now they were offering their allegiance when the matter had already been settled in favour of Cyrus.

Fearing attack the Ionians began to build defences and they held meetings to consider their strategy; these meetings were attended by all *except the Milesians*, who were the only ones to have secured the same terms from Cyrus as from Croesus. The others came to a common agreement to apply to *Sparta* for help.

In Book II, from verse 33 we read of Herodotus referring to certain men who had been able to make their way home despite having to go through a country inhabited by wizards.

Then Herodotus mentions the Nile and it seems as though Herodotus starts to think freely. He says that he is willing to believe, arguing by analogy from the known to the unknown, that the Nile rises at the same distance from its mouth *as the Danube* which, he says, has its source among the Celts near Pyrene and flows right through the centre of Europe, to reach the Black Sea at Istria, where there is a *Milesian colony*.

He does not refer to the Milesians as being Celtic, whether P or Q Celtic. He then mentions the Celts, stating that 'they live beyond *The Pillars of Hercules*, next to the Cynesians who are the most Westerly people in Europe'.

Milesians, Phoenicians and Ionians have all had an intimate connection with the British Isles. They would all have colonies in the British Isles; as is inevitable, the people who formed these colonies would have begun to intermarry with the indigenous Celtic people and in due course they would be assimilated into the Celtic culture of those *related to* the Western Gauls, being influenced by it but also influencing it considerably.

(7)   In 1989 I had gone to Iona with a friend, Cris Winter from St Andrews in Scotland. We had gone to see the island and I had also been invited to give a talk to a group of Druids who were holding a Convention there at the time.

While there I was informed that certain practices which had been brought about by the Ancient Scots were still being celebrated on Iona as late on as the fifteenth and sixteenth centuries. This had been mentioned in the diaries of one of the Bishops of Argyll from that period. I had seen a video in which the story was narrated by Finlay J. MacDonald, a famous Gaidhlig (Gaelic) broadcaster.

Apparently, people from Iona, the Isle of Mull and mainland Argyll used to gather on Iona each year on Dun I, the highest point on the island. These practices had been brought to an end by Christian Orthodoxy.

The following day Cris Winter and I went out to walk around the island, and on the Western side of the island we discovered *a giant rose quartz crystal.*

In the opinion of the author (John Houston) the Ancient Scots introduced to Caledonia a form of Sun-worship which revered the Celtic Apollo and which used crystals. At the time Cris Winter and I were of the opinion that the giant rose quartz crystal that we found was originally placed on top of Dun I, the highest point on the island. This was the origin of the practice of people gathering there for Religious Ceremonies until the fifteenth or sixteenth centuries.

(8) When Joan of Arc went out to fight the English army and save the French Crown, her personal bodyguard were Scots. Indeed, this *Garde Ecossaise* was, in due course, to become a famous fighting force within British ranks, and was known as *The Scots Guards.*

The flag which Joan of Arc carried had been given to her by a citizen of Glasgow, in Scotland.

Marie Stuart, Queen of Scots, had been brought up in France and, as was the custom she would marry the French Dauphin, the eldest French Prince.

(9) In October 1774, two years prior to American Independence, George Washington said,

> I am well satisfied that no such thing as independence is desired by any thinking man in North America; on the contrary, that it is the ardent wish of the warmest advocates of liberty, that peace and tranquillity on constitutional grounds should be restored and the horrors of civil discord be prevented.

(10) With the great Empires of the Ancient World the British Empire had little in common. The Empires of Egypt, Babylon, Assyria and Persia were Military Autocracies. They were founded by soldiers. They were sustained by the sword.

The rule of Rome was *despotic.* Rome had stood for world-unity, and that idea did not perish with the fall of the Western capital. The Human Race is *destined* to unite.

In connection with the British Empire, by the end of the reign of Queen Victoria, all the more important British colonies had attained the goal of responsible Government. As far as domestic affairs were concerned, they were *virtually* independent.

(11)  If the British Empire is to be compared with anything, then it should be compared with its *contemporaries*, not what exists *now*.

# 35: Life in Reverse

## I

The Human Race has emerged from a chaotic inflation which became a Cosmos. From amidst the animal kingdom, Humanity rose *above* those non-evolutionary circumstances such as we see in a jungle.

It is by means of these circumstances that an ecological stability is secured, by means of which animals are governed by an *Anti-pain Principle*. This means that they exist in a state of comparative slumber, or of *relative unconsciousness*. From this they are spurred into action either by danger signals or by the persistent craving for the satisfaction of basic physical needs.

Quite apart from the fact that we have possibly been *assisted* to rise above the level of animal behaviour, such an ascent involves a great deal of effort. If we are to rise to a level of Consciousness which is the stage *after this Human stage* in the evolution of Consciousness, then a certain amount of effort will be *necessary*, as birth-pangs.

This will involve *rising above* the level at which we presently exist. This is a level which is all too often content with soporific comfort; we can be lulled into not being bothered to think. This is a means of avoiding the full experience of psychic pain brought about by emotional distress.

The crucial thing for us is *understanding*, because if we do not understand then we can be tossed to and fro, this way and that, not knowing what to do or to believe. As such we are entrapped by our ignorance.

What we require to understand is that it is not actually a question of *belief* as such, for beliefs and teachings must never be viewed as an end in themselves. They should be seen as *stepping-stones* to True Knowledge or *Gnosis*.

This will involve the recognition that the evolution of Consciousness has reached the *Human* stage at this level of Consciousness within Absolute Consciousness. With the arrival of a Global Civilisation those powers presently latent within us will take a quantum leap *beyond* this present Human stage.

Ancient Wisdom informs us that it is by means of our corporeality, which is our *Humanity* that the soul, our Divine Essence which is a spark of *Celestial Fire*, is able to rise to greater levels of Consciousness. This is the reality of evolution, of *Homo erectus* evolving into *Homo sapiens sapiens* and so on. Sages of East and West taught that a *spirit-body* would develop. This was as fundamental to their teachings as were the doctrines of Pre-existence and Reincarnation. The Buddha radiated with an unearthly beauty, Krishna is physically beautiful to an *unlimited* degree and Hermes, too, is depicted as being exceptionally beautiful. There are parallels to this with the Biblical Moses.

Evolution takes place when that which is relatively unconscious is *further activated*. This process leads one to enter upon a *Suprapersonal* stage by means of *Rebirth*. Here we remember the exhortations of the New Testament that we be *born again*. This leads to a final integrated life which has been freed from opposites and from the *need* for Reproduction.

In practical terms, this will entail the end of the *robotic stage*, during which time we were heavily sedated, as the means of ensuring the continued survival of this aspect of the Universal Self. Now the Universal Self is preparing for the Human Race to emerge from our Human chrysalis as butterflies of Celestial Fire (1).

That which has reached *the Human stage* of evolution and which will soon take a Quantum Leap *beyond* the Human stage is a Psychic Principle which has been endowed with Its Humanity by Nature. This is to facilitate a specific interaction for the success of which the Human Race actually exists. As this is *Supra-Individual*, one has to be prepared to accept Destiny, as it does not stem from the conscious will. So-called individual lives are completely transcended by this.

In the Ancient World all Civilisations rested upon the assurance that there was an essential unity between Heaven and Earth, being to each other as microcosm and macrocosm. The link between them ensured that they were a part of each other. This was as true for the West as for the East.

In China, the great master Lu Yen, in *The Golden Elixir of Life*, informs us that Chinese philosophy, irrespective of tradition, is built upon the premise that, in the final analysis, the Cosmos and the Human Race obey the same law. The exact same principles apply to the one as to the other. They are as outer and inner worlds (2).

Chinese philosophers believed that by collecting the thoughts one can 'take flight and be born in Heaven', which is not the wide blue sky but 'the place where corporeality is begotten in the house of the Creative'. If spiritual development is maintained *another* body, a *spirit-body* appears, *quite naturally*. 'In the Beginning', in which everything is still One, which *appears* to us as the Highest Goal lies, in effect, 'at the bottom of the sea in the darkness of the Unconscious'.

To Confucianism, life is a Heaven-made law to which we must adapt. Taoists see it as a multi-coloured play of Nature which, although it cannot evade *The Laws of the Tao*, still happens to be pure coincidence. Chinese Buddhism sees it as the working out of *Karma* within an illusory world.

> Four words crystallise the Spirit
> In the Space of energy.
> In the sixth month white snow is suddenly seen to fly.
> At the third watch the Sun's disc
> Sends out blinding rays
> In the water blows the wind of the Gentle.

> Wandering in Heaven, one eats the
> Spirit energy of the Receptive.
> And the still deeper secret of the secret:
> The land that is nowhere,
> That is the true home. (3)

# II

Sages knew that there was a *pre-determined* aspect to the unfolding of the Human Race towards Its end and by means of which the Human Race becomes what It truly *is*, doing that for which It was created. Thereby the Human Race will be enabled to remember *why* It exists and why *living according to Its nature is all that is really required.*

A Collective Consciousness is awakening to Knowledge or Gnosis. Indeed the Human Race will recognise that this Awakening, this Quantum Leap in Consciousness, is Humanity's Truest Activity. This Knowledge is what really matters. This Gnosis cannot be found. It comes *to us* when we are able to receive it for it comes as *Recollection*.

That which is experimenting with *Form*, which has reached the Human stage in the evolution of Consciousness is actually endeavouring to create the circumstances for the Reproduction of our Ultimate Ancestor, the *Original Godhead*, as a Collective Consciousness; a change has to occur and Aristotle held that Change was possible by virtue of Matter, because *only that which is Material can change.* The Relation of Matter to Form is one of *potential* to act.

Matter manifests Possibility, which it expresses inasmuch as the Form is, robotically perhaps, endeavouring to realise that possibility. A child can become an adult because it is *Material*, a child being a *potential* adult. In all things two principles are present; these are a *Principle of Possibility* and an *Actualising Principle*.

Once again we are forced to realise that what we seek is that Reality which is *beyond* phenomena, which manifests Itself by means of phenomena. It has given life to phenomena for Its own good end.

It is as though this Principle is engaged in attempts to overcome individualisation or isolation, as though these were obstacles or opposites in a Process of *Becoming*. This culminates in the Self-Realisation *of* the Universal Oneness which means that the Godhead *has become* a Collective Consciousness.

According to certain teachers it is by means of a process of life after life that a certain level of Consciousness is reached. From this one it is possible to pass on to other levels in turn. This is made possible by means of sexual reproduction; 'we are deified by generation', says Hermes Trismegistus, *The Messenger of the gods*, no less (4).

At a more mundane level we can understand our lives as being historical and that, even with a noteworthy life, only a partial aspect of Truth can be seen or understood. If we were expecting to witness a display of the Omniscience or Omnipotence of God in these present surroundings then we are likely to be disappointed.

We need to come to terms with our finitude, but perhaps even more importantly, with the fact that we are inwardly divided and thus unable to *fully* appreciate anything which is purely spiritual in nature. We are able to congratulate ourselves that the Human Race has lordship over the beasts of the field but, on the other hand, it is humiliating to admit that we are *not* our own masters.

There is no such thing as push-button spirituality and, in truth, it will take a lot more than a simple decision to find ourselves in conformity with some well-intentioned, though possibly only presupposed, Cosmic purpose. We dare to assume that we are free to enter upon a pathway to Eternity, denying that within us an intense struggle is taking place. Whatever Destiny there may be for us, it is *not external*. It is *not* something, somewhere out there.

The life we live, which is governed by Nature, speaks to us neither of the love of God nor of the Omnipotence of God. It speaks to us of a level of experience which we will eventually leave behind us. We feel the urge to surrender, but this is not to the forces of Nature such as we see in our environment, but to an *Inner Reality* which presently manifests Itself *as a Human being*.

Nature can often terrify us because of its ambiguity and uncanniness. We resent being exposed to it, totally unprotected and, at a deeper level still, we realise that we are actually powerless in the face of it.

In time we will reach the stage where we realise, or remember, who and what we actually are. Knowledge will be ours. In the meanwhile, we have to contend with the Realisation that we are actually strangers to ourselves. Our Destiny is actually Self-Discovery with the corresponding Awakening of Innate Self-Knowledge.

Up until this point in time the Human Race has stood outside the realm where God can be seen or experienced *directly*. This demands the awakening of an Inner Reality. We must contend for a while longer with the burden of responsibility we are forced to carry and from which we seek to be relieved.

Hope is constantly rekindled, however, with the realisation of the possibility of this Awakening which will permit us to be *born again* and to become *new creatures*. It is then that we see that our fright, dread, loathing, solitude and anxiety are being experienced as passing away. Then we are refreshed by the expectation of the Dawn of Knowledge.

As such we see that we have no right to consider Nature and the historical development of our surroundings as the *revelation* of God, pure and simple. Our experiences may not fill us with confidence in God or in our fellow Humans. On the contrary, they force us to concede that restrictions and limitations have been placed on us. In time, though, from this chrysalis a butterfly will appear.

Our encounter with this world has disclosed to us that *we are not free* to serve either God or Mammon. We are *not* free to realise our inclinations. Something tends to get in the way. No matter, though, for the inclination lives on. We can shield it from others for a variety of reasons. In this we can be successful at times. Yet, in the final analysis we are the plaything of *Inclination*.

We see on the one hand that the barriers unnecessarily imposed between one Human and another, or between one community and another, cannot go unquestioned. Like all other things they are not there to be blindly accepted or uncritically adhered to. On the other hand, greatness and worth do exist and they should be recognised as such and revered accordingly.

# III

Life, in reverse, means that the end is the Beginning, or a New Beginning. That which we traditionally thought of as the beginning was really the beginning of a level of experience which would be transitory. Barbarism, the outcome of primitive conditions, with its prevailing ignorance, must therefore give way in time to the establishment of the Kingdom of God, which is Theocracy, with Justice as Its foundation.

The Kingdom of God will begin to arise within our communities when fellow Human beings, as a Collective Consciousness, begin to experience the happening of a growing sense of harmony. The Kingdom of God will be constituted by our activity *with* other Human beings because, when all is said and done, we are a Collective Consciousness and, as such, a part of each other.

Before the Kingdom of God can be established on Earth it has to be *germinated* within the minds of other Human beings. They will see it merely as the outcome of following *an Uncreated Vision* which will, by the grace of God, come to pass. They will not need to *make anything happen*. By collectively doing the will of God the whole of Creation can take a Quantum Leap.

Political stability, the end of injustice, and the satisfaction of the material needs of the Human Race are not an end in themselves. They will provide the infrastructure to enable the Human Race to contemplate upon that Ultimate Reality which is the *Awakening* of the Kingdom of God *within us*. That which presently rests at the Human stage of development will awaken to a higher state of Self-Realisation. The *Uncreated Vision* will guide us to this experience.

As this Great Transition grows closer and closer more and more will seek wisdom. They will turn from chaos and confusion and from those who are aggressive and self-seeking. They will contemplate upon a world which is harmonious for where Reason governs, nothing does or suffers wrong. Upon glimpsing it as the unfolding of *The Uncreated Vision* lives will be lived in the hope of realising it more and more fully. Every day people will fashion themselves into the demands made by its envisioned likeness.

*The True Religion*, which is the establishment of and the sustaining of the Kingdom of God, sparks off a whole host of perceptions which stem from the apprehension of the Divine in all things. This will make us all the more conscious of the Cosmos as a Divine Creation, but also of each other and how we are *inclined* to live.

It is precisely here that we come to consider *The Ancient Mysteries*. This Mythology is necessary in a positive way. It can free us from any preconceived notions. It throws us back upon ourselves, with all our experiences of life demanding an interpretation.

*The Ancient Mysteries* were never intended to be received *dogmatically*, but to throw light upon the appearance of life on Earth. They tell us of Hermes, the Son of God and *The Messenger of the gods*, who has invited the entire Human Race to walk in the light He provides, for *He* is that Light. He illumined the path our forefathers and mothers travelled and, unwittingly though it was, they set the stage for our *further evolution*, which is also the evolution of Consciousness.

The arrival of the Kingdom of God is a revolutionary situation. The establishment of Justice on Earth is neither a matter of abstract knowledge *nor* practical virtue. The Knowledge which leads to the understanding of *The Good* is not, as it were, a means to a practical end, as though such Knowledge were a criterion, a yardstick to assist in deciding what is either right or wrong, and for the shaping of circumstances.

This Knowledge is *Its own end* inasmuch as It provides the one who attains It with happiness and equips one completely for *citizenship*. The Kingdom of God is *not* an institution but exists among those who build and sustain It because, ultimately, the Kingdom of God exists *within their heads*. By means of the Kingdom of God, Humanity is able to live *according to Its nature*, which is *as a Collective Consciousness*.

Behind all our historical circumstances there is the desire to establish the Eternal and the Universal. Education will eradicate ignorance, in time, and that which is presently *dormant* within Human beings will become *dominant* in our communities.

At this time Humanity will realise the Eternal and Universal within Itself. From that time onwards all encounters will consciously be for the attainment of Perfection.

Until such time as life is no longer as we experience it now, which is *as the Human Race*, we should accept that we are *no independent phenomenon at all*, but part of the essential rhythm of the Universe; indeed we are nothing less than Its *Regulatory Principle*, now awakening.

Disentanglement from all that is transitory will have been our experience, springing from that Inner Awareness that we are *the means* whereby our Ultimate Ancestor, who is the Original Godhead, can consider Itself and interact with Itself, through the Godhead within us.

## NOTES

(1) According to authorities the new *spirit-body*, which is *the manifestation of a Psychic Principle*, is free to participate in an independent continuation of life. It has been freed from the energy system of the Human body which created it, leaving it behind in a way similar to a snake shedding skin.

(2) In the West, according to *Esoteric* Tradition, the Pyramids of Egypt were built to display the essential unity which links Heaven and Earth. They were built, once again according to Esoteric Tradition, in honour of *The Messenger of the gods,* Hermes Trismegistus, the Great Magician.

Initially, the Pyramids may have been of interest to Alchemists. Gods such as Prometheus, Thoth of the ibis beak, Idris, Mercury and so on, were all considered to be synonymous with Hermes, as *The Messenger of the gods* was known to the Greeks.

He was reputed to have been responsible for that first spark of Enlightenment which enabled Civilisation to take root on Earth. The Pyramids thus symbolised the *unity* of Heaven and Earth which Hermes, as the Representative of a Higher World, had undertaken to accomplish by *intervening* in Human affairs at crucial stages of development.

Great symbolism surrounds the Pyramids; those massive structures built in Antiquity and inalienably linked to the god who brought artificer's fire to Earth for our benefit. This involved a belief system which was kept out of reach, behind a veil of *secrecy*. The details were known only to *Initiates*.

This would explain the use of parables which would have had various depths of meaning. From Christian tradition, Jesus of Nazareth is depicted as saying that *the mustard seed* could be compared to the Kingdom of God, meaning that in some way the mustard seed had a mystical significance with the union of Heaven and Earth.

Those who were disciples of Pythagoras, in accordance with those traditions handed down from Antiquity, associated Fire, deemed to be *The First Element*, with the first figure of Solid Geometry, the *Tetrahedron*. In this formation the Element of Fire was believed to have its greatest significance.

Thus we see that, in a sense, the Pyramid and the Tetrahedron are basically synonymous, in spite of the fact that the Pyramid is not a regular Tetrahedron. They are related, however, with the Pyramid having four sides and a base.

The sacred structures of Antiquity were laid out in a special way. Their Measurements were related to *Gematria*, which is the Science of Numbers, because there had been a great Pythagorean influence upon The Ancient World, and philosophies were based on Measurements and Numbers.

Initiates would have learned that the Earth had been mapped out by a previous Civilisation, when the dimensions of the Earth were ascertained, depicting the place the planet Earth had in the Cosmic scheme of things. This was displayed in Architecture. Initiates learned that there was *a ratio* relating to both natural growth and celestial motion.

Traditional units of geodetic (land) measurement were to remain unaltered for many centuries. Inches, feet, yards and miles are all still familiar. They are also important fractions of the formal or ideal circumference of the Earth.

Egyptian, Greek and Roman geodetic measurements were based on the unit known as the *digit*, which was the equivalent of 0.729 inches, or one six-teenth of a Roman foot, or one hundred thousandth of a *nautical* mile.

The existence of such units and the fact that they are geodetic may be an indicator of the possibility of the Earth being mapped out by a *prehistoric* Civilisation such as Atlantis, which was mentioned by Plato.

The Pyramids were of importance to Alchemists, who deemed life to be the outcome of *the fusion of Mercury with Sulphur*. Mercury typified the Female or Dormant essence, which is activated by Sulphur, the Male or Activating Principle.

The outcome of the fusion of these two elements is *Magick*, the union of Heaven and Earth which, as can be seen from the Literature which emanated from Esoteric Schools, was symbolised by the *mustard seed* whose value in terms of Gematria, the science of numbers, is 1746.

The Pyramids had a connection with the element of Fire, the First Element, which Hermes as *The Messenger of the gods* had brought to Earth to assist the development of Human culture. Now the term *artificer's fire* has a numerical value of 2080, which is the equivalent of the numerical value of the Magic Square of Mercury. This is arrived at by adding together all the num-bers from 1 to 64 with 64 being 8 squared. Mercury had 8 as one of its spe-cial numbers.

Traditionally, the number of Mercury was taken to be the same as the number ascribed to the Holy Ghost which, in terms of Gematria, has a value of 1080.

Within the Pyramids it was believed that *the marriage of Heaven and Earth was consummated*. This would herald the appearance of God-like quali-ties within Humanity. When evaluated in terms of Gematria this is the equiv-alent of 1746, or 1080 plus 666. As it happens this is also the numerical value of the *mustard seed*.

(3)   *The Secret of the Golden Flower*. Published by Routledge & Kegan Paul. A Chinese Book of Life; Translated by Richard Wilhelm; Foreword and Psychological Commentary by Carl Jung. p. 53.

(4)   When considering this process, which is *experientially in reverse*, being often depicted as the negation of a negative, we should consider the salmon, a most potent symbol of Celtic spirituality.

This beginning to which we are *destined* to return is not an actual location, *per se*. It is a level of Consciousness which has been realised *through Experience* and which is, in effect, True Self-Expression for the One from whom everything emanates.

Here we are referring to a Person, the Ultimate Ancestor who has become the Supreme Personality of Godhead. Everything emanates from this Person who is the cause of everything.

This demands the *Perfection of Form*. Our Ultimate Ancestor seeks to discover a means of existence, a way of life which is conducive to the reproduction of the Original Godhead as a Collective Consciousness. This renders possible interaction with Itself, *as It and only It exists*, being the cause of everything. The Human Race exists for this purpose.

To the Celts, such as those Q Celts of Gaeldom, the salmon was referred to as *bradan*, which is pronounced as *bratan*. A corruption of this is *breadan*, which is pronounced as *bretan*, of which an Anglicisation is either *Briton* or *Britain*. This could suggest that there was from Antiquity among the peoples of the British Isles, a great reverence for the salmon and what the salmon *symbolised*.

The salmon is guided *internally*. It needs neither Politics, Philosophy nor Religion to find its way home. It would appear that Aristotle was correct when he asserted that some 'had read themselves into a state of ignorance'.

# 36: The Pre-Destined Kingdom

## I

When life began to make Its appearance on Earth it is probable that the chemical raw materials present were Water, Carbon Dioxide, Methane and Ammonia. When scientists attempted to imitate the chemical conditions of the Earth all those millions of years ago, Amino Acids were found to be in evidence. These are the *building blocks* of proteins, one of the two great classes of biological molecules.

Before these experiments were undertaken, naturally occurring Amino Acids were thought to be *diagnostic* of the existence of Life. Laboratory simulations have yielded Organic Substances called *purines* and *pyramidines;* these are the *building blocks* of the genetic molecule, *DNA*.

In the past a remarkable molecule was formed, some maintaining that this was *by accident*. This is the Replicator. As soon as It was born It spread Its copies throughout the seas. The process developed, with the result that smaller *building blocks* became more and more scarce, whereas larger molecules were formed all the more readily. This resulted in a population of Replicas which *were not identical* because, as it happens, this process is *not* perfect. Thus we have the profusion of life before us.

This is all in consequence of the emergence of the Original Godhead, our Ultimate Ancestor, who manifested Itself at the beginning of Time as the first atom of Pure Hydrogen. It is Hydrogen Fusion which is responsible for the birth of and the evolution of Consciousness.

The descendants of our Ultimate Ancestor are DNA molecules and, although it may appear strange, it is mistakes, so-called, in the process of copying which render evolution possible (1).

As miscopyings were propagated, the *primal soup* became filled with a population, *not* of identical Replicas, but by many varieties of replicating molecules, but *all* descended from our Ultimate Ancestor.

But where are they now? They are *in* you and me, for *they have created us to be their survival machines.* They have taken steps to ensure *their* survival, and the Ultimate Rationale of our existences is to ensure that *they* survive. These survival machines began as passive receptacles for genes, protecting them against the chemical warfare of their rivals, as well as the everyday life of molecular bombardment within the *primal soup*.

A major branch of survival machines, now referred to as *plants*, began to use sunlight directly in order to build up more complex molecules from more simple ones. Another branch of survival machines, now referred to as *animals*, discovered how to exploit the chemical labours of the plants, possibly by eating them. Others indulged in the practice of eating other animals.

These branches of survival machines developed more and more ingenious ways of increasing their efficiency in their means of survival. New *ways* of living appeared from there; sub-branches and sub-sub-branches developed. This has resulted in the situation such as we have at present, with life being witnessed in the sea, in the air, in the ground, underground, up trees and inside other bodies.

The so-called *Survival of the Fittest Theory* of Darwin is actually an aspect of a more general law which is known as *The Survival of the Stable*. The Universe is populated by stable objects. A stable object is a collection of atoms or molecules permanent enough or common enough to merit a name.

Darwin based his *Theory of Natural Selection*, the central component of his vision, on *two* observations. Firstly, plants and animals usually produce more offspring than their environment can sustain; secondly, these offspring differ slightly from each other, as they do from their parents (2).

All *ways* of living, including the Human Race, have evolved over a period of hundreds of millions of years by means of the process of *Natural Selection*. Within each species some individual members leave more offspring than others. This means that the inheritable traits, or genes, of the reproductively successful become more numerous in the next generation. This is *Natural Selection*.

All ways of living, trapped as they are in a robotic or hypnotically induced life, do what they do *out of necessity*. They exist within the context of an *all-embracing unity* of which they are unaware as they may have to fight and kill to survive. They are like cogs in a wheel. They will serve the purpose of the One and the All, *unwittingly* if need be.

As far as each so-called individual Human is concerned, each one will react instinctively to the appearance of the Christ, our Ultimate Ancestor who has had many guises. Yet each one who is *attracted* sees, hears, understands and loves this appearance in a slightly different way. Thereby they are empowered by *excitement* to follow *The Uncreated Vision*. This is how Human beings will be *guided* to a unity of purpose.

# II

The Universe *must* evolve and so must we as an integral part of it, the Knowledge of which has had considerable influence upon us. Evolutionary Theory was never intended to become a Religion, although some have sought to fashion it into a substitute for Popular Religion as it can be perceived as imparting a Knowledge somewhat removed from that of the Old Testament.

The Human Race, which is that which has *reached the Human stage* of evolution, shares a Common Origin with all other creatures. These other creatures have as much right to be here as the Human Race. Human beings are social mammals, endowed with an intelligence which effectively distinguishes us from all other *ways* of living.

Human beings require to live *meaningfully*. This is just as true for the individual Human, so-called, as for the Collective. As a Race, meaning that we are a Collective Consciousness, we must now take a step beyond the counter-productive stage of Tribalism.

The uniqueness of the Human Race consists quite fundamentally in an ability to accumulate knowledge and wealth, thus building upon the experience of former generations. This is impossible for other forms of life with whom we share a Common Heritage. They have been outstripped by Humanity because of the Human ability to use the tongue and the hands. Humanity possesses a consciousness of the past as well as an ability to anticipate the future.

*The Ancient Mysteries* proclaimed that something rather extraordinary had taken place for there had been a Divine intervention. This had enabled our Ancestors to rise above the level of animal or purely robotic behaviour, with the corresponding ability to employ the forces of Nature to our growing advantage (3).

The Old Stone Age, which is also known as *The Palaeolithic Period*, coincides with the geological period referred to as *Pleistocene* because, in geological terms it is the most recent (pleistos) chapter in the history of the development of the planet. *The Pleistocene Age* began about half a million years ago, witnessing four great advances of the Polar Ice Caps. During this time our Ancestors existed either in the open or in caves, where possible. For food they hunted game and gathered wild fruit and roots.

These cultures are essentially hand-axe cultures, with the remains produced for examination by Archaeologists being initially a display of ape-like creatures known as *Neanderthals*. The skeletons of Humans, as we employ the term, only begin to appear and become more numerous around the time of the Fourth Glacial Advance.

In connection with the earliest hominids, we cannot say whether they had any religious apprehension or not or whether they engaged in ritual practices. Archaeological evidence seems to suggest that *Neanderthals* practised interment of the dead. Graves discovered have shown flint implements placed near the hands. In Monte Circeo, in Italy, there is evidence of a *Cult of Skulls*.

Thus *prior* to the appearance of the Human Race as we understand the term, there is evidence of religious belief or apprehension. This may be related to the most spectacular find of all, the effigy of *The Dancing Sorcerer* in the cave of *Les Trois Frères* at Ariège. The Sorcerer, a dancing god and Lord of the Beasts, had a Human face, wolf ears, the claws of a lion, the tail of a horse and the antlers of a stag. In the late Palaeolithic Period when Humanity has certainly arrived, there is more extensive evidence of ritual practices.

Concerning Palaeolithic burial, there are certain main characteristics in evidence. At certain sites red ochre was sprinkled on the corpses, possibly to symbolise blood, hence life. Other graves contained necklaces and implements. There were also offerings for the deceased, indicating that there may have been the belief that, somehow or other, the deceased would live on. Some corpses had been bent into a huddled position prior to interment, which must have been done soon after death. It is possible that this may symbolise belief in Rebirth, either in another body here on Earth, or else in another world.

The story of the passage from Neolithic to History is not known in full detail but the likelihood is that it took place in the geographical area we now know as *Iraq*. This was the Civilisation of the Sumerians. Like all Civilisations it was the product of the mould into which the constituent parts were poured.

Archaeological evidence informs us that, at the outset of the period which merged into History, settlements had houses whose walls were constructed of adobe, with floors of clay and straw. Grain was stored in jars of unbaked clay sunk into the floor. There were large jars which seem to have contained the bones of deceased children, along with cups of *after-life* refreshment.

As settlements grew in size, cobbled streets start to appear and there is evidence of shrines and buildings for use by the entire community, possibly for worship. There is the appearance of seals denoting ownership and authority. Statues of a Mother Goddess are in evidence. She is depicted as squatting, with her arms encircling huge, heavy breasts.

# III

As we enquire into the Ancient Wisdom passed on from Initiate to Initiate down through the centuries, we discover what can only be described as an extraordinary account concerning the appearance of Civilisation on Earth.

It suggests that our Ancestors were far from being as primitive as we might have expected. It would appear from *The Ancient Mysteries* that our Ancestors possessed Knowledge involving Mathematics and Astronomy at a time when recently-held theories maintained that they could hardly fashion even the crudest of implements and nor had they invented the wheel.

Fundamental to *The Ancient Mysteries* was the belief that these beings had been able to transform our Ancestors into the Human Race as we know It now. This was by means of a process of insemination and mutation and this may have taken place around 250,000 years ago. There is *no* tangible proof in an archaeological sense that this is the case, although it does feature in legend. We can see this clearly in the Old Testament, in *The Book of Genesis* in particular. In Chapter 6, verses 1 to 4 we read,

When men began to multiply on the face of the ground, and daughters were born to them, the Sons of God saw that the daughters of men were fair; and they took to wife such of them as they chose. Then the Lord said,

'My spirit shall not abide in man for ever, for he is flesh, but his days shall be a hundred and twenty years.'

The Nephilim were on the Earth in those days, and also afterwards, when the Sons of God came into the daughters of men, and they bore children to them. They were the mighty men that were of old, the men of renown.

It is maintained that the Knowledge gained from these Extraterrestrials had moulded the religious and social customs in all parts of the planet. It is possible that such Knowledge emanated from one common point of origin, which could have been in the Atlantic, with Atlantis, or even earlier in the Pacific, with Lemuria.

Legends certainly abound concerning visitors from other worlds. There was Prometheus who, upon visiting Earth was smitten with compassion for our Ancestors as they were unable to cook food or build houses. According to legend, Prometheus went as far as to *sacrifice self-interest* for the benefit of our Race. For our advantage he *brought fire from Heaven*, which is to say he was the spark which produced the appearance of artificer's fire, so enabling Humanity to learn those skills which render life endurable.

The instruction received from Prometheus, depicted as the Representative of a Civilisation far in advance of anything we can yet appreciate, incorporated Architecture, Astronomy, the use of Letters, Medicine, Navigation, Metal Work and the Mystery of Prophecy.

Prometheus was also to be depicted as the embodiment of Human Knowledge striving with adamantine necessity. In time, those legends concerning Him, of which there were three major strands, were to provide the framework for Human Religion.

Hebrew prophecies, Greek philosophy, Christianity, Buddhism and Hinduism, *all* portray a Redeemer who, although Immortal and Divine, *voluntarily* undergoes a series of trials for the benefit of the Human Race. Most major Religions espouse belief in a *Person* who has come from another, higher world, as the Representative of that world which is benevolently disposed towards us.

There are also legends concerning Osiris, reputed to have been the first King of Egypt. From *The First Book of Diodorus*, and from the treatise entitled *On Isis and Osiris*, we read of how these Beings had redeemed the inhabitants of Egypt from barbarism by providing them with instruction in Agriculture and other Sciences.

In hieroglyphics Isis, who was to become the principal Egyptian goddess, is depicted as having a small fish-tail in her head-dress. Some suggest that this fish-tail could indicate *the salmon*, these Beings being, like the salmon, *destined to return*, as in their case to Earth until their task has been completed. Her true home was deemed to be on a planet which orbits *Sirius*.

The same notion applies to the legends from the Babylonians, who venerated a semi-daemon known as Oannes. He is also reputed to have established Civilisation on Earth although his actual home was on a planet which orbits Sirius.

From our standpoint, proto-History merges into History with the Neolithic Age in Iraq and those mysterious people known as the Sumerians. They have been generally attributed with the distinction of being the first to put a developed script to use (4).

The Sumerians were excellent astronomers and, according to *Esoteric* Tradition, they possessed Knowledge concerning the revolutionary periods of *all* the planets of the Solar system. This included both Uranus and Neptune, neither of which are visible from Earth except by means of a very powerful telescope. For ordinary *uninitiated* Humanity they are only *recent* discoveries. The Sumerians were responsible for dividing the day into the length of 86,400 seconds, which takes the form of 24 hours of 60 minutes with 60 seconds in each minute.

In The Ancient World it was commonplace for Knowledge to be transmitted *orally*, and only after a process of *Initiation*. This continued for many centuries because, when we come to the Christian Era, which is also *The Age of Pisces*, we find that Proclus, the last of the Classical Greek philosophers, may have possessed knowledge of the Solar system which was in contradiction to the officially-held theories of the day.

Proclus insisted that planets had moons and that planets were satellites of stars. He also insisted that there existed in space certain objects which were invisible to the naked eye but which were of considerable importance to us. There is every possibility that this could be an allusion to the planet which orbits Sirius for, as one *initiated into The Ancient Mysteries*, he would have been aware of the legends concerning the gods who came from there to instruct our

Ancestors in Astronomy and Mathematics, the basics of which have been preserved in The Orphic and Pythagorean Traditions.

Proclus was an Initiate into *The Ancient Mysteries of Egypt and Babylon*, concerning the actual details of which he would have been sworn to secrecy. His beliefs would have involved rites to do with the invocation of Hecate, the goddess who is a symbol for *Sirius*.

Pythagoras still exerts considerable influence over us, although somewhat less well-known than the Theorem concerning right-angled triangles are what are referred to as *The Orphic Mysteries* which, as well as other considerations, involve beliefs relating to Sirius.

Pythagoras instructed *orally* and *in secret*. This involved a *Doctrine of Numbers* and, ultimately, all things were Numbers. Knowledge of Reality was gained through an understanding of the significance of Numbers. This was fundamental to a process which was for the purpose of *Katharsis*, or Purification.

Those who possess even the most rudimentary knowledge of Chemistry can appreciate this to a certain extent. The Universe is evolving and is comprised of around 100 Elements. These Elements can be likened to a long alphabet which is used to construct words and sentences.

The Universe, or the Cosmos, is essentially a means of *natural data processing*, with Hydrogen as the most elementary letter of the alphabet. This process also has a preferred shorter alphabet of only four letters; these are known to us as Carbon, Hydrogen, Oxygen and Nitrogen.

# IV

We live in an evolving Universe with the process of evolution evidently having taken place in various stages. There was the formation of stars and planets with the subsequent appearance of intelligent life. This was all brought about by the creation of the very first atom of Hydrogen and then the process of Hydrogen fusion which has given us our environment as well as our bodies.

We tend to think of the objects around us as solid and tangible, or as *material*; although these are certainly *not* hallucinations they are real only in a *relative* sense. This certainly applies to our bodies, or our corporeality, the psycho-physical organism which constitutes the so-called individual. Our bodies should be viewed as the *coagulated*, as the *crystallised*, the *material* consciousness which is derived from the past. It is the *Active Principle of Consciousness* which, as *effect*, steps into visible appearance.

With the majority of Human beings, their consciousness has *not* progressed *beyond the past* from which their visible form has sprung. The body, therefore, belongs to the present and corresponds to an existing state of *Mind*.

If Science has anything to teach us here, then it is that *The Ultimate Unit of Reality* is what is known as *Planck's Constant*, a positive and negative electrical flow in a Universe which is formed of electricity. This may imply the necessity of a *closed* Universe, which may be easier to accept than any other hypothesis (5).

If the Myths from the Ancient World are to be understood properly, they may be informing us that these two opposites are not engaged in some kind of conflict, but that they actually *require each other to produce a higher level of union* which is, in fact, the good end of a process of *Reproduction*.

This Reproduction is the goal of the evolution of the Cosmos, which is endeavouring to discover the most perfect Form for Itself. This will be neither Positive nor Negative but the perfect balance of the two. Until such time as this is attained, that which is Immortal in and of Itself must continually reproduce Itself. It has to learn, or remember, the secret of rendering Reproduction unnecessary by attaining Realised Immortality.

This process, if *The Ancient Mysteries* are properly understood, demands a process of evolution by means of sexual reproduction, for it is a *biological* process. It also requires the *experience* of this process of evolution to be *witnessed* and undergone by such as the Human Race.

In this process, the Human Race is *the means* for this balance to be attained, indeed in the process of the evolution of the Universe the Human Race is the *Regulatory Principle*. Humanity exists to witness the Cosmic Drama and, in participating in it, actually channels the energies of the planets and of the heavens towards their end. This will be the union of all worlds and, thereby, the union of all Humanities, the scene set for the creation of Heaven.

# V

Legend informs us that from Immemorial Antiquity there have been attempts to establish a Kingdom of God on Earth, thus unifying the Human Race. Yet this Kingdom was never viewed as an end in Itself, but *as a landmark* on the pathway to the realisation of Human Destiny.

The legends continue: there is evidence to suggest that there was a Civilisation on Earth which was to collapse around 3000 BC. This is what is known as *UR III*. It was from this Civilisation that the impetus came to see the establishment of Civilisation in the Ancient Near East.

Recent research informs us that, in Egypt, the beginnings of Civilisation there date from 2900 BC, approximately (6). In Mesopotamia, with Sargon of Akkad in particular, we see the beginnings of Sumerian Civilisation around 2700 BC.

A great *Aryan* Civilisation had been displaced. The embers of that Civilisation would ignite the growth of Civilisation elsewhere. This Aryan Civilisation was ruled by a warrior and priestly caste who were themselves the custodians of *The Ancient Mysteries of Atlantis*, of which our present *Ancient Mystery Tradition* is but a facet.

Over many long and bloodthirsty centuries, *unwittingly though it may have been*, the task of the Human Race has been to resurrect the Atlantean Civilisation, only this time on a global scale. The seeds that Atlantis had been left to germinate and produce fruit, and this is why we see the development of Imperial Endeavour. It happened with the Sumerians and the Egyptians; it was to develop, and in due course there was the Empire of the Greeks and then the Empire of the Romans.

Yet these are only *stages in the reappearance of Atlantis*. Then, it is believed, the Human Race will be able to be assimilated into the Galactic Confederation; that is, Humanity will be reunited with those who were responsible for the appearance *not only* of the Atlantean Civilisation but of the Human Race as we know it now.

Here we ask a very important question: *how* will the Kingdom of God, which is the Atlantean Civilisation on a global scale, be resurrected? What are the steps to be taken as this Kingdom seeks to make its appearance?

It is here that we must now consider *The British Empire* which, to date, has been the largest Empire the world has ever seen and whose language, which is English, and whose Protestantism have spread all over the planet.

Nowhere in history's record of imperial endeavour is there any-thing to compare with the British Empire. It was unique. In size it was paramount, ruling the largest area and the most people. Its acquisition was the most haphazard, its holdings the most varied, its motives and benefits the most mixed. It rose, flour-ished and declined in less than four centuries, and its effects upon modern history are almost incalculable. (7)

Yes, it flourished and declined in less than four centuries but, as it hap-pens, 2003 was the four-hundredth anniversary of *The Union of the Crowns* when James VI, King of Scots, became James I, King of Great Britain and Ireland. There was *no* British Empire *until* the King of Scots ruled the British Union.

What will happen now? Will that Empire which was the most liberal of all the Empires be able to resurrect itself? Will we see a new and radical unity appearing from the great British Diaspora all over the planet? Could the English-speaking nations, such as the United Kingdom, Canada, the United States of America, Australia and New Zealand, with others, really come together for the sake of a Common Purpose?

Whatever happens, *if* it is to succeed, it has to be in accordance *with the will of God*. If the will of God is *not* adhered to then, whatever Humanity seeks to achieve will come to nothing and time and energy will have been wasted. This is not to say that doing the will of God is easy. Here we need to remind ourselves of what Niccolo Machiavelli had to say in *The Prince*.

There is nothing more difficult to carry out, nor more doubt-ful of success, nor more dangerous to handle, than to initiate a New Order of things. For the reformer has enemies in all who profit by the Old Order, and only luke-warm defenders in all those who would profit by the New Order. This luke-warmness arises partly from fear of their adversaries, who have the Law in their favour; and partly from the incredulity of Mankind, who do not truly believe in anything new until they have had actual experience of it.

Indeed, however far Science pushes its discovery of the Essential Fire, or how capable it may one day become of reshaping and perfecting the Human Element, it will still find itself confronting the *same* problem: how to give final value to all and to each of the Elements in grouping them *within the unity of* the organised whole.

Should we look to Plato we would see that he understood things as being about *the city*, the *entire* city itself and how *the city* may orient itself towards itself and *other cities*.

All our great Religions inform us that we are able to call upon God, who is our Ultimate Ancestor, for the sake of whom everything exists, in order that we may *do* the will of God.

The Power who guides us has a task to fulfil, and for this to be rendered possible, the Human Race exists. The New Testament implores us to always remember that it is not the will of the Human Race which matters. *It is the will of God which matters.* Whatever will the True Pilgrim has, the true pilgrim is exhorted to surrender that will to the will of God so that progress may be experienced. This is why it is our Christian duty that *we offer ourselves as living sacrifices to God*, thereafter, in due course, spiritual progress is made until such time as it is *no longer I* who live but *Christ* who dwells within.

There is more to it than this; we see that we have been created by God for the purposes of God and that everything is predestined or predetermined.

For by grace are ye saved
Through faith
And not of works
Lest any man should boast.
For we are God's workmanship
Created unto good works
*Which God has afore ordained*
That we should walk in. (8)

So how will the Kingdom of God be established on Earth?

# VI

When at the crossroads of Human Destiny, when the British stand leaderless, *Arthur will appear*. This will be a clarion call to the great British Diaspora in general, and to the Scots in particular for in the future Kingdom, *the Scots will be the Royal Nation*.

Eventually all the nations of the Earth will attach themselves to the Commonwealth. Indeed, in this process one of the great landmarks of all will be the *restoration of the United States of America to the British Union*.

Here we bear in mind that *karmically*, the United States of America is *British*; the United States of America began life as thirteen British colonies, built on the English language and on Protestantism, and whose greatest and most successful citizens have been the Scots (9).

*If* it is the will of God that a Kingdom should be established on Earth then it *will* happen. It will happen because God *wants* it to happen. People will start to dream of it; people will be brought together to begin to establish it. In *the Bhagavad-Gita*, Lord Krishna says,

In reality, action is entirely the outcome of all the modes of Nature's attributes; moreover, only he whose intellect is deluded by egotism is so ignorant that he presumes, 'I am doing this.'

The relationship between the United States of America and the United Kingdom is very special indeed. There has always been a great deal of misunderstanding when considering this special relationship and *how* the American Revolution blew apart what is referred to as The *First* British Empire (10). At any rate, people could be easily forgiven for thinking that from the time of the American Revolution onwards, the British Empire and the United States of America were bitter enemies, although this is hardly the case.

Much has been said of the curious relationship between the British Empire, which became the Commonwealth and the United States of America.

In 1765, John Dickinson said,

Many states and kingdoms have lost their dominions by severity and an unjust jealousy. I remember none that have been lost by kindness and a generous confidence. Evils are frequently precipitated by imprudent attempts to prevent them. In short, we can never be made an independent people, except it be by Great Britain herself; and the only way for her to do it is to make us frugal, ingenious, united and discontented.

In 1815 John Adams said,

What do we mean by the Revolution? The war? That was no part of the Revolution; it was only an effect and consequence of it. The Revolution was *in the minds of the people*, and this was affected from 1760 to 1775, in the course of fifteen years before a drop of blood was shed at Lexington.

After 1759, when the war with the French Empire was won, it appears that the Americans felt that they were ready to become independent. The English-speaking Protestant people had been victorious and *The Declaration of Independence* in 1776 was correct to say that 'Governments derive their just powers from the consent of the people'.

But how was the special relationship between the United States of America and the British Empire conducted? It would appear that, when all was said and done they remained *allies*, and correctly so.

Geography, historical circumstance and political tradition intersect to condition all nations, and the United States in the nineteenth century was no exception. The world was so large, the oceans so wide and their own continent so vast and empty it was impossible for the Americans to be much concerned with foreign affairs.

Furthermore, it was a settled assumption of British foreign policy, from *The Treaty of Ghent* (1814) onwards, that a war with the United States was always likely to be more trouble than it was worth; and while America was at peace with the British Empire (its greatest neighbour) it was buffered against interference from other quarters. The English and the Americans might have their tiffs, for there was always plenty to dispute about; but they were *at one* in the view classically expressed in *The Monroe Doctrine*, that the New World was to be preserved against the ambitions of the other great powers. The profits of trade and industrialisation from Canada to the Falkland Islands were to be reserved to the English-speaking world; and although the competition between its two principal components, as they built up their ascendancy in the Caribbean and further south, was intense, it never led them to break with each other and so let in the rival pretensions of the Spanish, the French or the Germans. There was, in fact, *a partnership* between England and the United States; but it was so informal, and punctuated by so many rows, that most Americans never detected it. Their notion of Anglo-American relations remained that which had emerged from the Revolution, been strengthened by the war of 1812 and been strengthened again by the Civil War; John Bull was an obsolete bully, but Uncle Sam could handle him. (11)

The Revolution came and went. Peace was restored. Indeed, by 1789, the year that the French Revolution broke out, approximately one-third of the value of all British commercial transactions was with the United States.

Meanwhile, the United Provinces (Holland), though still a substantial trading power, was falling behind in the race with the more powerful British and French. By 1739, in fact, it was rumoured that twice as many ships unloaded their cargoes in London as in Amsterdam. The Dutch, however, still held their own over the British and French in banking and international financial operations. In 1777, the Dutch owned 40 percent of the British national debt.

The Bill on Amsterdam was to the eighteenth century what the Bill on London was to become in the nineteenth century. (12)

British supremacy was to continue, with the British being the most powerful of the nineteenth-century powers. The United States of America, being English-speaking and predominantly Protestant like its British relatives, was to dominate the twentieth century. Now the entire planet is at the crossroads, requiring a new direction now that a New Millennium has dawned. Furthermore, 2003 saw the four-hundredth anniversary of the Union of the Crowns, which gave rise to the British Empire, which produced Canada, the United States of America, South Africa, Australia and New Zealand, among others!

The British Empire and the United States of America have both dominated the world. Both have made some terrible mistakes, but *both did a lot of positive things as well* and we should not forget that. In the nineteenth century the British had to fight the entire world, and won. The British Empire took on the other Empires and won the day. Not only did the British Empire survive to become the Commonwealth but *their survival ensured the survival of the fledgling United States of America.*

We should never lose sight of the fact that when the United States was developing and growing territorially they sought to quickly establish frontiers with Mexico, then the west coast. The last states to join the American Union were those which bordered Canada, which was part of the British Empire.

In 1842 the United States of America laid claim to the whole of that portion of the Pacific Coast which lay between California, which was Mexican until 1849, and Alaska, which was Russian until 1867. This was known as *The Oregon Question*. Had the American claim been conceded, Canada would have been cut off from the Pacific Ocean and there would have been no British Columbia. At first the Americans refused arbitration but later accepted it. In 1846 the boundary between the United States and Canada was fixed at the 49th parallel. The British also received Vancouver Island.

Always behind the scenes there was intrigue with other powers, especially the Catholic powers seeking to undermine the British Empire as well as the United States of America. The British Empire was born of conflict with Catholic Spain; thereafter Catholic France was the greatest enemy of the British Empire. However, the British were to survive and build up their supremacy as they were able to secure help from other quarters (13).

It is claimed that there is a secret history of Catholic attempts to undermine the United States of America. President Lincoln, speaking of the American Civil War, is reputed to have said,

This war would never have been possible without the sinister influence of the Jesuits. We owe it to Popery that we now see our land reddened with the blood of her noblest sons. Though there were great differences of opinion between the South and the North on the question of slavery, neither Jeff Davis nor any of the leading men of the Confederacy would have dared attack the North, had they not relied on the promises of the Jesuits that, under the mask of democracy, the money and arms of the Roman Catholics, even the arms of France, were at their disposal if they would attack us. (14)

**It may be true that the good end of the entire imperial endeavour over the millennia since the appearance of the Human Race will be the restoration of the United States of America to the Commonwealth. This could very easily take place early on in the New Millennium. *If* it is the will of God then it *will* happen.**

In addition to this, those rulers of *UR III* who were backed by priests and priestesses initiated into *The Mysteries of Atlantis*, who migrated when *UR III* came to an end around 3000 BC, did not die out. They were to be the progenitors of the Pharaohs of Egypt. Lord Krishna would have been one of them. They would have arrived in the British Isles in considerable numbers by around 1500 BC. They would have moved to what would eventually be known as Scotland early in the Christian Era.

It was *for them* that the British Union, then the British Empire, then the United States of America, have all existed and been exalted by God. It is because *of them* that the Scots will be the Royal Nation in the Kingdom yet to emerge. Indeed, when the time is right *God will give the Kingdom* to the one prepared by God to rule over the Earth. He will be the King of Scots but he will also be the King of Kings and the Lord of Lords and His Kingdom shall *never* end as long as there is a planet Earth.

## NOTES

(1) The DNA molecule is a long chain of building blocks, of small molecules called *nucleotides*. Just as protein molecules are chains of amino acids, so DNA molecules are chains of nucleotides.

(2) Darwin borrowed this idea from Thomas Malthus, a British economist.

(3) From around 17 million years ago, the process of the evolution of Consciousness undergone by our Race is supplied here. The information here is from an article entitled 'The Bones of Our Ancestors', from *Science* 1984, April edition. The aim here is not scientific as such, but simply to indicate roughly *how* Consciousness has evolved to the *Human* stage.

## Straipithecus

Existed from about 17 million years ago until possibly 8 million years ago. Hominid lineage may be traced back to *Siraptibecus*, or to its close relative *Ramapithecus*. In appearance it was like an Orang Utan. It could be the common ancestor of all apes and hominids.

## Australopithecus afarensis

Existed between 3 and 4 million years ago. This is the first generally accepted hominid. Here Human and ape lineage diverge. A specimen was found which lived in Tanzania about 3.6 million years ago. The head is ape-like but the body is more Human. *Afarensis* walked on two legs but without a fully strident gait.

## Australopithecus africanus

Lived between 2 and 3 million years ago. At one point this was hailed as *the missing link*. It has a blend of traits which link apes with Humans.

## Australopithecus robustus

Approximately 2.2 million years ago the process of evolution diverged and produced two species. There was *africanus*, who was to be the ancestor of Humans; then there was *robustus*, who thrived for a million years before extinction. In appearance it was like a gorilla.

## Homo habilis

*Habilis* is the first to have the term *Homo* conferred upon it. In this sense this is the first *Human*. It marks a trend towards bigger brains. Skeletal remains show that the differences between *habilis* and *africanus* are not great. *Habilis* lived on Earth from 2.2 million years ago until around 1.5 million years ago.

## Homo erectus

The first *Human* to migrate out of Africa. This is the earliest known hominid to have been able to control fire. Its period of operations probably lasted until about half a million years ago.

## Homo sapiens (early)

The transition from *erectus* to *sapiens* was gradual indeed. *Sapiens* may have appeared as long ago as 400,000 years, although scientific work on placentas and by geneticists would tend to suggest that every Human being has a common ancestor who lived in Africa 250,000 years ago, approximately.

*Homo sapiens neanderthalensis*

It is believed that they first made their appearance around 130,000 years ago. They were *not intellectually dull* as was previously supposed of them and they seem to have had a spiritual sense. They are the oldest known hominids to have practised interment of the dead. Ritual objects are known to have been buried with the deceased.

In comparison to us they are believed to have been much more robust. Some believe that they were to become extinct for some reason, the possibility being that they were wiped out by our Race to avoid competition for food. Others disagree with this.

The consensus is that *they did not evolve into Humanity as we employ the term*. There are others who say that early Human beings are like modern Humans, that is, they come in different shapes and sizes.

*Homo sapiens sapiens*

This is the most recent development of our Race as this is *ourselves*. The process of evolution is *not yet over* and it will be interesting, to say the very least, to see what develops from here.

(4)   We tend to think of Civilisation as beginning to appear in Ancient Egypt around 2900 BC, or in Mesopotamia with the Empire of Sargon of Akkad around 2700 BC.

While most of us are aware of the legends concerning the Civilisation of Atlantis, believed to have been in the Atlantic Ocean, and even earlier in the history of our planet with Lemuria in the Pacific Ocean, very few have heard of what Archaeologists tend to refer to as *UR III*.

This was an *Aryan* Civilisation, whose origins are unknown to us but which collapsed around 3000 BC. This was still in the *proto-literate* period. Thereafter in what is the Ancient Near East we see Civilisation being ignited by the smouldering embers of *UR III*.

(5)   In the past, however, the acceptance of the possibility of a *closed* Universe was hindered by a problem brought about by the fact that without at least 100 times as much mass as was then detectable, the Universe could not be *closed*. Within the Scientific Community this was referred to as *The Mystery of the Missing Mass*.

There are many types of sub-atomic particle, but most of them do not exist in sufficient quantity in Nature. For this reason, there are no more than six forms of sub-atomic particle which, effectively, constitute the mass of the Universe. These sub-atomic particles are Protons, Neutrons, Electrons, Photons, Gravitons and Neutrinos.

The answer to this *Mystery of the Missing Mass* may be found, apparently, with the Neutrinos which seem to pass through the Universe as though there were nothing there. To them the planet Earth is like an empty space.

At one stage in 1980, experiments in the USA and in the then Union of Soviet Socialist Republics were construed as demonstrating that Neutrinos have a *rest mass* of perhaps 0.0001 of that of an Electron and 0.000000055 of that of a Proton. This means that 99.3 percent of the Universe consists of Neutrinos.

Protons and Neutrons make up the mass of the rest of the Universe, such as Stars and Planets, which constitute 0.7 percent of the mass of the Universe.

With the inclusion of the Neutrinos into the equation we have approximately 165 times as much mass in the Universe as had been previously realised. This, therefore, is sufficient to *close* the Universe.

If Space-Time is finite but *without boundary* then there are implications here. We could describe the Universe by using a mathematical model determined by *The Laws of Science*, and them alone. No supplement for boundary conditions would be required.

The Form of those *Laws* is not yet known precisely, however. As yet, we have only partial *Laws* which govern the behaviour of the Universe under all but the most extreme conditions. These *Laws* are all part of an as-yet undiscovered Unified Theory.

Progress continues to be made but, in the meanwhile, the Scientific Community considers it to be too speculative to make any predictions about the Universe.

There are two reasons for this. There is *The Uncertainty Principle* which states that certain quantities cannot be exactly produced, but only their *probability distribution*. Then there is the complexity of the equations, which makes it fundamentally impossible to solve anything other than the simplest problems.

(6)  David M. Rohl, *A Test of Time. The Bible – From Myth to History*. On which the television series *Pharaohs and Kings* was based. Published in 1995 by Book Club Associates by arrangement with Century Publishing

Ltd, London. See p. 24. David M. Rohl mentions the overall view of the Conventional Egyptian Chronology. He states that the Late Pre-Dynastic Period merges into the Early Dynastic Period around 2920 BC.

(7)  *The Horizon History of the British Empire*. The American Heritage Publishing Co. Inc. A subsidiary of McGraw-Hill, Inc. Published in 1973. From the Introduction.

(8)  *The Epistle of Paul to the Ephesians*, Chapter 2: 9f.

(9)  In 1976, on the bicentenary of the United States of America, a survey was completed of 200 ethnic minorities within the United States to see who had been the most successful. The answer provided by the survey was unambiguous: *the most successful minority was the Scots.*

These days many Americans are asking themselves a very important question: *what is the United States of America really about?* The answer to this question is, yet again, unambiguous: it is not a question of *why* does the United States exist! Since the United States of America is *karmically British*, the question we should be asking is: *why did the British Empire exist?* The answer to this question is, quite simply, that *the British Empire existed for the Scots to be spread throughout the world*.

The Ancient Scots would have had as the inner circle of their ruling classes a Priesthood who were *Initiates* into *The Mysteries of Atlantis*, and who would have existed in *UR III* in pre-History. They had given their name to Scotland and their genes have been passed on into the gene pool of the Scots in the modern sense. It is for this reason that the Scots are to be the Royal Nation in the approaching Kingdom of God.

(10)  The First British Empire is the term used to describe the British Empire up until the disruption caused by *the American Revolution*. The Second British Empire started after the American Revolution and coincided with the Napoleonic Wars. It lasted until what was referred to as the New Imperialism with the British controlling large swathes of Africa. This was superseded by the Commonwealth.

(11)  Hugh Brogan, *Longman History of the United States of America*. Guild Publishing, London. 1987 reprint. p. 448 f.

(12) George Rude, *Revolutionary Europe 1783 to 1815*. Fontana History of Europe. Published by Fontana Press in 1964. p. 10.

(13) This again is part of what could be described as *a secret history* of the British Empire. Evidence for what I am going to say here is anecdotal.

With the defeat of the Spanish Armada the English started to plan the British Empire. At this time the Scots were the allies of France, a state of affairs which lasted from 1295 until 1595. The Scots referred to this as *The Auld Alliance* whereas even to this day the English are often referred to as *The Auld Enemy*. With the Reformation both Scots and English went over to Protestantism and it was only a matter of time before there was a Union of the Crowns, which took place in 1603. *There was no British Empire until the King of Scots became King of Great Britain and Ireland.*

Because the British had been excommunicated, as it were, from the Catholic world, they were unable to secure loans to do what they sought to do. They wanted to establish colonies for the purpose of trade. Here also we should bear in mind that the British were rather late in building an Empire; the Spanish and the Portuguese had been establishing colonies for over a century.

How would the British finance their operations, since they were unable to obtain loans from the Catholic world which saw the British Protestants as mortal enemies? There is a secret history that they were able to receive help from the Jews. At this time there was no love lost between the Jews and the Vatican.

Later on it was obvious that the British Empire was going to be very successful, for it was to become the largest of the European Empires. The British Empire was built on the supremacy of the Royal Navy; this meant that the British Isles and the colonies were able to become very successful.

At the beginnings of the British Empire, James VI, King of Scots, was on the throne. His mother, Marie Stuart, Queen of Scots, had been a Catholic and had allies in France and Spain. In due course, for whatever reason, the Stuarts were forced from the throne and it was given to a Dutch King, William III, Prince of Orange.

The Stuarts tried to regain the throne and enlisted the help of the Catholic powers, but to no avail. Perhaps it was part of the arrangement for the British Empire to receive loans that the Stuarts be replaced by a Dutch Protestant, especially when we bear in mind that Holland, being tolerant for the time, was the headquarters of European Jewry. Indeed it was the Dutch who, more than anyone else in the eighteenth century in particular, owned the British National Debt.

The British, in becoming Protestant, had incurred the wrath of the Catholic world, who would have liked nothing better than to see English-speaking Protestantism brought to its knees. Thus we see that the British Empire was involved in a battle which involved Religions, with Religions providing support for different Empires in the hope that, thereby, they would gain greater influence across the globe.

Should it be the case that the Jews did help the British to build their Empire against incredible odds then Jews and the British are *linked karmically* in a positive manner. Even in the seventeenth and eighteenth centuries, before the British were able to become the most powerful Empire, it is remarkable to see that building an Empire, even then, was impossible without loans to build navies and equip armies to fight, should the occasion arise.

(14)  Charles Chiniguy, *Fifty Years in the Church of Rome*. Chick Publications, Chino, California, USA. Published in 1985.

# 37: The Necessity of Monarchy

## I

In the chapters of *The Sacred Ibis Speaks* prior to this one, consideration has been given to the *Form* which Human communities should take. This is no easy task because all communities, indeed all nations, are comprised of various *strands* and, inevitably, there is competition between groups and between individuals within groups, and all for the sake of gaining power and status.

In mid-October 1999, while walking to work, I met a young man with whom I had been on a Training Scheme around 1991 to 1992. He was a keen Socialist Republican, something to which I can relate quite easily as I was once a Socialist Republican myself, a member of the Young Communist League and later on, for a brief period, the Communist Party of Great Britain. During our conversation we arrived, in due course, at what we both recognised as the very real crux of the matter: which is more important, *Order* or *Rights*?

There has always been a struggle for power between tribes, nations, empires, and all this brought about because Human beings are very competitive. So what is the *best* way for a nation, for example, to orient itself towards other nations? Once again we ask the question: which is more important, *Order* or *Rights*?

The answer is Order. *Without Order there are no rights*! Without Order there is *no* recourse to the Law. Without Order it is every man for himself, every tribe for itself and every nation for itself. Without Order, tribes and even nations will tear themselves apart and maybe even go out of existence altogether.

If we consult the Bible we see that in Ancient Israel, which was ruled Theocratically by the Priesthood, real power within the nation resided in the Temple with the Priesthood. From the earliest of times it was known that the religious life of Israel would be regulated by the Levites. The reason for this was that when we are dealing with the *unity* of the nation then, if power was to be *given consensually* to a particular family or caste, it would *end competition* for the power which resided, by agreement, with the Levites. The other tribes would be expected to engage themselves in other matters for the upkeep of the nation. *Internal competition was restricted by consent for the sake of Order.*

Here we have the beginnings of an understanding of *why* there can never be any real alternative to Monarchy, although it has to be understood that, historically, not all Monarchies were alike. This is clearly seen when we consider the British Monarchy and then compare it to the Absolute Monarchy of France.

Let us look at the British Monarchy, which has come in for all sorts of criticism for various reasons. Some say that it is an undemocratic anachronism, and not only this but there are better and more gifted people who would be better suited to the position.

> A hereditary Monarchy is *not* democratic or classless. It is not a job that is open to everyone or awarded to the best qualified. If those are the ultimate tests of the value of an institution then Monarchy fails abysmally. *But there are other standards* and to understand the role of the hereditary principle in the British Monarchy it is important to examine them even if you do not accept them or consider them as valuable as the more democratic virtues.

> If an office is not hereditary, it must be open to election in some form. A successor has to be appointed or chosen. This can leave a vacuum at the top when the old leader dies, and can provoke damaging competition.

'In an elective Monarchy', wrote the historian Edward Gibbon, in *The Decline and Fall of the Roman Empire*, 'the vacancy of the throne is a moment big with danger and mischief'. Gibbon was writing just before 1789, but the French experience of replacing a hereditary form of Government with an elective one by revolution did not contradict his pronouncement. And even in a stable modern Republic like the United States of America, the last year or two of a President's second term, the 'lame-duck' period, are well recognised as a time of creeping Governmental paralysis. A hereditary system avoids all these problems. (1)

Maintaining Order need not be easy but there is nothing more important. Behind the everyday calm of the modern Nation-State there are those who are hungry for power, prestige and status. Some people are so determined to improve their status that they do not consider the likely cost to themselves, to the honour of their nation or to the planet.

During the 1980s, Lord Stockton, formerly Sir Harold MacMillan, one-time Prime Minister of the United Kingdom, appeared on a programme for BBC 2 Scotland entitled *Open to Question*. During the programme, Lord Stockton answered questions from a number of schoolboys and schoolgirls. One young Scottish schoolgirl asked Lord Stockton a rather important question: *who was the nicest person you met in politics?*

Lord Stockton remained silent for a moment. Then he replied, maintaining that 'there are *no* nice people in politics'. He described politics *as a jungle* and said that, in a jungle, *only wild animals can survive.*

Later on, as a member of *The Scottish Green Party* and as a member of Its National Council, the author (John Houston) came to a similar conclusion. At this time in the United Kingdom the majority of people in politics are there on an ego-trip. Their main concern is their own self-advancement. As far as the majority of people in politics in the United Kingdom are concerned, they believe *solely in being elected.* They are not really there to defend principles, but for power.

Before we can take steps towards considering how best to re-structure Human communities, we have to recognise that there is an incessant and unquenchable thirst for power within members of the Human Race. Any attempts to redistribute wealth and power must take this into consideration.

There is a fashionable view that status-seeking and status displays are in some way undesirable or unworthy, but the truth is that status is *universal* to our species and to every species of social animal. You can choose what sort of system you will have, but you cannot choose *not* to have one.

The comrades who founded The Soviet Union swept away all the ranks and privileges of the Tsars, but a new system grew up which was every bit as subtle and pervasive as the one it replaced. The privileges of the *Nomenklatura*, the inner group of The Communist Party, were as significant as those of The Court of the Romanovs.

Canada decided to abandon the British Honours system as an undemocratic anachronism, but soon realised the need to replace it and invented *The Order of Canada* complete with companions, officers and members.

Badges of status are visible all over the world and in every walk of life; very obviously in the Armed Forces, for example, but no less clearly, if you know where to look, in the modern corporation. Managers do not wear pips or stripes or medals, but their status is affirmed in a dozen different ways; the car they drive or in which they are driven, the place where they park it; the size of their office, the floor level it is on, the quality of furnishing, whether they share it with another manager or their secretary, or have no secretary, or three in an office outside; where they eat and wash, whether they have flowers in the office and a drinks cabinet, a butler, porcelain tea service or vending machine in the corridor, and a hundred other subtle distinctions and gradations.

Status is one of the ways a species keeps order. If everyone knows their place, internal squabbles are avoided. Often the order has to be established by squabbles but, once it is fixed, peace can reign and discipline can be maintained. It is no coincidence that the word *order* has three meanings; first, a command; second, a pecking order; and third, the opposite of chaos. Nor is it a coincidence that the different kinds of honour are called *orders*. (2)

# II

Within Human communities there is a very real and unavoidable stratification. In the early 1940s, beginning in the United States of America, there was the advent of a period of abundance which by the 1960s had reached considerable proportions. Prior to this period it was widely assumed that prosperity could eliminate, or at least greatly reduce, *class differences*. If everyone could enjoy the good things in life, as defined by the Mass Merchandisers, class distinctions would eventually disappear.

P. D. Ouspensky recognised that there were divisions within Human communities and that these divisions were *quite natural*. This is why Ouspensky, in *The New Model of the Universe*, states that there is nothing more absurd and ridiculous than the concept of *the evolution of the masses*.

For Ouspensky this would be like expecting a tree to transform all its molecules of wood-fibre, leaves and flowers into fruit. Yet this is not the case. *Only a tiny fraction* of the molecules which constitute a tree *become fruit*.

Not only are people divided into certain groups but those of a certain type seem to prefer those who are most like themselves.

> Racial segregation is much more sweeping in new development-type towns than in established, old-fashioned-type communities. *The Commission on Race and Housing* charges that the mass builders have done much to intensify racial segregation in America.

> The result of this clustering by kind is the creation of many hundreds of one-class communities unparalleled in American history. Each mass-produced community has its own shopping centre and community centre. There is no need to rub elbows with fellow Americans of a different class.

> There is, however, another factor behind the growth of one-layer towns, which at least abets the developer's vested interest in homogeneity. This is our own habit of seeking out our own kind … people prefer to live near others as much like themselves as possible … They do not seem interested in the possibility of new stimulating associations with people different from themselves. (3)

In 1976, which was the year prior to which I went to Glasgow University, I was working as a window cleaner. One day while washing the windows in a hotel at Glasgow Airport I was listening to the radio and to a very interesting programme which featured Mohammed Ali, who was visiting the United Kingdom for one reason or another.

Like many of the other boys in my class at Netherton Primary School in Glasgow, Scotland's largest city, Muhammad Ali, or Cassius Clay as he was known when the public at large first became acquainted with him, had been one of my boyhood heroes. There had been great interest in the fight he had with Sonny Liston. Cassius Clay had been the underdog. When I was getting up to go to school the first thing my mother said to me that day was 'Guess who won?' I was so pleased, as were many others.

Muhammad Ali talked about his youth in Louisville, Kentucky. In due course the conversation arrived at the topic of *segregation*. As I listened I was impressed by the honesty of Muhammad Ali. I could tell that he was not in the business of trying to impress the listeners.

What he stated was that segregation had never been a problem to him because *he had always been in favour of it*. He added that he felt that sincere do-gooders could create a lot of problems by *forcing* people to mix. Muhammad Ali said that if people wanted to mix then they will mix. If they don't want to mix then *they should not be forced*. He stated that, in his experience, people prefer their own kind.

There is a lesson here for Government of today. They are elected to represent *others*. Surely it is time for Government to ask us what we, the people, want. Here we think of Aristotle in *The Politics*.

> Therefore, one mode of good Government is taken as being to obey the Laws *as laid down*, but an *alternative* is to lay down well those Laws that the people abide by …

# III

Already we have asked the question: which is more important, *Order* or *Rights*? Yet, when we recognise that Order is *more* important than Rights, that is not to say that Rights are of no consequence for if a nation is *not* just then it cannot be *efficient*. If a general state of inefficiency is permitted to continue then that nation may end up at the mercy of other nations.

Otherwise there could be a revolution. A ruling class might find that their power and authority has been undermined by a band of subversives bent on gaining power by manipulating the situation by calling for people's *Rights* either to be defended or increased.

Revolutions have taken place in Europe in the twentieth century. Why did they take place?

> A traditional list of causes for all this trouble would not be hard to compile. Peasants, handicraft workers and factory hands were everywhere living in appalling poverty and neglect. Better-off classes were in all countries excluded from Government, for in the Autocracies of Eastern Europe it was only a small section of the Aristocracy which had any influence and, in the more liberal States of Western Europe; only an upper crust of the bourgeoisie had any real power. (4)

> Yet, there were some Statesmen, notably Guizot and Metternich, who persisted in believing that Government would have reigned secure but for the subversive activities of a few malcontents. In a memorandum addressed to Tsar Alexander I in 1820, Metternich delivered himself of the studied opinion that revolutions were never the work of great masses of people.

> They were stirred up by small groups of ambitious men, almost all of whom came from the lower middle classes ... 'the agitated

classes' as he called them … and which he enumerated as 'paid state officials, men of letters, lawyers and individuals charged with public education'. Of the whole collection, the most dangerous, he thought, were the lawyers.

There is a natural reluctance to agree with Metternich, if only because he was insufferably conceited. In one of his letters from Teplitz in 1819, he told his wife that he always saw much further than other men.

Yet it is interesting to note that the arch-revolutionary Blanqui, with very different sympathies from those of Metternich, came similarly to the conclusion that the masses neither could nor would make a revolution. A study of the attitudes and behaviours of the major classes of the population supports the view. The masses were often angry and unruly, but the elements plotting the violent removal of existing Government were few and small. (5)

# IV

The Human Race needs to *unite* for action. We need to restructure our communities in anticipation of *a quantum leap* in Consciousness. We need to inaugurate a process of *Co-operation* between the nations of the Earth on a scale which is without precedent. Such co-operation would have to be global in extent.

Our problems are global. For these to be dealt with effectively, before there can be any global action there will have to be *Global Order*. Here, quite specifically, we have to come face to face with a most important series of questions, such as: *who* rules? In what *manner*? For what *purpose*?

A *New Vision* would have to begin to unfold itself. This could involve the New Millennium, of course; alternatively, it could also have something to do with the fact that 2003 was the 400th anniversary of the Union of the Crowns, the event which heralded the birth of the British Empire and the subsequent appearance of nations such as Canada, the United States of America, South Africa, Australia and New Zealand, among others.

Could we be about to witness the dawn of the next stage in the unfolding of an Ancient Saga whose previous chapter began almost 400 years ago? On the 5th of March 1603, James VI, King of Scots and son of Mary, Queen of Scots, left Edinburgh to become James I, King of Great Britain and Ireland.

Should there be a rebirth of British culture then it will not be restricted to the British Isles as was the case in 1603. It will be felt by the great British Diaspora in general and by the Scottish Diaspora in particular. Indeed, should the English-speaking nations, which are those which are *karmically* British, come to an understanding about greater co-operation between them by means of the Commonwealth then, just possibly, by means of the Scots, the British in general could provide *leadership* for others to follow.

Eventually, *all* the nations of the Earth will *voluntarily* attach themselves to the Commonwealth. Within the Commonwealth each nation will be *autonomous*. Each nation will be part of the Human Commonwealth, a global *family* of nations. The King of Scots will be the leader of the Commonwealth and within the Commonwealth the Scots will be the *Royal Nation.*

All the nations of the Earth will *serve* the Scots; in turn the Scots will *serve* the other nations of the Earth. The Scots will rule on Earth as *The Inner Sanctum* of the great British Diaspora.

## NOTES

(1)   Anthony Jay, *Elizabeth R. The Role of the Monarchy Today.* Published in 1992 by BCA Books, a division of BBC Enterprises Ltd., London W12 0TT. p. 62f.

(2)   as above. pp. 111-112.

(3)   Vance Packard, *The Status Seekers.* A Pelican Book. Published by Penguin in 1959. See pp. 84-85. Vance Packard stated that there are basically five classes and that the class system operates on a two-dimensional basis. The class system is as follows:

*The Real Upper Class.*
Daughters go to finishing schools. Sons attend boarding school, then college.

*The Semi-Upper Class.*
Confident, energetic and ambitious. Men have college degrees. Wives power charity drives. With the *Real Upper Class* these people constitute *the Diploma Elite.*

*The Limited-Success Class.*
They want to be seen as respectable, proper, cultured and *above* the working masses. They have high-school diplomas and they form the lower ranks of the white-collared people.

*The Working Class.*
Family heads left school early. They are the backbone of industrial unions. Their work is boring and repetitive and not a source of pride.

*The Real Lower Class.*
Other people look down on them. They work erratically at unskilled tasks. They lack initiative and ambition.

Vance Packard talks of a *two-dimensional* class system. The *horizontal* levels are based on prestige derived principally from such social-class functions as wealth, job, education and life-style. The *vertical* divisions are based on seeming differences of people arising from *ethnic background* as well as religious affiliation.

(4)    If harvests were poor, or even mediocre, there was widespread famine. In 1817, 1831 and 1839, peasants starved to death all over Europe. In 1847 *whole populations* perished in Flanders, Saxony, Silesia and Central France as well as a fifth of the Irish. In parts of Germany and Northern Italy people ate manure and the bark of trees.

In Ireland, the disaster between 1845 and 1851 caused a million deaths and forced one and a half million others to emigrate. During the previous half-century the population in Ireland had doubled. Irish dependence on the potato was greater than ever before. The fungus which destroyed the crop was unknown and no antidote was discovered until 1882. Harvests were bad for those on the British mainland too, especially in 1846, this leading to a financial crisis in 1847.

(5)    Irene Collins, *Revolutionaries in Europe: 1815-1848*. Published by *The Historical Association*, London. 1984 reprint. p. 1f.

# 38: Inclination

Inclination gains Self-Expression by means of Sensory Perception; the Sensory Perception we refer to here is the *Relationship of Sensory Perception* which is the Human Race. The Human Race exists within the context of the All, the *Relationship* of everything that *is*.

Consider the salmon, a potent symbol of Celtic spirituality! As far as the salmon is concerned, its journey is *pre-ordained*; as far as the salmon is concerned, its journey is *pre-arranged*.

The salmon exists *to make the journey*; indeed the salmon exists to make the journey *possible*. But what is the *purpose* of the journey? This has to do with the *necessity* of its nature which has been made *manifest*.

*All* manifestation is the activity of our Racial Memory. Whatever happens, or whatever is manifested, there will be those drawn to it. *Inclination* is what is at play here. Inclination is the beginning and end of everything. Nothing begins but for the *Inclination* for it. The end is reached when we are *inclined* to arrive at a new place. This is true of The Universal Self, that Collective Consciousness which has evolved from the Original Godhead.

If a Collective Consciousness is involved then it comes down to *Sociobiology*, whereby the manifestation of a *Super Organism* (God) is regulated in accordance with *Its Purpose*.

Manifestation is necessary. Form is about the manifestation of *having to comply* with Inclination; thus we see that *Inclination* is the *necessity* of our nature. We exist for the sake of the Inclination which is fundamental to our nature. We exist so that the Inclination which is fundamental to us can gain Self-Expression. We are the means to an end for the

Inclination which is fundamental to our nature and *for* the Self-Expression of which we exist.

We do not need to search for that Inclination which we *feel* so powerfully *within* ourselves. Indeed we cannot avoid it. It uses *us* for Its good end. All we can do is to *surrender* to It in the knowledge that this is the power of God *within us* preparing us for *Rebirth*.

Ancient Wisdom informs us that there were people who knew about these things. As it happens some of them were Chinese.

> Who would have expected that the Self-Nature is fundamentally pure and clean?
>
> Who would have expected that the Self-Nature is fundamentally beyond birth and death?
>
> Who would have expected that the Self-Nature is fundamentally complete in Itself ?
>
> Who would have expected that the Self-Nature is fundamentally immutable?
>
> Who would have expected that the Self-Nature can create all things? (1)

## NOTES

(1)  *Ch'an and Zen Teaching*. Edited, translated and explained by Lu K'uan Yu (Charles Luk). Published by Rider & Co., London. 1969 edition. p. 25.

# 39: Our Milesian Foundation

## I

It is now widely recognised that it was in what we now refer to as the Steppes of Southern Russia that the earliest Indo-European development took place.

Millennia have now passed since the Aryans separated to the North, South, East and West. New languages were to emerge. Empires would be built and new philosophies would appear.

The original mother-tongue of the Aryans has long since passed away. The language which, on the whole, has preserved the Aryan language is Sanskrit, albeit in a somewhat primitive state. This is *not* the parent of other languages which have developed as they have retained forms which Sanskrit has lost.

From the great Aryan family the Milesians would emerge. Initially Milesius, a Milesian leader was to marry Scota, the daughter of a Pharaoh, and their son, Gaidheal Glas (pronounced *Gael Glas*), was the first Scot in the classical sense. There would have been colonies of Milesians all over the Mediterranean Sea and beyond. In modern Scots Gaidhlig, there is still a word *sgod* (pronounced as *scot* and could just as easily be spelt as such) which means *fragment*. These Milesians were indeed a fragmented people.

The Milesians from whom the Ancient Scots emerged reached the British Isles in considerable numbers around 1500 BC. There would also have been colonies in the Middle East. They were in Egypt when the Kingdom of Zedekiah fell.

Miletos was one of the chief cities of Asia Minor. It was the southern-most of the famous twelve Ionian cities. Its founder was the fabled Miletos who led Cretan refugees there. Miletos was to be the centre of a great revolt of the Ionian cities against the dominion of Persia.

Miletos had been the focus for Literature and Philosophy. Thales, reck-oned to be the founder of Milesian Cosmology, lived there. So did other phi-losophers such as Anaximander and Anaximanes. The historians Kadmos and Hecateus were also citizens.

As philosophy developed we begin to see the significance of Thales. Eudemos, who was a disciple of Aristotle, was responsible for the first History of Mathematics; he maintained that it was Thales who introduced Geometry to the Greeks.

The possibility is that he had learned the elementary rules of mensuration in Egypt. He is said to have taught the Egyptians how to measure Pyramids by their shadows. He had developed a method of establishing the distance of a ship out at sea. The peoples of the Near East knew that a triangle whose sides were as 3:4:5 always had a right angle. It has been suggested that he invented some applications of this primitive science and this was the begin-ning of rational science. (1)

So how did Thales view his world?

> According to Aristotle, Thales said that the Earth floats on water, and he doubtless thought of it as a flat disc ...

> It sounds primitive enough but, in reality, it marks a notable advance. The whole history of Cosmology at this date is the story of how the solid Earth was gradually loosed from its moorings. Originally sky and Earth were pictured as a lid and bottom of a sort of box; but from an early date the Greeks, as was natural for them, began to think of the Earth as an island surrounded by the River Okeanos. To regard it as resting on water is a fur-ther step towards a truer view. It was something to get the Earth afloat. (2)

Next in the Milesian Tradition was Anaximander. He held that all life began in the sea and that the present form of animals was the result of adaptation to a fresh environment. He recognised that the young of the Human Race require a prolonged period of nursing, while those young of other species soon find food for themselves. For Anaximander, *if* Humans had always been as they are now, they would *not* have been able to survive.

With the Fall of Miletos in 494 BC *The Milesian School* came to an end. The philosophy of Anaximanes continued to be taught in other Ionian cities. At this time those Teachings relating to Orpheus were beginning to spread in every direction.

The greatest contribution of all by the Milesians to Human Knowledge is that it was they who gave the world the concept of what we call *Matter*; in due course, Pythagoreans were to supplement this by a correlative conception of *Form*.

# II

Pythagoras of Samos was an *Ionian*, reckoned by many to be the first man to unite Science with Religion. He was to prove, as did others, that *all* great advances come from *individuals* rather than the collective work of a School.

It is generally accepted that Pythagoras brought his ascetic practices and mystical beliefs from his Ionian homeland. He would have been greatly influenced by *The Orphic Mysteries*, which were concerned with Orpheus. This would have come from a genuine Ionian source. As far as Pythagoras was concerned it was *Apollo* who was revered above all the other gods.

Pythagoras taught Rebirth or Transmigration. These teachings were prevalent in the Celtic world and were certainly known to the Druids. Legend states that Pythagoras was instructed by Druids, but he was also to be greatly influenced by *The Orphic Mysteries*. (3)

For Pythagoras the things perceived by the senses *remind* us of things we knew when the soul was *out of the body*, thus able to perceive Reality directly. We have never seen equal sticks or stones but we still know what equality is; by comparing the things of sense with the Realities of which they *remind* us we judge them to be *imperfect*.

It must have been obvious to Pythagoras that the Realities with which he was dealing were *not* perceived by the senses. Furthermore, the Doctrine of

Reminiscence follows easily upon the Doctrine of Rebirth.

> Aristotle tells us that the Pythagoreans represented the world as inhaling *air* from the boundless mass outside it, and this *air* is identified with *The Unlimited*.
>
> On the other hand, Pythagoras seems to have learned from Anaximander that the Earth is not a flat disc … As soon as the causes of eclipses came to be understood, it was natural for them to infer that the Earth was a sphere, and we may possibly attribute that discovery to Pythagoras himself. With this exception his general view of the world seems to have been distinctly *Milesian* in character.
>
> When, however, we come to the process by which things are developed out of *The Unlimited*, we observe a great change. We hear nothing of *separating out* or even *rarefaction* and *condensation*. Instead, we have the theory that *what gives Form to The Unlimited is The Limit*. (4)

At this time, for many a new solution was sought to the Age-old Milesian problem of *opposites*. For many of those alive at the time, *The Unlimited* and *The Limit* were as opposites. The discovery of *The Mean* suggested such a solution.

Anaximander regarded the encroachment of one opposite upon another as *an injustice*. He would no doubt have held that there was a point which was fair to both. This, however, he had no way of determining.

The discovery of *The Mean* suggested that it could be found in a blend of opposites. This *blend* could be numerically determined just as high and low notes of the octave had been.

The convivial customs of the Greeks made such an idea natural for them. The Master of the Feast used to prescribe the proportion of wine to water to be poured into the mixing-bowl before it was served to guests. In Plato's *Timaeus* the Demiourgos uses a mixing-bowl. For Pythagoras, it may have seemed that, if we could discover the rule for blending such apparently elusive things as high and low notes, the secret of the world would be uncovered.

# III

Zeno, too, had an interest in *The Unlimited*, or in *The Continuous* as the Eleatics called it. For Zeno, however, *The Unlimited* could not be composed of *units*, no matter how small or how many.

We can always bisect a line; every bisection leaves us with a line that can, itself, be bisected. *We never come to a point or to a unit.*

It follows that, if a line is made up of units or points, there must be an infinite number of such points on a given terminated straight line.

If these points have magnitude every line will be of infinite length. If they have *no* magnitude every line will be infinitely small. Again, if a point *has* magnitude, the addition of a point to a line will make it longer whilst its subtraction will make it shorter.

If the points have *no* magnitude, neither their addition nor their subtraction will make a difference to a line. That to which the addition or subtraction makes *no* difference is *nothing at all*.

If *Number* is a *sum* of units (and no other account has yet been suggested) there is an impassable gulf between the Discrete and the Continuous, between Arithmetic and Geometry.

For Zeno, things are *not* numbers. For Zeno, Geometry cannot be reduced to Arithmetic so long as the number *One* is regarded as the beginning of the numerical series. For Zeno what really corresponds to the point is *Zero*.

> What Zeno actually does prove is that *Space and Time cannot consist of points or moments which themselves have magnitude*, or that the Elements of a Continuum cannot be units homogenous with the Continuum constructed out of them. He shows, in fact, that there must be more points on a line, more moments in the shortest lapse of Time, than there are members of the series of natural numbers or, what comes to the same thing, although every Continuum is infinitely divisible, infinite divisibility is not an adequate criterion of Continuity. (5)

As it says in *The Parmenides*,

> One as being is a Whole, and parts are only parts as parts of the Whole, and the parts are contained *in* the Whole. Now that which *contains* is a *Limit*. But if it is Limited, it will have Extremes and, if it is a Whole, it will have beginning, middle and end.

> Further, since all the parts which make up the Whole are contained in the Whole, it must be *in Itself*; and since the Whole is not contained in the parts, it must, regarded as a Whole, be *in something else*. Therefore, it will be both at Rest and *in Motion*.

# IV

Perhaps we are now face to face with what was often referred to as *The Chief Secret of the Ancients*, which referred to Knowledge about *why* the Human Race exists.

If the Platonic maxim is correct that 'Man is the measure of things that are, that they are, and of things that are not, that they are not', then does this not in some way imply that the Human Race is a Regulatory Principle, a yardstick in fact?

Indeed, the author (John Houston) is of the opinion that, all other things aside, the Human Race must now *know Itself* on a level *above* the need for Self-Preservation in the world.

The reason for the end of unnecessary struggle is quite simple: in the attainment of this end the Human Race will be free to receive guidance from other inclinations. The so-called evolution of the Human Race is actually the evolution of *Inclination* which is innate within Humanity and for the sake of which Inclination, Humanity actually exists.

Perhaps now, as was true in the days of the wise Socrates, *we* need to *know ourselves* as beings endowed with Inclination sufficient to take us to where our Inclination will guide us.

The answer to our problems can only come from within us. In reality there is *no* external world, *no* external Universe. *Mind* is all there is.

Anaxagorus looked to the microcosm, *the inner world*, for a suggestion as to the source of Motion. He was to find such a source for his purpose. He called it *Mind* as Mind was the source of Motion as well as of Knowledge *within us*.

What else can we do? Einstein's *Special Theory of Relativity* prohibits the transmission of Matter or even Information faster than the speed of light. *Quantum Mechanics* dictates that our knowledge of the micro realm will always be uncertain. *Chaos Theory* confirms that even without *Quantum Indeterminacy* many phenomena would be impossible to predict. *The Incompleteness Theorem* of Kurt Godel denies us the possibility of constructing a consistent mathematical description of Reality.

Beginning in the 1950s, Charles Wheeler had grown increasingly intrigued by the philosophical implications of Quantum Physics.

The so-called Orthodox Interpretation was also known as *The Copenhagen Interpretation* which was set forth by Niels Bohr in the 1920s. This *Copenhagen Interpretation* held that sub-atomic particles such as Electrons have *no* real existence. They exist in a state of comparative limbo where many super-imposed states are possible until *forced* into a single state by an act of *observation*.

The Electrons or Photons may act like waves or like particles depending on how they are experimentally observed. The Electrons *seem* to know *in advance* how physicists will observe them.

Charles Wheeler was one of the first prominent physicists to propose that Reality might not be wholly physical. In some sense our Cosmos might be a participatory phenomenon, *requiring* an act of observation, thus Consciousness, Itself.

In the 1960s Charles Wheeler helped to popularise *The Anthropic Principle*. This *Anthropic Principle* holds that the Universe must be as it is because, if it were otherwise, we might not be here to observe it.

Then there was James Lovelock who popularised the concept of *GAIA*. The basic idea behind Gaia is that the Biota, the sum of all life on Earth, is locked in a symbiotic relationship with the environment. This includes the atmosphere, the seas and other aspects of the Earth's surface. Biota regulate the environment to promote the survival of Biota (6).

There is also Stuart Kauffman whose book *At Home in the Universe* spells out his theories on biological evolution. Here we have a set of models which say that the emergence of life might be *a natural phenomenon*. We are not incredibly improbable accidents at all. Life could very easily exist elsewhere.

For Kauffman the order displayed by biological systems does *not* result from the hard-won success of natural selection but from pervasive *order-generating* effects. For Kauffman, order is not only spontaneous; it is also *free*.

Edward Wilson is another fascinating character. He maintains that Sociology could only become a truly scientific discipline if it were submitted to the Darwinian Paradigm. For Edward Wilson warfare, male dominance, altruistic tendencies and so on could well be understood as adaptive behaviour stemming from our primordial compulsion to propagate our genes.

For Wilson, further advances in Evolutionary Theory as well as in Genetics and Neuroscience would enable *Sociobiology* to account for a wide variety of Human behaviour. Wilson believes that *Sociobiology* would subsume Sociology as well as Psychology, Anthropology and others. He was criticised for saying that the Human condition was somehow *inevitable*. Critics argued that this represented an updated version of Social Darwinism. It was felt that this could be used as a scientific justification for Racism, Sexism and Imperialism.

At any rate, for Edward Wilson, to maintain our species indefinitely we are compelled to drive towards Total Knowledge, right down to the level of the Neuron and the Gene.

## NOTES

(1)   As John Burnet says in *Greek Philosophy*, pages 4-5,

> If the Egyptians had possessed anything that could rightly be called Mathematics, it is hard to understand how it was left for Pythagoras and his followers to establish the most elementary propositions in Plane Geometry; and if the Babylonians had any real conception of the Planetary System, it is not easy to see why the Greeks had to discover bit by bit the true shape of the Earth and the explanation of eclipses ...

> It is true, of course, that in Hellenistic times, a certain number of Egyptian priests applied the methods of Greek science to the traditional lore of their own country. The Hermetic Literature proves it, and so does the elaborate Astrological System the later Egyptians erected on a Stoic foundation. All that, however, throws no light on the origins of Greek Science. On the contrary, if the Egyptians of these days adopted the contemporary

Greek Science and philosophy, it is only another indication of their own poverty in such things.

There is always the possibility that although the Egyptians and by the same token the Babylonians or the Assyrians, were knowledgeable in certain matters that does not mean that this Knowledge was freely dispersed among the people and thus readily available. Such Knowledge would not have been available to those who were not Initiates. That Knowledge would have been prevented from becoming common Knowledge by an elite group, thus protecting Sacred Knowledge from any profane influence.

By way of an explanation, in *The Phaedrus* of Plato we read that,

> At the Egyptian city of Naucratis, there was a famous old God, whose name was Theuth; the bird which is called *the ibis* is sacred to him, and he was the inventor of many Arts, such as Arithmetic, Calculation, Geometry, Astronomy, Draughts and Dice, but his greatest discovery was the use of Letters. Now in those days the God Thamus was the King of the whole country of Egypt; and he dwelt in that great city of Upper Egypt which the Hellenes called Egyptian Thebes, and the God himself is called by them *Ammon*. To him came Theuth and showed his inventions, desiring that the *other* Egyptians might be allowed to have benefit of them.

The Milesian Tradition is one of the noblest of all Philosophical Traditions. By means of the embers of *UR III* Civilisation was germinated elsewhere. This was ultimately established by *Initiates* who saw their mission as the civilising of the Human Race in anticipation of a Quantum Leap in Consciousness.

(2)   John Burnet, *Greek Philosophy*. A standard book for Greek Philosophy. Published by the MacMillan Press Limited. First published in 1914. 1981 reprint. p. 15.

(3)   The word *metempsychosis* is inaccurate. For J. Burnet that would mean different souls entering the same body. A better and older word, apparently, is *paliggenesia*, which means 'being born again'.

(4)  ibid. p. 34.

(5)  ibid. p. 68.

(6)  When James Lovelock was bringing the concept of *GAIA* together he was assisted by Lynn Margulis who has an interest in *Symbiosis*.

All *Multicellular Organisms*, such as ourselves, consist of *eukaryotic* cells. Margulis proposed that *eukaryotes* may have emerged when one *prokaryote* absorbed another, smaller one which, in due course, became the nucleus. She suggested that such cells should not be considered as individual organisms but *as composites*.

Give up all varieties of Religion
And just surrender to Me
And I will protect you
From all sinful reactions
Therefore you need have no fear

This confidential Knowledge
Will not be revealed
To those who are not austere
Or dedicated
Or engaged in devotional service
Or to one who is envious of Me

For the one who reveals
This Supreme Secret
To the devotees
Devotional service is guaranteed
And at the end
He will come back
To Me

*Hare Krsna*

# About John Houston

I was born on the 26th of July 1950 in the Southern General Hospital in the south of Glasgow, Scotland's largest city.

On that day my father had gone to work in the shipyard as usual. Not long after he had gone to work my mother started to have contractions. In due course she was taken by ambulance to hospital.

The very first thing I remember saying to my mother when still very young was that I had lived before. Who I had been or where I had lived remained a mystery to me; I was able to recount experiences which I had had whilst *out of the body*.

Psychologically speaking it was a dream-like state, as though I were a *neuron of memory*; then I remember beginning to transcend my physical form and looking out of my eyes. I heard a voice saying to me 'this is your next task'. I was eight months old. My mother was changing my clothes. This is John Houston's first experience.

Years passed. I lived my life in expectation of meeting people whom I had known before. Then when I was eight years old and walking to primary school in the area of Castlemilk in Glasgow, *the vision came to me*. Right there and right then I realised that there was going to be a great transition for the Human Race. It was because of *the necessity* of this transition that I had come here *to the Earth* because I would be involved in this transition. That was what my life would entail.

One year later, while in class at Netherton Primary, I realised that I would have to be transformed. It was as though I was looking down on myself from a distance. I could see my crown chakra. It was being activated. I realised that

I would have to be transformed, like a butterfly emerging from a chrysalis. How I was then was one thing; yet how I was then was not the way I truly was for there was a power within me which demanded an awakening *within* me and *of* me.

I experienced a great restlessness during adolescence, but I had seen the vision and I was thereby empowered to deal with anything that came my way.

It wasn't until early January 1980 that things really started again. I saw the thousand-petalled lotus of Krishna and, thereafter, the writings began *to come to me.* I wrote them down as I was inspired to do.

I didn't go looking for this Truth or this Knowledge, because it came to me.


I am who I am and I will be whom I will be.